HATE CRIMES

HATE CRIMES

VOLUME 2

The Consequences of Hate Crime

Barbara Perry, General Editor
Paul Iganski, Volume Editor

PRAEGER PERSPECTIVES

Westport, Connecticut
London

Library of Congress Cataloging-in-Publication Data

Hate crimes / Barbara Perry, general editor.
    p. cm.
  Includes bibliographical references and index.
  ISBN 978–0–275–99569–0 (set : alk. paper) — 978–0–275–99571–3
(vol. 1 : alk. paper) — 978–0–275–99573–7 (vol. 2 : alk. paper) — 978–0–275–99575–1
(vol. 3 : alk. paper) — 978–0–275–99577–5 (vol. 4 : alk. paper) — 978–0–275–99579–9
(vol. 5 : alk. paper)
  1. Offenses against the person.   2. Hate crimes.   3. Violent crimes.   4. Genocide.
I. Perry, Barbara, 1962–
  K5170.H38   2009
   364.15—dc22   2008052727

British Library Cataloguing in Publication Data is available.

Library of Congress Catalog Card Number: 2008052727
ISBN: 978–0–275–99569–0 (set)
      978–0–275–99571–3 (vol. 1)
      978–0–275–99573–7 (vol. 2)
      978–0–275–99575–1 (vol. 3)
      978–0–275–99577–5 (vol. 4)
      978–0–275–99579–9 (vol. 5)

First published in 2009

Praeger Publishers, 88 Post Road West, Westport, CT 06881
An imprint of Greenwood Publishing Group, Inc.
www.praeger.com

Printed in the United States of America

The paper used in this book complies with the
Permanent Paper Standard issued by the National
Information Standards Organization (Z39.48–1984).

10 9 8 7 6 5 4 3 2 1

Contents

Set Introduction by Barbara Perry   vii

Introduction: Hate Crime as a Scholarly Domain

by Paul Iganski   xiii

CHAPTER 1   How Hate Crimes Hurt More: Evidence
             from the British Crime Survey   1
             Paul Iganski and Spiridoula Lagou

CHAPTER 2   The Psychological Harms of Hate:
             Implications and Interventions   15
             Kellina M. Craig-Henderson

CHAPTER 3   Homophobic Hate Crimes in Sweden:
             Questions and Consequences   31
             Eva Tiby

CHAPTER 4   Body Maps: Envisaging Homophobia,
             Violence, and Safety   49
             Gail Mason

CHAPTER 5   The Psychological and Social Effects
             of Antibisexual, Antigay, and Antilesbian
             Violence and Harassment   73
             Monique Noelle

CHAPTER 6   Beyond the Immediate Victim:
             Understanding Hate Crimes
             as Message Crimes   107
             Helen Ahn Lim

CHAPTER 7   Crime and Prejudice: Needs and Support
             of Hate Crime Victims   123
             Peter Dunn

CHAPTER 8   Identity, Otherness, and the Impact
             of Racist Victimization in the English
             Countryside   143
             Neil Chakraborti and Jon Garland

CHAPTER 9   The Harms of Verbal and Textual Hatred   161
             Nicole Asquith

CHAPTER 10   Hate Crime as a Human Rights Violation   175
             Barbara Perry and Patrik Olsson

About the Editor and Contributors   193

Index   197

Set Introduction

Barbara Perry
General Editor

The twentieth century appeared to close much as it had opened—with sprees of violence directed against the Other. The murder of Matthew Shepard, the lynching of James Byrd, the murderous rampage of Benjamin Smith, and post-9/11 anti-Muslim violence all stand as reminders that the bigotry that kills is much more than an unfortunate chapter in U.S. history. Racial, gender, ethnic, and religious violence persist. It is a sad commentary on the cultural and social life of the United States that a series such as this remains timely as we enter the twenty-first century. The dramatic cases cited earlier are but extreme illustrations of widespread, daily acts of aggression directed toward an array of minority communities. I use the term *communities* purposefully here since these acts are less about any one victim than about the cultural group they represent. Hate crime is, in fact, an assault against all members of stigmatized and marginalized communities.

Clearly this is not a new phenomenon, even in the United States. It is important to keep in mind that what we currently refer to as hate crime has a long historical lineage. The contemporary dynamics of hate-motivated violence have their origins in historical conditions. With respect to hate crime, at least, history does repeat itself, as similar patterns of motivation, sentiment, and victimization recur over time. Just as immigrants in the 1890s were subject to institutional and public forms of discrimination and violence, so, too, were those of the 1990s; likewise, former black slaves risked the wrath of the Ku Klux Klan (KKK) when they exercised their newfound rights in the antebellum period, just as their descendants risked violent reprisal for their efforts to win and exercise additional rights and freedoms in the civil rights era; and women who demanded the right to vote on the eve of the twentieth century suffered the same ridicule and harassment as those who demanded equal rights in the workplace later in the century. While the politics of difference that underlie these periods of animosity may lie latent for short periods of time, they nonetheless seem to remain on the simmer, ready to resurface whenever a new threat is perceived—when immigration levels increase; or when relationships between groups shift for other political, economic, or cultural reasons; or in the aftermath of attacks like those on 9/11. Consequently, hate crime remains a crucial indicator of cultural fissures in the United States and around the globe. This set, then, remains similarly relevant in the current era.

Hate Crimes offers interested readers a comprehensive collection of original chapters surveying this phenomenon we have come to know as hate crime. Interestingly, the field of hate crime studies is interdisciplinary, so the contributors here represent a variety of disciplines, including law, sociology, criminology, psychology, and even public health. Moreover, since it is also a global phenomenon, we have invited not just American scholars, but international contributors as well. This comparative/cross-cultural approach adds an important element to the set. It reminds readers that hate crime is a universal problem and that approaches taken elsewhere might be of use to North Americans.

The volumes included in this set have been divided into five distinct focal areas. Volume 1, *Understanding and Defining Hate Crime*, is edited by Brian Levin of California State University, San Bernardino. He has collected a series of chapters that lay a strong foundation for the volumes that follow. The pieces here provide an introduction to what it is we mean by the term *hate crime*. There is ongoing debate about such things as whether the term is even appropriate, what behaviors ought to be included in our understanding of hate crime, and what classes of victims should be included. The relevant chapters, then, offer diverse definitions, ranging from legal to sociological approaches.

One consequence of the varied and divergent definitions used to conceptualize bias-motivated crime is that the confusion also complicates the process of gathering data on hate crime. Berk, Boyd, and Hamner (1992) astutely observe that "much of the available data on hate motivated crime rests on unclear definitions; it is difficult to know what is being counted as hate motivated and what is not" (p. 125). As a result, while both academic and media reports make the claim that ethnoviolence represents a "rising tide," the truth is that we don't know whether in fact this is the case or not (Jacobs & Potter, 1998). Thus Levin also includes a number of chapters that attempt to address the issue of data collection and measurement of hate crime.

The limitations of definition and measurement highlighted previously help to explain the limited attempts thus far to theorize hate crime. In the absence of empirical information about bias-motivated violence, it is difficult to construct conceptual frameworks. Without the raw materials, there is no foundation for theorizing. Additionally, the relatively recent recognition of hate crime as a social problem (Jenness & Broad, 1998) also contributes to the lack of theoretical accounts. This volume, however, includes chapters that begin to offer compelling models to help us make sense of hate crime.

The second volume, *The Consequences of Hate Crime*, is a particularly valuable contribution to the literature on hate crime. Editor Paul Iganski of Lancaster University in the United Kingdom has brought together a unique collection of chapters that explore both the individual and the social impacts associated with this form of violence. Running through much of the literature—even through court decisions on hate crime—is the assumption that such offences are qualitatively different in their effects, as compared to their non-bias-motivated counterparts. Specifically, Iganski (2001) contends that there are five distinct types of consequences associated with hate crime: harm to the initial victim; harm to the victim's group; harm to the victim's group (outside the neighborhood); harm to other targeted communities; and harm to societal norms and values. The first of these has been the subject of considerable scholarly attention. Research suggests that first and foremost among the impacts on the individual is the physical harm: bias-motivated crimes are often characterized by extreme brutality (Levin & McDevitt, 1993). Violent personal crimes motivated by bias are more likely to involve extraordinary levels of violence. Additionally, the empirical findings of studies of the emotional, psychological, and behavioral impacts of hate crime are beginning to establish a solid pattern of more severe impact on bias crime victims, as compared to nonbias victims (see, e.g., Herek, Cogan, & Gillis, 2002; McDevitt et al., 2001). Several chapters in this volume explore these individual effects.

Additionally, however, this volume includes a number of chapters that begin to offer insights into other often overlooked consequences of hate crime: community effects. Many scholars point to the "fact" that hate crimes are "message crimes" that emit a distinct warning to all members of the victim's community: step out of line, cross invisible boundaries, and you, too, could be lying on the ground, beaten and bloodied (Iganski, 2001). Consequently, the individual fear noted previously is thought to be accompanied by the collective fear of the victim's cultural group, possibly even of other minority groups likely to be victims. Weinstein (as cited by Iganski, 2001) refers to this as an *in terrorem* effect: intimidation of the group by the victimization of one or a few members of that group. It is these effects that contributors such as Monique Noelle and Helen Ahn Lim address.

Barbara Perry, editor of volume 3, *The Victims of Hate Crime*, introduces this volume with the caveat that little empirical work has been done on the distinct experiences of different groups of hate crime victims. Much of the literature has more or less assumed a homogeneous group known as "victims." However, this occludes the fact that the frequency, dynamics, motives, and impacts of bias-motivated violence differ across target communities. Thus the volume draws on emerging theoretical and empirical work that explores manifestations of hate crime within diverse communities. Especially novel here is the inclusion of pieces that address hate-motivated crime directed toward women and the homeless community. Consideration of these groups, in particular, forces us to expand our traditional characterization of hate crime victims, which is often restricted to race, religion, ethnicity, or sexual orientation.

Volume 4, *Hate Crime Offenders*, brings us to a consideration of the second half of the equation: perpetrators of hate crime. Randy Blazak from Portland State University has gathered an intriguing collection of chapters. The authors here have been set the task of responding to Blazak's opening question, Who are the hate mongers? Many would respond to this question by reference to members of the KKK or a skinhead group, for example. This is a very common myth. In fact, fewer than 5 percent of identifiable offenders are members of organized hate groups. Recognizing this, Blazak has asked his contributors to explore both individual perpetrators and those involved in hate groups. Thus this is an engaging and diverse collection of chapters, which explore issues ranging from women's involvement in hate crime, to typologies of hate crime offenders, to white power music. He even includes an interview with a hate offender.

Frederick Lawrence, editor of volume 5, *Responding to Hate Crime*, has solicited work from his contributors that gives us food for thought with respect to how we might respond to hate crime. Clearly there are diverse approaches available: legislation, social policy, community organizing, or education, to name just a few. In the extant scholarship, there have been relatively few concentrated analyses of such efforts to respond to or prevent bias-motivated crimes. In large part, such recommendations come by way of a conclusion and are thus not fully developed. Hence the chapters in Lawrence's volume explicitly present interventions intended to ameliorate the incidence or impact of hate crime. While the emphasis is on criminal justice responses (legislation, policing, prosecution), Lawrence also includes chapters that explore preventative measures, restorative justice initiatives, and the role of organizations like the Southern Poverty Law Center.

I speak for all of the editors when I say that we are very pleased to have been asked to develop this collection of hate crime literature. It was a unique opportunity to share emerging perspectives and analyses with a diverse audience. It is hoped that what we offer here will provide the insights that readers are seeking, but also inspiration for further explorations and interventions into this disturbing class of violence.

REFERENCES

Berk, R., Boyd, E., & Hamner, K. (1992). Thinking more clearly about hate-motivated crimes. In G. Herek & K. Berrill (Eds.), *Hate crimes: Confronting violence against lesbians and gay men* (pp. 123–143). Newbury Park, CA: Sage.

Herek, G., Cogan, J., & Gillis, R. (2002). Victim experiences in hate crimes based on sexual orientation. *Journal of Social Issues, 58*, 319–339.

Iganski, P. (2001). Hate crimes hurt more. *American Behavioral Scientist, 45*, 626–638.

Jacobs, J., & Potter, K. (1998). *Hate crimes: Criminal law and identity politics.* New York: Oxford University Press.

Jenness, V., & Broad, K. (1998). *Hate crimes: New social movements and the politics of violence.* New York: Aldine de Gruyter.

Levin, J., & McDevitt, J. (1993). *Hate crimes: The rising tide of bigotry and bloodshed.* New York: Plenum.

McDevitt, J., Balboni, J., Garcia, L., and Gu, J.,. (2001). Consequences for victims: A comparison of bias- and non-bias motivated assaults. *American Behavioral Scientist, 45*, 697–713.

INTRODUCTION: HATE CRIME AS A SCHOLARLY DOMAIN

Paul Iganski

Hate crimes involve expressed animus toward some aspect of the victim's identity and manifest either in an offender's actions or in his or her words, or both. Offenders are commonly acting out strands of bigotry that are intricately threaded into the social fabric—pursuing bigotry to its logical violent conclusion. Such understanding about the motivating impulses of hate crime offenders, however, provides a necessary, but not a sufficient, condition for distinguishing hate crimes from similar, but otherwise motivated (or "parallel," Lawrence, 1999, p. 4) crimes. Arguably, the common denominator that separates hate crimes from other crimes concerns the harms inflicted on targeted victims and society more broadly. While all crime hurts in one way or another, the very essence of a hate crime is that it hurts more than a parallel crime. The additional hurts inflicted by hate crime have provided the justification for penalty enhancement for offenders convicted of such crimes. Assertions that such harms occur have been evident in the policy and scholarly literature in the United States and elsewhere for some decades. They were also fundamental to the landmark case that settled the constitutional challenges against hate crime laws in the United States—*Wisconsin v. Mitchell* (1993).

Understanding of the hurts involved not only provides a critical evidential basis in support of the provisions of hate crime laws, but understanding is also vitally important to inform effective intervention with victims and the provision of appropriate support. And in the same way that it might arguably be appropriate to think in terms of *perpetrator communities* (Sibbitt, 1997), with offenders serving as proxies for the sentiments and values shared by the communities from which they are drawn, it is also appropriate to think in terms of victimized communities, as the harms of hate crime spread beyond the targeted individual to the communities of which victims are a part. And wider still at the societal level, hate crimes offend against a respect for, and a commitment to, diversity. Each act of hate crime therefore inflicts numerous hurts and involves many victims (Iganski, 2001; Noelle, 2002).

The fact that hate crimes hurt has not been a matter of dispute. But the nature and extent of the hurts of hate crime have, to date, not been fully understood. And claims that hate crimes hurt more than parallel crimes have not been convincingly evidenced, limited often by constraints affecting the design of the research into the matter. This is not to downplay the ever accumulating research literature on the harms of hate crime, but there is clearly a need for a greater and more nuanced understanding of the harms involved. Consequently, this volume aims to take a major step forward in that understanding by gathering much of the available evidence between its covers. It presents a collection of chapters written by many of the influential authors in the research literature to date on the harms of hate crime.

It has been argued that hate crime can be thought of as a policy domain: an arena in which elements of the political and criminal justice process have converged and focus on the substantive issue of offences and incidents, where some bigotry against the victim plays a part (Jenness & Grattet, 2001). Hate crime might also be regarded as a scholarly domain in which there is an analytical coalition between scholars in once disparate fields of study concerned with oppression, discrimination, and bigotry in various guises. It is such a coalition that this book provides. In a truly collaborative international enterprise, scholars from Australia, Canada, Greece, Sweden, the United Kingdom, and the United States have contributed chapters: Some provide original research findings, others offer new theorizing, and some indicate the interventions and support needed for victims. As a collection, the chapters present the major thinking in the literature to date on the harms of hate crime—serving therefore as a valuable reference text—and they also take that thinking forward with new research and ideas. This book is therefore not only a source for reference: it is also at the cutting-edge of research in hate crime studies. The enterprise is also truly interdisciplinary, with scholars employing analytic tools and perspectives grounded in criminology, psychology, psychotherapy, and sociology. It is also multimethod in that a range of research approaches spanning qualitative and quantitative strategies have been employed by those contributors offering research findings. And to reassure readers, especially those who are interested in knowledge to inform policy and other interventions against hate crime, and who are interested in supporting victims, all of the contributors are involved in applied research, and for some, the perspectives they offer are informed by their professional practice with victims.

The authors most eloquently present their perspectives and evidence here. It is hoped that the reader will critically engage with the ideas presented by the volume and join the analytical coalition of scholars found between the volume's covers.

REFERENCES

Iganski, P. (2001). Hate crimes hurt more. *American Behavioral Scientist, 45*, 626–638.

Jenness, V., & Grattet, R. (2001). *Making hate a crime: From social movement to law enforcement.* New York: Russell Sage Foundation.

Lawrence, F. M. (1999). *Punishing hate: Bias crimes under American law.* Cambridge, MA: Harvard University Press.

Noelle, M. (2002). The ripple effect of the Matthew Shepherd murder: Impact on the assumptive worlds of members of the targeted group. *American Behavioral Scientist, 46*(1), 27–50.

Sibbitt, R. (1997). *The perpetrators of racial harassment and racial violence* (Research Study No. 176). London: Home Office.

Wisconsin v. Mitchell, 113 S. Ct. 2201 (1993).

CHAPTER 1

HOW HATE CRIMES HURT MORE: EVIDENCE FROM THE BRITISH CRIME SURVEY

Paul Iganski and Spiridoula Lagou

THE HARM OF HATE CRIME

What distinguishes hate crime from other types of crime is that hate crimes generally hurt more than parallel crimes. The notion that hate crimes inflict greater harm on their victims is a fundamental dimension in conceptualizing the meaning of hate crime. In now well-known arguments, critics of hate crime laws contend that the additional punishment of hate crime offenders over and above the punishment that can be meted out for a parallel, but otherwise motivated crime amounts to the state criminalizing the expression of certain thoughts, opinions, and values (cf. Bruce, 2001; Gey, 1997; Hurd, 2001). Against such criticisms, however, supporters of hate crime laws argue that speech and other expressions and the thought behind the crimes, or the offender's motivation, are not being punished (see Iganski, 2001), or that particular categories of victims are not being proffered special treatment. Instead, they propose that the laws impose greater punishment for the greater harm they believe is inflicted by hate crimes (cf. Weinstein, 1992; Lawrence, 1999; Levin, 1999). Assertions that such harm occurs were fundamental to the landmark case that settled the constitutional challenges against hate crime legislation in the United States: *Wisconsin v. Mitchell* (1993). From this standpoint about the harm of hate crime, the nature and extent of the harm inflicted by an offense are critical for determining the appropriate punishment, and in the case of hate crime, the motives of the offender are only relevant to determine whether the particular offense committed is a type of crime that inflicts greater harm than a similar but otherwise motivated crime. From this perspective, the harsher punishment of hate crimes simply provides the just desserts for the greater harm inflicted by such crimes. This argument, though, hinges perilously on the evidence of the extent and type of harm inflicted, and much of the evidence for the supposed greater harm caused by hate crime has been equivocal.

THE SPATIAL IMPACT OF HATE CRIME

One particular type of harm allegedly caused by hate crime concerns the spatial or terroristic impact that such crimes can inflict on individuals and communities. For instance, the effect that racist attacks can have on a community are elaborated on by Paul Gordon (1994) in the early scholarly literature on racist violence in the United Kingdom:

> Once attacks go beyond the isolated, the exceptional, they act as threat, an attack, not just against those individuals who are themselves the victims, but the whole group of people who consider themselves to be, who are at risk. In the same way that potentially all women are affected by rape or other violence against particular individual women, so all black people are affected by attacks on particular black people. When we speak of racist attacks, in other words, we are speaking of a form of violence against a group or a community. . . . The reality behind these figures is a Britain in which, in some areas, black people will not venture out after dark. Where even during the day black people will take cabs to work or to the shops, where black schoolchildren have to be escorted to and from their schools. (p. 48)

The processes involved in the spatial consequence of racial attacks were outlined by Rai and Hesse (1992), drawing from their research in the London borough of Waltham Forest in the 1980s:

> Asian and Black people form mental maps of the distribution of racial harassment . . . people begin to perceive social spaces in "racially" particular ways. That is as locations which allow freedom of movement and those which inhibit; and locales which are "no go areas" or are relatively safe to live. In this sense the movements of people are shaped by the mental maps they "carry in their heads." (p. 177)

The impact on the spatial mobility of people from victimized communities can be considerable. According to Rai and Hesse (1992),

> Their social behaviour may be restricted in the local environment because they have to live with not only ineffective responses from statutory agencies when reporting their experiences, but the reality of the harassment recurring. . . . As a consequence the spatial mobility of people becomes restricted. Not only does this interfere with everyday life (e.g. going shopping, going to work, etc.), it also restricts access to the use of public facilities. (p. 177)

However, arguably, much of the evidence behind these assertions has been questionable on the matter of whether hate crimes produce greater behavioral harm than otherwise motivated crimes. It is instructive to turn to the British Crime Survey (BCS) and some of the questions put to respondents who reported crimes (racially motivated and non–racially motivated), concerning their behavioral reactions following incidents.

The BCS samples the experiences of adults aged 16 and over in households living in private residential accommodation in England and Wales. The survey includes a "nonwhite" boost sample, as the number of respondents from black and Asian minority ethnic communities would otherwise be insufficient, given their small representation in the population of England and Wales, to enable a robust analysis of their specific experiences. (Even the boost sample in any one year's sweep of the survey provides insufficient numbers of minority ethnic respondents for a rigorous analysis. Consequently, the data used in the discussion that follows combine three annual sweeps of the BCS for 2002–2003, 2003–2004, and 2004–2005.)

Respondents are asked screening questions early on in the survey interview about whether they themselves, or a member of their current household, has been a victim of a "crime or offense" within the 12 months before the date of the interview, and if they have, on how many occasions. To prompt their memory, they are asked about a range of offenses, from theft or damage to a motor vehicle to bicycle theft, burglary, theft from the person, threats, and violence. In the case of threats, for instance, respondents are asked, "Has anyone threatened to damage things of yours or threatened to use force or violence in any way that - actually frightened you?" In the case of assault, the respondent is asked, "Has anyone, including people you know well, deliberately hit you with their fists or a weapon of any sort, or kicked you or used force or violence in any way?"

More detailed questions are asked about all of the incidents reported in response to the screening questions, including whether they believe that the reported incidents were "racially motivated." Unfortunately, respondents were not asked if they thought incidents occurred because of the victim's sexual orientation, because of his or her religion, or because of a disability that the victim might have. Therefore the analysis here is necessarily confined to incidents that were perceived to be racially motivated.[1]

The majority of incidents reported in the survey are "one-off" events. However, in a substantial minority of cases, respondents reported being victimized more than once. If a respondent reports more than six incidents in the 12 months prior to the interview, and they are different types of incidents, the incidents are prioritized in order, and only the first six in the order of priority are followed up with detailed questions. If a person has experienced the same type of incident more than once, the incidents are classified as a "series." In such cases, detailed questions are asked only about the most recent incident in the series.

It is useful to note some descriptive observations about the reported racially motivated incidents to set the context for the data on the harm of such incidents that follow. Incidents were reported by respondents from each of the minority ethnic groups and the white groups. However, the proportions reported by respondents from the black and Asian minority ethnic groups greatly exceeded the white groups (Table 1.1). Almost 1 in 5 crime incidents reported by Asian or Asian British Bangladeshi respondents, for instance,

Table 1.1 Percentage of Incidents Believed to Be Racially Motivated by Ethnic Group

	Percentage of all incidents believed to be racially motivated	All incidents reported (N)
Mixed: white and black Caribbean	12.2	378
Mixed: white and black African	24.8	141
Mixed: white and Asian	11.1	207
Mixed: any other mixed background	7.9	290
Asian or Asian British: Indian	13.9	1,899
Asian or Asian British: Pakistani	16.7	1,380
Asian or Asian British: Bangladeshi	19.4	360
Asian or Asian British: other Asian background	16.4	567
Black or black British: Caribbean	7.6	1,215
Black or black British: African	13.7	1,056
Black or black British: other black background	12.0	108
Chinese	12.1	257
Other ethnic group	10.2	787
White: British	0.8	52,557
White: Irish	1.5	600
Other white background	3.5	2,161

Source: British Crime Survey 2002–2003, 2003–2004, and 2004–2005. The data from the British Crime Survey reported in this chapter are material from Crown copyright records made available through the Home Office and the UK Data Archive and used by permission of the Controller of Her Majesty's Stationery Office and the Queen's Printer for Scotland. Those who carried out the original analysis and collection of the data bear no responsibility for the further analysis or interpretation provided in this book. The data from this table and the other tables in this chapter were first published in Paul Iganski (2008) *Hate Crime and the City*, Bristol, UK: Policy Press.

Note: The table uses data from variables Ethnic, RaceMot, and NumInc. Numbers of incidents include all "one-off" incidents and up to the first five where there are series of incidents. The data exclude incidents where respondents answered "other," "don't know," or declined to answer.

were believed to be racially motivated, compared with less than 1 in 100 incidents reported by white British respondents.

A prominent criticism of crime victimization surveys is that they provide a static and "decontextualized" picture of crime that conceals the processes behind incidents (cf. Bowling, 1993). The BCS provides just a small insight into the processual dynamics of many racially motivated incidents as the data show that such incidents were more likely, for the minority ethnic and white groups alike, to be part of a series of incidents, compared with those incidents that were not believed to be racially motivated (Table 1.2). The extent of repeat victimization was slightly greater for the minority ethnic groups

Table 1.2   Percentage of Reported Incidents that Were the Most Recent in a Series of Incidents: Racially Motivated Compared with Non–Racially Motivated Incidents

	Racially motivated		Non–racially motivated	
	Series (%)	All incidents (N)	Series (%)	All incidents (N)
Mixed: white and black Caribbean	45.5*	22	20.2	247
Mixed: white and black African	53.3**	15	16.9	83
Mixed: white and Asian	41.7*	12	13.4	149
Mixed: any other mixed background	30.8	13	23.5	179
Asian or Asian British: Indian	31.9***	160	15.5	1,298
Asian or Asian British: Pakistani	35.6***	132	17.5	868
Asian or Asian British: Bangladeshi	28.9	45	17.1	222
Asian or Asian British: other Asian background	30.9**	55	13.5	392
Black or black British: Caribbean	27.6*	58	16.4	884
Black or black British: African	28.9***	97	13.3	753
Black or black British: other black background	0.0	13	13.3***	75
Chinese	31.3	16	12.4	185
Other ethnic group	21.4	56	12.7	575
White: British/Irish/other white background	28.8***	302	17.5	41,320

Source: British Crime Survey 2002–2003, 2003–2004, and 2004–2005.

Note: The table uses data from variables Ethnic, RaceMot, and Pincid. The data exclude incidents where respondents answered "other," "don't know," or declined to answer.

*p < .05; **p < .01; ***p < .001.

combined compared with whites for both racially motivated and non–racially motivated incidents.

It is notable that statistically significant higher proportions of minority ethnic and white victims of incidents they believed to be racially motivated, compared with victims of non–racially motivated crimes, reported that they had "started to avoid walking in/going to certain places," and higher proportions of victims of racially motivated crime reported having moved home (Table 1.3).

The data are limited, however, with respect to evaluating the greater harm inflicted by hate crime. As they concern the reactions of individual victims of crime, they do not provide an indication of any wider behavioral impact, or the "ripple effect" (Noelle, 2002) of incidents beyond the initial victim. Furthermore, as the noted behavioral changes were reported by only a small minority of victims of racially motivated incidents, they undermine the justification for hate crime laws on the basis of the greater harm inflicted, as almost half of respondents reported no behavioral harm.

THE EMOTIONAL HARM INFLICTED BY HATE CRIME

Much more compelling evidence of the greater harm inflicted by hate crime compared with parallel crimes is apparent in the case of psychological and emotional harm. Assertions that such harm occurs have also been evident in the policy literature on racist violence in the United Kingdom. For instance, the 1989 Home Office report *The Response to Racial Attacks and Harassment* states,

> Take, for example, the family which is racially harassed by neighbours on a local authority housing estate. The mental and physical health of the family members may suffer; the children's physical and social development may be affected if they cannot be allowed outside to play; and older children may under-perform at school because of stress at home, or they may miss school altogether because their parents keep them at home or move house to avoid the problem. Such a family may need support and practical help from the housing department, the police, community groups, the local tenants' association, the children's school, doctors and social workers. (U.K. Home Office, 1989, para. 185)

In support of such observations, a substantial body of research from the United States has been published over the last two decades. The early research on the psychological and emotional impact of hate crimes indicated the effects on individual victims, but due to the design of the research and the nature of the samples of respondents involved, the findings were equivocal on the question of whether hate crimes hurt more than parallel crimes. For

Table 1.3   Reported Behavioral Reactions Following Racially Motivated and Non–Racially Motivated Crime

	Minority ethnic groups		White groups	
	Racially motivated (%)	Non–racially motivated (%)	Racially motivated (%)	Non–racially motivated (%)
Types of action taken after incidents				
Improved home security	5.6	10.7***	6.1	11.5***
Improved vehicle security	3.4	7.0***	0.7	5.7***
Started carrying personal security devices	2.0**	0.5	1.0	0.3
Started to avoid walking in/going to certain places	13.4***	2.6	15.3***	2.7
Started to avoid parking in certain places	5.5	6.8	3.4	6.0**
Moved house/flat	3.8**	1.6	5.4**	1.5
Changed jobs	1.1*	0.4	1.4	0.3
Tried to be more alert/not so trusting of people	17.3***	12.0	11.5**	8.2
Make sure valuables are always secure/locked away	2.7	13.4***	1.7	11.0***
No longer carry valuables/money when out	1.1	2.5***	0.7	1.4
Make sure valuables/money are secure when going out	0.8	6.0***	1.0	4.2***
None of these	45.0*	41.0	45.1	41.0
Number of incidents (N)	655	5,607	295	39,368

Source: British Crime Survey (BCS) 2002–2003, 2003–2004, and 2004–2005.

Note: The table uses data from variables TryPreA–TryPreP from the 2002–2003 BCS and TryPre2A–TryPre2R from the 2003–2004 and 2004–2005 BCS. Data are for incidents that occurred in England and Wales and exclude incidents where respondents answered "other," "don't know," or declined to answer.

*$p < .05$; **$p < .01$; ***$p < .001$.

instance, from a small purposive sample of hate crime victims, Barnes and Ephross (1994) reported feelings of anger, fear, sadness, powerlessness, suspicion of others, and bad feelings about themselves. But they also observed that "to some extent the predominant emotional responses of hate violence victims appear similar to those of victims of other types of personal crime"

(p. 250). But in the absence of a comparison group of parallel crimes, it was not possible to determine whether the psychological harm experienced by hate crime victims in the sample is indeed the same or worse than others. The absence of a comparison group of victims of parallel crimes affected the findings of subsequent research that further illuminated the emotional harm experienced by hate crime victims (cf. Hershberger & D'Augelli, 1995; Otis & Skinner, 1996). But more recently, Herek, Gillis, and Cogan (1999) compared a purposive sample of lesbians and gay men who had been victims of hate crime in the last five years ($n = 69$) with a sample ($n = 100$) who had been victimized on other grounds than their sexual orientation. They observed that the hate crime victims recorded statistically significant higher scores on measures of depression, traumatic stress, and anger. However, while their data revealed that *on average*, victims of hate crimes suffered more emotional harm, the evident variation in the scores indicated that not all victims experienced harm to the same extent, and potentially, that some victims of parallel crimes suffered greater emotional harm than some victims of hate crimes.

Arguably, one of the most comprehensive studies to date on the psychological harm of hate crime was conducted by McDevitt, Balboni, Garcia, and Gu (2001) and involved a mail survey of a purposive sample of victims of assaults reported to the Boston Police Department and victim advocacy agencies for the years 1992–1997. The survey included victims of both hate crime and parallel crimes. The survey questionnaire was designed to measure the psychological postvictimization impact of "intrusiveness" and "avoidance" reactions, according to Horowitz's Psychological Scale, utilizing a 19-item scale. Six of the items presented statistically significant differences between victims of hate crime and victims of parallel crimes, with the former reporting stronger reactions on measures of depression, nervousness, lack of concentration, unintentional thinking of the incident, and thoughts of futility regarding their lives (McDevitt et al., 2001).

The research clearly demonstrated the psychologically intrusive nature of hate crime and indicated the victims' struggles postvictimization. While the use of a control group of assault victims in parallel crimes was an advance on much of the earlier research, the design of the study had some limitations, as McDevitt and colleagues (2001) acknowledged. It is instructive, therefore, to turn to the BCS on the matter. Respondents were asked whether they had an "emotional reaction" following an incident. For each of the major types of crime reported, it is notable that higher proportions of victims who believed that incidents were racially motivated reported an emotional reaction compared with incidents that were not believed to be racially motivated (Table 1.4).

The pattern of greater harm holds when the black and Asian minority ethnic groups combined and the white groups combined are examined as two

Table 1.4   Percentage of Respondents Reporting Emotional Reactions After Incidents by Offence Type: Racially Motivated Compared with Non–Racially Motivated Incidents, Minority Ethnic Groups and White Groups Combined

Type of crime (Home Office code)	Racially motivated incidents		Non–racially motivated incidents	
	%	N	%	N
Assault and attempted assault	92.4*	262	86.8	3,717
Robbery and theft from person	91.8	49	88.7	2,264
Burglary and attempted burglary	97.3***	37	84.3	6,267
Theft and attempted theft	91.9***	74	82.8	17,892
Criminal damage	93.9***	228	86.6	11,481
Threats	91.2*	294	88.0	3,343

Source: British Crime Survey 2002–2003, 2003–2004, and 2004–2005.

Note: The table uses data from variables Ethnic, RaceMot, EmotReac, and Offence (re-coded). The data exclude incidents where respondents answered "other," "don't know," or declined to answer.

$^{*}p < .05;\ ^{**}p < .01;\ ^{***}p < .001.$

separate groups of victims, with stronger emotional reactions consistently reported for racially motivated incidents (Table 1.5).

Additional variables in the survey further reveal the greater mental impacts of race-hate crime compared with parallel crime. Statistically significant higher proportions of victims in incidents that were believed to be racially motivated, compared with other crimes, reported feelings of shock, fear, depression, anxiety, and panic attacks; feelings of a loss of confidence and of vulnerability; difficulty sleeping; and crying (Table 1.6).

It is notable that feelings of "fear" manifest the highest differential in the types of emotional reactions reported. It is instructive to observe, therefore, that for each major category of crime, higher proportions of victims of racially motivated crime, compared with victims of non–racially motivated crime, reported being "worried" or "very worried" about future victimization (Table 1.7). (Worry about rape provides the only exception to the trend, as equal proportions of minority ethnic respondents were worried about future victimization, irrespective of whether or not they were victims of racially motivated crime.)

In the case of victims of non–racially motivated crime, it is also notable that the same pattern applies: for each major crime type, higher proportions

**Table 1.5   Respondents Reporting Being Affected "Very Much":
Racially Motivated Compared with Non–Racially Motivated Incidents**

	Minority ethnic groups		Whites	
	Racially motivated (%, N)	Non–racially motivated (%, N)	Racially motivated (%, N)	Non–racially motivated (%, N)
Assault/attempted assault	51.8 (164)	44.8 (328)	41.0* (78)	29.4 (2,896)
Robbery/snatch theft/ theft from person	59.3** (27)	36 (456)	38.9 (18)	23.2 (1,551)
Burglary/attempted burglary/theft in dwelling	88.5*** (26)	37.4 (685)	90.0*** (10)	27.3 (4,595)
Theft/attempted theft	50.9*** (53)	24.2 (2,090)	53.3** (15)	17.5 (12,711)
Criminal damage	56.2*** (169)	22.8 (1,004)	34.1* (44)	17.9 (8,939)
Threats	40.1 (172)	35.9 (262)	29.2 (96)	23.7 (2,674)

Source: British Crime Survey 2002–2003, 2003–2004, and 2004–2005.

Note: The table uses data from variables Ethnic, RaceMot, HowAff1, and Offence (re-coded). The data exclude incidents where respondents answered "other," "don't know," or declined to answer.

$^*p < .05$; $^{**}p < .01$; $^{***}p < .001$.

**Table 1.6   Types of Emotional Reaction Reported Following Racially
Motivated and Non–Racially Motivated Crime**

	Minority ethnic groups		White groups	
	Racially motivated (%)	Non–racially motivated (%)	Racially motivated (%)	Non–racially motivated (%)
Types of emotional reaction				
Anger	66.1	64.7	67.9**	62.9
Shock	46.4***	35.5	41.5***	24.2
Fear	38.9***	17.0	32.8***	12.0
Depression	20.7***	10.1	14.3***	6.3
Anxiety/panic attacks	16.8***	7.8	14.7***	6.1
Loss of confidence/ feeling vulnerable	32.9***	17.4	32.1***	14.5
Difficulty sleeping	19.2***	10.2	16.2***	8.6

Table 1.6 Types of Emotional Reaction Reported Following Racially Motivated and Non–Racially Motivated Crime (*continued*)

	Minority ethnic groups		White groups	
	Racially motivated (%)	Non–racially motivated (%)	Racially motivated (%)	Non–racially motivated (%)
Crying/tears	13.5***	8.4	12.8**	7.8
Annoyance	42.8	49.8***	49.4	58.6**
Number of incidents (N)	614	4,861	265	33,560

Source: British Crime Survey 2002–2003, 2003–2004, and 2004–2005.

Note: The table uses data from variables WhEmotA–WhEmotL. The data are for incidents in which respondents reported experiencing an emotional reaction. They exclude incidents where respondents answered "other," "don't know," or declined to answer.

*p < .01; **p < .001.

Table 1.7 Worries About Future Crime Victimization: A Comparison of Victims of Racially Motivated and Non–Racially Motivated Crime

	Minority ethnic groups		White groups	
Worry about . . .	Racially motivated (%, N)	Non–racially motivated (%, N)	Racially motivated (%, N)	Non–racially motivated (%, N)
Burglary	69.7 (535[a])	65.4 (3,990)	62.1 (227)	55.4 (27,050)
Mugging	62.2 (535)	58.3 (3,983)	55.9 (227)	40.8 (27,022)
Car theft	66.8 (367)	64.5 (2,993)	63.3 (147)	54.8 (21,613)
Theft from car	69.5 (367)	66.2 (2,986)	59.2 (147)	53.9 (21,580)
Rape	41.6 (461)	41.6 (3,983)	38.0 (208)	27.1 (24,603)
Physical attack	69.9 (535)	56.1 (3,983)	55.5 (227)	40.6 (27,016)
Insult	69.3 (536)	49.1 (3,986)	49.8 (227)	34.4 (26,995)
Racial attack	71.6 (535)	43.3 (3,974)	43.1 (197)	11.0 (22,249)

Source: British Crime Survey 2002–2003, 2003–2004, and 2004–2005.

Note: The table uses data from variables WBurgl, WMugged, WCarStol, WFromCar, WRaped, WAttack, WInsult, and WRaceAtt. The data exclude incidents where respondents answered "don't know" or declined to answer.

[a]Number of respondents. *p < .05; **p < .01; ***p < .001.

of minority ethnic respondents reported worries about future victimization compared with white respondents (Table 1.7). The greatest differentials between minority ethnic and white victims, and between victims of racially motivated and non–racially motivated crime, are evident in the case of worry about physical attack, insults, and racial attack.

CONCLUSION: HURTS CAUSED BY OFFENDERS' EXPRESSED VALUES

Could it be that it is the values expressed by offenders that account for the more severe psychological and emotional impacts of hate crime revealed by the BCS? Frederick Lawrence (2006), author of the book *Punishing Hate*, argued in a recent paper that victims of race-hate crime experience attacks as a form of racial stigmatization and that an incident "carries with it the clear message that the target and his [or her] group are of marginal value" (p. 3). The idea clearly proposed by Lawrence is that it is the message conveyed by the offender that inflicts the psychological and emotional damage: in short, it is the offender's expressed values that hurt. From this perspective, the emotional harm experienced by a hate crime victim arguably occurs as a consequence of the victim's aversion to the attacker's animus toward their group identity. In essence, it is the values of the attacker—painfully evident in his or her actions—striking at the core of the victim's identity, that hurt more.

NOTES

This chapter is adapted from P. Iganski, *Hate Crime and the City* (Bristol, UK: Policy Press, 2008).

1. The British Crime Survey (BCS) has included a question since 2005/2006 on whether victims of crime thought the incident was religiously motivated. A question was also introduced on an experimental basis in the 2007/2008 BCS to ask whether crimes were perceived to be motivated on account of the victim's sexual orientation, disability, or age. To date, however, there are insufficient sweeps of the BCS with these questions included to enable a robust analysis.

REFERENCES

Barnes, A., & Ephross, P. H. (1994). The impact of hate violence on victims—emotional and behavioural responses to attacks. *Social Work, 39*, 247–251.

Bowling, B. (1993). Racial harassment and the process of victimisation: Conceptual and methodological implications for the local crime survey. *British Journal of Criminology, 33*, 231–250.

Bruce, T. (2001). *The new thought police.* New York: Three Rivers Press.

Gey, S. G. (1997). What if Wisconsin v. Mitchell had involved Martin Luther King Jnr? The constitutional flaws of hate crime enhancement statutes. *George Washington Law Review, 65*, 1014–1070.

Gordon, P. (1994). Racist harassment and violence. In E. A. Stanko (Ed.), *Perspectives on violence* (pp. 46–53). London: Quartet.

Herek, G. M., Gillis, J. R., & Cogan, J. C. (1999). Psychological sequelae of hate-crime victimization among lesbian, gay, and bisexual adults. *Journal of Consulting and Clinical Psychology, 67,* 945–951.

Hershberger, S. L., & D'Augelli, A. R. (1995). The impact of victimization on the mental health and suicidality of lesbian, gay, and bisexual youth. *Developmental Psychology, 31,* 65–74.

Horowitz, M. J., Wilner, N. R., & Alvarez, W. (1979). Impact of Event Scale: A measure of subjective stress. *Psychosomatic Medicine, 41,* 209–218.

Hurd, H. (2001). Why liberals should hate "hate crime legislation." *Law and Philosophy, 20,* 215–232.

Iganski, P. (2001). Hate crimes hurt more. *American Behavioral Scientist, 45,* 626–638.

Lawrence, F. M. (1999). *Punishing hate: Bias crimes under American law.* Cambridge, MA: Harvard University Press.

Lawrence, F. M. (2006). *The hate crime project and its limitations: Evaluating the societal gains and risk in bias crime law enforcement* (Working Paper No. 216). Washington, DC: George Washington University Law School.

Levin, B. (1999). Hate crimes: Worse by definition. *Journal of Contemporary Criminal Justice, 15,* 6–21.

McDevitt, J., Balboni, J., Garcia, L., & Gu, J. (2001). Consequences for victims: A comparison of bias and non-bias motivated assaults. *American Behavioral Scientist, 45,* 697–713.

Noelle, M. (2002). The ripple effect of the Matthew Shepherd murder: Impact on the assumptive worlds of members of the targeted group. *American Behavioral Scientist, 46*(1), 27–50.

Otis, M. D., & Skinner, W. F. (1996). The prevalence of victimization and its effect on mental well-being among lesbian and gay people. *Journal of Homosexuality, 30,* 93–122.

Rai, D. K., & Hesse, B. (1992). Racial victimization: An experiential analysis. In B. Hesse, D. K. Rai, C. Bennett, & P. McGilchrist (Eds.), *Beneath the surface: Racial harassment* (pp. 158–195). Aldershot, England: Avebury.

U.K. Home Office. (1989). *The response to racial attacks and harassment: Guidance for statutory agencies.* Report of the Inter-Departmental Racial Attacks Group. London: Home Office.

Weinstein, J. (1992). First Amendment challenges to hate crime legislation: Where's the speech? *Criminal Justice Ethics, 11,* 6–20.

Wisconsin v. Mitchell, 113 S. Ct. 2201 (1993).

CHAPTER 2

THE PSYCHOLOGICAL HARMS OF HATE: IMPLICATIONS AND INTERVENTIONS

Kellina M. Craig-Henderson

Intergroup and interpersonal conflicts have a long history of occurrence throughout the world and within the United States (Levin, 2002). In the United States, when these conflicts are instigated by bigotry and involve illegal behaviors, they are called *hate crimes*. Hate crime is defined in the 1994 Crime Act as crimes in which a perpetrator intentionally selects a victim because of his or her actual or perceived race, color, gender, disability, national origin, or sexual orientation (Gondles, 1999).

The Federal Bureau of Investigation (FBI; 2006) of the U.S. Department of Justice (DOJ) reported that 7,163 hate crimes occurred in 2005.[1] Of these incidents, by far the greatest proportion of them were instigated by racial animus (3,919), and more than one-third (37%) of these incidents were directed at blacks. Racial and ethnic biases are among the most frequent motives for hate crime (Garofalo, 1997).

As further evidence of this, since the 9/11 attacks in the United States, and in the context of the continuing war in Iraq, the Civil Rights Division of the DOJ reports an increase in the number of hate crimes targeting people who are perceived to be Arab, Muslim, or Middle Eastern. Furthermore, there were numerous examples of incidents driven by anti-Arab motives during the Gulf War (Kleinfield, 1992), and some attribute current anti-Arab sentiment to the ongoing war in Iraq.

Although the Bureau of Justice Statistics data are limited to hate-motivated incidents targeting individuals, groups, and property because of race, ethnicity, religion, sexual orientation, gender, and physical or mental disability status, victims of hate crime can also include the homeless, migrant workers, immigrants, and refugees. Victims can span the gamut and have little in common with one another other than the misfortune of having elicited a perpetrator's extreme bias.

Hate crimes are both a national and a global problem and represent a distinct form of interpersonal and intergroup aggression. Although intergroup violence has a long history in the United States, it is only within the last two decades that the label hate crime has been applied to these particular acts of intergroup aggression and violence (Jenness & Broad, 1997; Levin & McDevitt, 1993). Public attention that galvanized legislators' concerns focused on two of the more egregious hate crimes involving the slaying of an African American man in Texas and a gay youth in Wyoming.[2]

Not all people who have been targeted by bias are actual victims of crime.[3] Indeed, no matter how offensive the incident may be, if it does not reach the level of illegality, it is not recorded or reported as a hate crime (Wallace, 1999). Thus it can be argued that the numbers of hate crimes and victims appearing in uniform crime reports are conservative relative to the numbers of bias incidents that actually occur. Most advocacy groups report that hate-motivated incidents are on the rise (e.g., Anti-Defamation League, 2002; National Gay and Lesbian Task Force, 2003; Moser, 2004). Furthermore, international organizations that monitor incidents such as hate crimes throughout the world overwhelmingly suggest an increase in activity (e.g., Amnesty International, 2004; Human Rights Watch, 2004).

Most forecasts portend the continuance of hate crime activity and note that these incidents correspond to changes in demographic, political, and economic events domestically and abroad (Herek & Berrill, 1992; Levin & McDevitt, 1993). Consequently, mental health professionals and others who provide services to crime victims (e.g., social workers, first responders) will be increasingly likely to encounter people who are targeted because of an ascribed status characteristic (e.g., race, nationality, or sexual orientation). As such, they must be especially sensitive to the distinctive aspects of this form of victimization.

This chapter describes the psychological impact of hate crime victimization. It draws largely from the criminal justice and social work literatures as well as from the important perspectives of social and clinical psychology that address the problem of intergroup violence and victimization in general. Suggestions are also provided for those most likely to encounter and interact with victims of hate crime. Researchers who study hate crimes have suggested a variety of negative consequences for communities that experience hate crime, including an increase in suspicion and fear, a decline in the quality of intergroup relationships, and the increased potential for retaliatory intergroup aggression (Craig, 1999; Garofalo, 1997; Sanchez & Castenada, 1994). Because researchers and legislators alike predict an increase in the possibility of widespread community unrest following a hate crime (e.g., Wisconsin v. Mitchell, 1993), a brief discussion of community-level strategies aimed at preventing subsequent unrest in the wake of a hate crime is also included.

CRIME VICTIMS AND OFFENDERS

In general, victims of crime can incur a number of different "costs" following a victimization experience that involve physical, financial, and psychological liabilities (Craig-Henderson & Sloan, 2003; Janoff-Bulman & Frieze, 1983). At the time of the crime, the most obvious cost is that which is associated with the victim's actual physical well-being. Victims of assault will suffer greater risk of physical injury than will victims of property crime (e.g., burglary).

Hate crime offenders are distinguished from perpetrators of nonbias crime in a number of important ways. Sociologists Levin and McDevitt (1993) have offered a profile of the typical hate crime offender. Their compilation has been adopted by the Cook County State's Attorney's Office (1994), which states in their prosecutorial guide to hate crime that the "typical offender matches the following profile: male, between the ages of 14 and 24, with no prior record, neither impoverished nor chronically unemployed" (p. II-5). According to Levin and McDevitt (1993), most perpetrators, who are often juveniles, are otherwise not involved in the criminal justice system.

That most descriptions of hate crime offenders indicate that they are young, male, and tend to perpetrate offenses in groups, rather than alone, suggests that it is more likely that when the hate crime involves a physical assault, it is especially brutal. Some of the more recent well-known and publicized hate crimes reflect greater brutality than nonbias assaults. Although the focus throughout this discussion is on the psychological impact of hate crime victimization, it is important to note that physical costs may be severe and, in the extreme, can result in the victim's death.

In addition to any injury sustained, the victim of a physical or threatening assault is likely to undergo a number of bodily reactions, which "may include increased heart rate, hyperventilation, shaking, tears, numbness, a feeling of being frozen or experiencing events in slow motion, dryness of the mouth, enhancement of particular senses such as smell, and a 'fight or flight' response" (United Nations Office for Drug and Crime Prevention, 1999, p. 4). These physiological responses can inhibit rational decision making or accurate recall following the incident. First responders who interact with hate crime victims should not only be aware of this, but should engage victims in ways that ensure that they understand questions they are being asked to answer.

Beyond the physical bodily reactions, victims of crime experience a disruption of normal life and the activities associated with their daily routine. In many ways, this disruption constitutes a life crisis for them (Sales, Baum, & Shore, 1984). The theoretical approach known as *crisis theory* provides a useful way of understanding the "postcrisis" period for victims of crime. The theory predicts the initial experience of an intense immediate affective reaction to an extreme negative stressor like criminal victimization. This is followed by a gradual decrease in symptoms and a return to the victim's normative state before the victimization. The utility of this theory lies in its ability to separate healthy functioning in response to the victimization from those whose reactions are characteristic of enduring psychopathologies or illnesses present before the incident occurred (Rapoport, 1965; Sales et al., 1984).

When criminal victimization occurs, its impact is initially so profound as to alter the victim's sense of reality. Presumably, there is nothing in their experience or skill set that can prepare them for this traumatic event. Their "equilibrium" (i.e., sense of physical and psychological well-being) is altered. The victim responds to this state of affairs with an almost immediate suspension of his or her ordinary, characteristic way of behaving. The onset of this state of crisis is rapid and intense (Bloom, 1963).

To experience a "crisis" is to experience a number of intense, overwhelming emotions simultaneously over a period of time or, in some cases, as intermittent disruptive experiences. Although the details and context in which the incident occurred differ for victims, it is generally assumed among those who counsel victims that most will experience a common series of emotional reactions (e.g., Kubler-Ross, 1969). In fact, it is fair to say that reactions to highly stressful events like criminal victimization are relatively predictable (Sales et al., 1984; Wiseman, 1975). Generally, the crisis experience is assumed to progress through at least three stages. In stage 1, the crisis is acute, and the victim's immediate reaction is one of denial. A sense of disbelief that this is really happening characterizes this stage. The second stage occurring in the wake of the acute experience can take place as early as 24 hours after the incident to as late as six months or a year afterward. During this time, the victim experiences a series of different emotions, including fear, anger, shame, guilt, and frustration, at different times. At one point, the victims may blame themselves for the incident that has befallen them, and moments later, they may suddenly find themselves raging against the perpetrator and the violation dealt them. In the final stage of "reintegration," the victim resumes his or her normal life. The memories of the incident cease to intrude as frequently or as intensely. This stage can also vary in terms of when it occurs: as early as a week after the initial incident to as much as a year later (Office for Victims of Crime, 2000).

According to Bard and Sangrey, authors of *The Crime Victim's Book*, "there is nothing more isolating than the pain of violation" (as cited in Office for Victims of Crime, 2000). Unfortunately, most mental health practitioners and counselors do not receive substantial training in victimization issues. While the topic is addressed briefly in counseling curricula, rarely are mental health and victim service providers well trained in crisis intervention techniques. A report commissioned by the American Psychological Association Task Force on the Victims of Crime and Violence and chaired by the first author of *The Crime Victim's Book* offered several recommendations regarding psychologists' involvement in service delivery to victims of crime. The recommendations included greater involvement of psychologists in the criminal justice system, more specialized training and collaboration with victim services agencies, and active endorsement of legal issues supporting victims' rights.

HATE CRIME VICTIMIZATION

In 1993, the U.S. Supreme Court justice Rehnquist drafted an opinion that would impact the sentencing of subsequently convicted hate crime offenders. In deciding whether the First Amendment rights of a perpetrator had been violated, the justice ruled that hate crimes were distinct in their effects. According to the justice, hate crimes were far worse than similarly egregious crimes. The justice's rationale was based in part on the belief that hate crime breeds retaliation, particularly in the wake of a highly publicized incident. The norm of reciprocity provides a convenient way of considering such motives. According to this, much of human behavior is governed in a quid pro quo manner; that is, people respond to others in ways and to a degree that resembles the other person's initial response (Gouldner, 1960). Research suggests that the recipient of a harmful act tends to respond to its provider with a harm that is comparable in both quantity and quality (Youngs, 1986). This possibility was investigated in an experimental study (Craig, 1999), and the findings, though mixed, suggest that retaliatory efforts will differ according to the victim's specific social group. Thus, whether retaliation is likely following a hate crime seems to depend largely on the group to which the victim belongs. In the case of racist hate crimes, Garofalo (1997) presents evidence of reciprocity between African American and white perpetrators and victims. There may be a greater willingness for retaliation between these two groups than among other groups.

Much of the existing research examining effects of hate crime victimization has been limited to examinations of the postvictimization experiences of victims of antigay crimes and wartime genocide (Chalk & Jonassohn, 1990; Herek & Berrill, 1992; Herek, Gillis, Cogan, & Glunt, 1997; Noelle, 2002). For example, in the case of the antigay criminal victimization, Herek and colleagues (1997) demonstrated that victims of hate crime experience long-term posttraumatic stress disorder (PTSD) symptoms. Results of an interview study including 147 gays, lesbians, and bisexuals revealed higher levels of depression, anxiety, and anger among those who were targeted because of their sexual orientation than among those who were not. Herek and colleagues also found that the hate crime victims needed almost twice as much time to overcome the effects of their experiences compared to those who were victims of nonbias crime, and in some cases, this amounted to as much as five years.

As further evidence of the debilitating effects of antigay hate crime victimization, Ehrlich (1992) reported results of a study in which he compared the victimization experiences of hate crime victims to victims of other types of crimes. As was the case in Herek and colleagues' (1997) research, the findings suggest that victims of hate crimes generally suffer more traumatic effects following victimization than do victims of other crimes involving assault. Thus the hate crime in which the victim sustains a broken collarbone is worse than a mugging resulting in the same type of injury because in the former case, the victim knows that they were assaulted precisely because of their perceived membership in a particular social group.

Additional research by Garofalo (1997) has examined the postvictimization experiences of victims of other forms of hate crime. That study, conducted in New York City and Baltimore County during the 1980s, involved a small telephone survey of victims of bias and nonbias crimes. According to Garofalo (1997), "some clear patterns of differential effects emerged" (p. 141). Results of a comparison of 30 bias crime victims to 28 comparison crime victims revealed that the hate crime victims were more likely to rate their crimes as "very serious"; to report being "frightened" and "very upset," rather than "angry or mad," after the incident; and to say that the incident had a "great deal" of effect on their lives in the short and long term.

The National Center for Victims of Crime (2008) notes that the postvictimization experience for hate crime victims may be particularly debilitating. In one report currently available on line, they wrote,

> A sense of anger is one of the common responses to being a victim of a hate crime, but so is a deep sense of personal hurt and betrayal. Victims experience feelings of powerlessness, isolation, sadness and suspicion. Fear is another pervasive victim response.

PSYCHOLOGICAL IMPACTS

Whereas only some forms of victimization involve physical or financial losses, almost all victimization experiences will entail psychological costs. This is certainly the case for hate crime victims. One of the primary goals of the present discussion is to examine the psychological costs incurred by victims of hate crimes. Research on the experience of victimization reveals that although all victims will perceive the experience to be negative, there is considerable variability in the psychological resources victims are able to muster in response to the victimization (Norris, Kaniasty, & Thompson, 1997). Criminal victimization is "taxing" for all victims, and people differ in their psychological responses to the experience, and this has direct implications for their ability to cope with the effects of the crime (Lazarus & Folkman, 1984). Although it is recognized that the postvictimization experience will differ according to whether the victim was targeted because of their race, ethnicity, sexual orientation, or other social group status, page constraints prohibit consideration of the specific differences in postvictimization experience across the different types of hate crime victims.

When victims are unable to manage the stress of their experience, they develop clinical symptoms. Findings from research reviewed previously, examining the effects of hate crime victimization, underscore the likelihood of this type of outcome. Because of the volume of research examining the postvictimization experience of victims of rape, it is useful to refer to that literature at this point. In their study of rape victims, Sales and colleagues (1984) note that long-term healthy functioning in the wake of a rape is evident in the victim's return to her previous level of function involving social activities and interpersonal involvement. Somewhat paradoxically, however, they suggest that this "normal" response may be at the expense of symptom elevation; that is, although the victim may appear to have achieved behavioral "normalization" and function, there is evidence of continued emotional distress.

Extended Emotional Distress

In the case of hate crime victims, although they may return to their normal routine after enough time has passed, they may be especially likely to continue to ruminate about the incident. This is because hate crimes, unlike other similarly egregious offenses, are perpetrated because victims of hate crimes are almost always members of negatively stereotyped or stigmatized social groups. The stereotypes associated with these groups are pervasive and resistant to change. Many victims of hate crime are familiar with the more commonly experienced daily acts of discrimination that occur in a variety of areas including, though not limited to, housing, the criminal justice system, and employment. Thus, for some victims, the experience of hate crime victimization is likely to compound the alienation that their stigmatized status chronically affords them. An assault on a salient part of their identity and one over which they have no control resonates deeply with their identity as a member of an out-group; their ideas about self and community; and their feelings of security.

Shattering of Assumptions

When a hate crime occurs, its target must find a way to understand his or her vulnerability and come to terms with the reality of having been victimized. This is somewhat "contrainstinctual," given that it contradicts the "illusion of invulnerability," which operates in most people's self-concept.

A long-standing tenet in social psychology, the illusion of invulnerability involves people's day-to-day belief that "it can't happen to me" (Weinstein & Lachendro, 1982). The illusion of invulnerability rests on our assumptions about the world as an orderly and predictable place. To make sense out of the events that happen, it helps to create personal theories that provide prediction and control, and the illusion of invulnerability aids us in dong this. For example, we believe we can avoid certain misfortunes that befall others by exercising greater caution and can take heart in believing that people get what they deserve. In a similar vein, Lerner's (1970) *just world theory* holds that one of the social laws most people endorse is that the world is a just place; bad things happen to bad people, and good things happen to those who are good.

The illusion of invulnerability is shattered and the corresponding belief in a just world is compromised when an individual experiences a hate crime. The world as they know it no longer makes sense; their experience just doesn't fit with their vision of the universe (e.g., "people don't get attacked because their skin color is different, but I did!"). The resulting experience and shift in identity is characterized by a sense of vulnerability and search for meaning. Not only are victims fearful and anxious, but they also lack any comprehension for their misfortune. This loss of comprehension is particularly likely for victims who regard themselves as practical, decent individuals who take care of themselves. According to researchers Janoff-Bulman and Frieze (1983), along with a shattering of these basic assumptions about invulnerability and a just world, criminal victimization (as in a case of hate crime) is apt to dislodge another assumption that operates as a core postulate within individuals' conceptual systems. Most healthy people maintain a relatively high regard for themselves. Victimization leads to serious questioning of these positive self-perceptions. Victims generally see themselves as weak and ineffective, and they may feel particularly powerless. Early work on crime victims has noted that feelings of powerlessness are typical following victimization, as the victim wrestles with the fact of having been singled out for misfortune (Peterson & Seligman, 1983). Victims are left with a less than positive image of themselves.

Feelings of Deviancy

In the wake of a hate crime, victims' views of themselves are especially likely to be deflated relative to their esteem before victimization. Not only is the hate crime victim likely to feel powerless in the wake of the incident, but because they know that they have been deliberately singled out, they are apt to experience a sense of deviance. Their misfortune establishes them as different from others, and this self-perception of deviance contributes to a negative self-image. Whereas victims of other types of crime are encouraged to take comfort in knowing that what happened to them could have happened to anyone, victims of hate crimes recognize that what happened to them could have happened only because of their distinctive feature or social status (e.g., skin color, religion, sexual orientation). Following the initial shock period, as hate crime victims come to terms with their experience, they begin to absorb the full reality of what has actually happened to them. This means recognizing and understanding that they were victimized because of a distinctive status characteristic (e.g., their ethnicity or sexual orientation).

Errors in Attribution

Research on attributional processes and biases predicts additional psychological effects for victims of hate crime. Attributions represent the explanations people hold for the causes of events. Rarely are these explanations exact representations of reality. Instead, they are determined by the experiences, expectancies, and biases of the individual and vary between individuals. An attributional analysis can shed light on the specific way that the hate crime victim reconciles his or her experience in deciding on its causes. For example, according to the theoretical perspective known as the ultimate attribution error, people attribute socially undesirable actions of out-group members to internal factors such as motives or dispositions (Pettigrew, 1979). Victims of hate crimes may be especially likely to make these types of attribution about the behaviors of others. To the extent that this error in information processing occurs with the victim, he or she will perceive harmful intent on the part of others who merely resemble the perpetrators because of shared group membership, and the individual will believe that victimization is especially likely for any other person who is a member of his or her group (Craig-Henderson & Sloan, 2003).

Another error that often occurs in the attributional process and that would seem to have some relevance for hate crime victims is the fundamental attribution error (Ross, 1977). This involves the individual's tendency to attribute causality to dispositional factors (i.e., internal causes), rather than situational causes. In the context of a hate crime, the individual is beset with a compelling need to explain his or her own victimization (i.e., "why was I targeted?"). The fundamental attribution error occurs when the victim attributes their victimization to some specific detail they associate with themselves, rather than is really the case, to the antisocial penchant of the offender. The cause for the victimization lies with factors outside of the victim, and an accurate attributional analysis attributes the victimization to factors outside of the individual and out of his or her control.

Effects on the Victim's In-group

Importantly, the psychological effects of hate crime victimization extend well beyond the immediate victim. This aspect of the hate crime is what makes it so problematic for people who are in no way involved in the incident and who are unacquainted with the victim, but who happen to share membership in the social group that was targeted (i.e., victim's in-group). Members of the victim's in-group who hear about the incident and learn that the victim was targeted because of his or her membership in a shared social group are likely to experience any number of negative reactions, including fear, anger, and despair. What's more, a hate crime targeting a member of an individual's in-group reminds them that they could be next. For example, findings from a small study of gay and bisexual respondents in the wake of Matthew Shepard's murder reveal a "vicarious traumatization effect." According to Noelle (2002), the brutal antigay assault and murder evoked particular concerns among the respondents who, because of their status as sexual minorities, identified most strongly. Indeed, the researcher concluded that the assault challenged the respondents' worldviews concerning benevolence, justice, and their place in the world.

IMPLICATIONS AND INTERVENTIONS

Following the hate crime, victims have psychological, physical, and legal needs. Informal, formal, and legal remedies can address many of these needs. This final section outlines several strategies that can assist victims, mental health service providers, and first responders in addressing the needs of victims of hate crime. These strategies are based on the recommendations of governmental agencies, community advocacy groups, and existing research in the area (e.g., Coates & Winston, 1983; Frieze, Hymer, & Greenberg, 1987; Taylor, 1983; Umbreit & Coates, 2000).

A common response among victims is to turn to others, including friends and family, for support. In addition to mental health service providers, those who are part of the victim's social network can be especially useful (Krupnick, 1980). The degree of informal support that victims can expect to receive from these informal social networks is likely to be related to friends' and family's education and awareness about the problem of hate crime. How informed members of the victim's social group are is important because it is well established that people who receive social support function better immediately and well after the incident in comparison to those who do not (e.g., Norris & Feldman-Summers, 1981; Ruback, Greenberg, & Westcott, 1984). The degree of support others provide victims is not only related to their awareness about the occurrence of hate crime, but it is also associated with their beliefs about the victim's culpability, among other things. In an early study, Craig (2000) investigated the impact of individuals' knowledge about hate crime on their responses and reactions to victims of heterosexist hate crime. Forty-three college students completed mood inventories before observation of a videotaped interview of a victim of hate crime. The interview was described as having been filmed at a university counseling center and included two white men, one describing his experience as a victim of a brutal hate-motivated assault to the other. During the interview, the victim recounted a harrowing tale in which he was brutally beaten, robbed, and taunted with antigay epithets. The interview concluded with his description of his hospitalization and extensive recuperation following the incident.

Among the findings from that study, several have implications for predictions about victims' likelihood of receiving support from others. For example, more than 25 percent of participants expressed sorrow or sadness following observation of the video containing the victim's testimony. Furthermore, the more angry observers perceived the perpetrators to be, the less justified they regarded their actions, and the more reliable, truthful, mature, and innocent they judged the victim. On the other hand, the more they blamed the victim, the more they judged the perpetrators to be justified in carrying out the assault. This latter finding underscores the relative importance of victims' need for informal social support networks. Reactions of others affect the social support available to victims of crime in general, and hate crime in particular. The more compassion others have for victims of crime, the more support they will be willing to offer. Findings from this study convincingly suggest that less blaming of the victim is associated with greater compassion for them, and correspondingly, more blame for the perpetrator. Importantly, more recent research by Lyons (2006) and Saucier, Brown, Mitchell, and Cawman (2006) explicates the way in which victims' social status influences others' attributions of blame.

Mental health providers who interact with victims of hate crime can ensure effective counseling and treatment of victims by employing a variety of strategies. At the outset, it should be recognized that counseling must be focused on the criminal incident. To ensure that the service provided is "trauma-specific," victims should be assessed for such things as PTSD, depression, and anxiety (United Nations Office for Drug Control and Crime Prevention, 1999).

Although most researchers who have studied victims' responses to victimization generally agree that victims should be encouraged to reconstruct their beliefs about safety and well-being, there are many different strategies for doing so. For example, written materials about the incidence of hate crime can be very helpful for victims. This will better position victims to effectively incorporate what has happened to them into their personal life stories. Mental health professionals can provide them with information, including documentation, detailing hate crime frequency rates and offender profiles.

Effective postvictimization counseling involves helping victims to reconnect with others and to become socially integrated again. Because victims see themselves as "deviant" and because many nonvictims may have trouble providing the support victims need, social integration can sometimes be best achieved by participation in peer support groups. Peer support groups offer victims the opportunity to meet and talk with other victims. Mental health service providers working with victims of hate crime can refer them to appropriate support groups and encourage them to participate in them.

For the victim, full recovery from the crisis of victimization requires revisiting of the incident either by physically returning to the scene or by psychologically returning to it through memory. Although this may be difficult and painful for the victim, it is essential to long-term recovery. It is at this stage that mental health service providers can be especially useful in guiding the victim through this stage of the postvictimization experience.

The likelihood that the victim's postvictimization experience will conclude with a criminal justice response will depend on apprehension and indictment of the offender as well as the victim's allegations and complaint. First responders and law enforcement personnel should inform victims about the different treatment and processing of hate crime offenses within the criminal justice system. The processing of hate crime offenses is determined by federal legislation and varies according to relevant state and local legislation. As a result of a bias motive present in any hate crime, the penalty for these offenses may be enhanced. Whether this occurs is determined by several factors, including evidence of the perpetrator's bias, the prosecutor's experience and familiarity with hate crime statutes, and the judge's philosophy about the appropriateness of such penalties. Victims can benefit from a thorough explanation of these options and their contingencies. Communication between victims and first responders who may or may not be law enforcement personnel is essential in preventing *secondary victimization*. Secondary victimization occurs after the criminal offense, when the victim interacts with the criminal justice system, which may not be perceived to be sympathetic or concerned with the victim's plight. In its most basic form, secondary victimization occurs as a result of the inherent difficulties in a system that strives to balance the rights of the victim against the rights of the accused (Symonds, 1980).

Communities that experience hate crime are believed to be susceptible to any number of negative consequences. According to the Community Relations Service (CRS) of the DOJ (2001), what may be most problematic are hate crimes that are unresolved. Unresolved hate crimes create additional levels of friction and tension between social groups, which can give rise to community-wide conflict and civil disturbance. In cases such as this, the CRS recommends systematic communication between representatives of social groups whose members were involved in the incident as victims and perpetrators. Establishment of a human rights commission can facilitate such discussions.

Local government clearly has a role to play. Local governments can establish ordinances against hate crime that are modeled on existing state-level legislation. Swift and deliberate punishment consistent with the local statutes should follow determination that a hate crime has occurred. A wide array of strategies can be enacted to ensure compliance. According to CRS (U.S. Department of Justice, 2001), some examples include additional training for law enforcement personnel to enforce existing statutes, imposing penalties when statues have been violated, and providing incentives or awards.

Local governments that are committed to the eradication of hate crime activity in their community can utilize resources from law enforcement, schools, advocacy groups, and the media. Each of these distinct representatives of the community can contribute to eliminating the problem of hate crime. For example, public school settings often reflect the diversity of their neighborhoods, and when rapid immigration shifts occur, they are likely to be more visible in the classroom. To be sure, hate crimes can occur in schools as well as in neighborhoods. School and police officials can work cooperatively to diffuse tensions through regular communication with parents and students. The Office for Juvenile Justice and Delinquency Prevention of the DOJ provides information and resources on preventing hate crimes in schools.

When incidents occur in communities, they are often fueled by rumors. This has the effect of aggravating the situation, which in turn leads to more widespread community unrest and intergroup conflict. Given their ability to influence public attitudes, the media can play a critical role by disseminating useful and accurate information. Local officials should maintain open channels of communication with the media. One way of accomplishing this is by designating an official point of contact or liaison for hate crime information or incidents.

Finally, CRS offers a number of different services to communities that have experienced hate crime, including mediation; training of law enforcement, residents, and students; public education; technical assistance; and event contingency planning. It is worth noting that these can be incorporated into existing community and school-based policies and programs. Only with a multitiered approach that incorporates victim perspectives, mental health service providers' assistance, and law enforcement and legislative commitment will hate crime and its corresponding psychological impacts be eliminated.

NOTES

This chapter draws from an earlier article by the author that provided recommendations for psychologists working with victims of racist hate crime. The views contained herein do not represent those of the National Science Foundation.

1.   Variability in terminology exists across the literature and contexts. In some cases, these incidents are referred to as bias crimes, and in others, they are referred to as hate crimes or, lacking illegality, simply hate-motivated incidents. Throughout the present discussion, the terms are used interchangeably, except where otherwise noted.

2.   In the first case, James Byrd was dragged by a car to his death by two white men who were affiliated with neo-Nazi groups, and in the second case, Matthew Shepard, an openly gay college student, was brutally beaten and left to die by two males who claimed he had bothered them.

3.   For example, consider the case of the bigoted shopkeeper who "hates" a customer because of his racial status and, in the course of completing the transaction, mutters an offensive racial epithet.

REFERENCES

Amnesty International. (2004). *Annual report.* New York: Author.

Anti-Defamation League. (2002). *Audit of anti-Semitic incidents, January–May 2002.* New York: Author.

Bloom, B. L. (1963). Definitional aspects of the crisis concept. *Journal of Consulting Psychology, 27,* 21–28.

Chalk, F., & Jonassohn, K. (1990). *The history and sociology of genocide: Analyses and case studies.* New Haven, CT: Yale University Press.

Coates, D., & Winston, T. (1983). Counteracting the deviance of depression: Peer support groups for victims. *Journal of Social Issues, 39,* 169–194.

Cook County State's Attorney's Office. (1994). *A prosecutor's guide to hate crime.* Chicago: Author.

Craig, K. M. (1999). Retaliation, fear, rage: African American and white responses to racist hate crimes. *Journal of Interpersonal Violence, 14,* 138–151.

Craig, K. M. (2000). *An eye for an eye? Examining public beliefs and reactions to hate crime.* Paper presented at the Hate Crime Symposium of the annual meeting of the Society for the Psychological Study of Social Issues, Los Angeles, CA.

Craig-Henderson, K. M., & Sloan, L. R. (2003). After the hate: Helping psychologists help victims of racist hate crime. *Clinical Psychology: Science and Practice, 10,* 481–490.

Ehrlich, H. J. (1992). The ecology of anti-gay violence. In G. M. Herek & K. T. Berrill (Eds.), *Hate crimes: Confronting violence against lesbians and gay men* (pp. 105–122). Newbury Park, CA: Sage.

Federal Bureau of Investigation. (2006). *Hate crime statistics 2005.* Washington, DC: U.S. Department of Justice.

Frieze, I., Hymer, S., & Greenberg, M. (1987). Describing the crime victim: Psychological reactions to victimization. *Professional Psychology: Research and Practice, 18,* 299–315.

Garofalo, J. (1997). Hate crime victimization in the United States. In R. C. Davis, A. J. Lurigio, & W. G. Skogan (Eds.), *Victims of crime* (pp. 134–145). Thousand Oaks, CA: Sage.

Gondles, J. A. (1999). Hate crimes: Not new but still alarming. *The Free Library.* Retrieved September 29, 2008, from http://www.thefreelibrary.com/Hate crime: not new, but still alarming.-a055503296

Gouldner, A. W. (1960). The norm of reciprocity: A preliminary statement. *American Sociological Review, 25,* 161–178.

Herek, G. M., & Berrill, K. T. (Eds.). (1992). *Hate crimes: Confronting violence against lesbians and gay men.* Newbury Park, CA: Sage.

Herek, G. M., Gillis, J. R., Cogan, J. C., & Glunt, E. K. (1997). Hate crime victimization among lesbian, gay and bisexual adults: Prevalence, psychological correlates and methodological issues. *Journal of Interpersonal Violence, 12*, 195–215.

Human Rights Watch. (2004). *Human Rights Watch publications catalogue.* Washington, DC: Author.

Janoff-Bulman, R., & Frieze, I. H. (1983). A theoretical perspective for understanding reactions to victimization. *Journal of Social Issues, 39*, 1–18.

Jenness, V., & Broad, K. (1997). *Hate crimes: New social movements and the politics of violence.* New York: Aldine de Gruyter.

Kleinfield, N. R. (1992, January 27). A hatred up close: The tension in New York. *New York Times*, p. A1.

Krupnick, J. (1980). Brief psychotherapy with victims of violent crime. *Victimology, 5*, 347–354.

Kubler-Ross, E. (1969). *On death and dying.* New York: Rockefeller Center, Touchstone.

Lazarus, R. S., & Folkman, S. (1984). *Stress, appraisal and coping.* New York: Springer.

Lerner, M. J. (1970). *The belief in a just world.* New York: Plenum.

Levin, B. (2002). Cyberhate: A legal and historical analysis of extremists' use of computer networks in America. *American Behavioral Scientist, 45*, 958–988.

Levin, J., & McDevitt, J. (1993). *Hate crimes: The rising tide of bigotry and bloodshed.* New York: Plenum.

Lyons, C. J. (2006). Stigma or sympathy? Attributions to fault to hate crime victims and offenders. *Social Psychology Quarterly, 69*, 39–59.

Moser, R. (2004, Summer). Age of rage. *Intelligence Report.* Montgomery, AL: Southern Poverty Law Center.

National Center for Victims of Crime. (2008). Trauma of Victimization. Retrieved from http://www.ncvc.org/ncvc/main.aspx?dbName=DocumentViewer&DocumentID=32371, retrieved May 13, 2008.

National Gay and Lesbian Task Force. (2003). *Hate crimes against gay, lesbian, bisexual and transgendered Americans.* Washington, DC: Author.

Noelle, M. (2002). The ripple effect of the Matthew Shepard murder: Impact on the assumptive worlds of members of the targeted group. *American Behavioral Scientist, 46*, 27–51.

Norris, F. H., Kaniasty, K., & Thompson, M. P. (1997). The psychological consequences of crime. In R. C. Davis, A. J. Lurigio, & W. G. Skogan (Eds.), *Victims of crime* (pp. 146–166). Thousand Oaks, CA: Sage.

Norris, J., & Feldman-Summers, S. (1981). Factors related to the psychological impact of rape on the victim. *Journal of Abnormal Psychology, 90*, 562–567.

Office for Victims of Crime. (2000). *Bridging the systems to empower victims: Mental health and victim services training guide.* Retrieved August 23, 2007, from http://www.ojp.usdoj.gov/ovc/publications/infores/student/student.pdf

Peterson, C., & Seligman, M. P. (1983). Learned helplessness and victimization. *Journal of Social Issues, 39*, 105–118.

Pettigrew, T. E. (1979). The ultimate attribution error: Extending Allport's cognitive analysis of prejudice. *Personality and Social Psychology Bulletin, 5*, 461–476.

Rapoport, L. (1965). The state of crisis: Some theoretical considerations. In H. J. Parad (Ed.), *Crisis intervention: Selected readings* (pp. 22–31). New York: Family Services.

Ross, L. (1977). The intuitive scientist and his shortcoming. In L. Berkowitz (Ed.), *Advances in experimental social psychology* (Vol. 10, pp. 174–221). New York: Academic Press.

Ruback, R. B., Greenberg, M. S., & Westcott, D. R. (1984). Social influence and crime-victim decision making. *Journal of Social Issues, 40*, 51–76.

Sales, E., Baum, M., & Shore, B. (1984). Victim readjustment following assault. *Journal of Social Issues, 40*, 117–136.

Sanchez, S., & Castenada, C. J. (1994, March 7). Hate crime report: Blacks targeted most. *USA Today*, (Nationline).

Saucier, D., Brown, T., Mitchell, R., & Cawman, A. (2006). Effects of victims' characteristics on attitudes towards hate crimes. *Journal of Interpersonal Violence, 21*, 890–909.

Symonds, M. (1980). The "second injury" to victims. In L. Kivens (Ed.), *Evaluation and change: Services for survivors* (pp. 36–38). Minneapolis, MN: Minneapolis Medical Research Foundation.

Taylor, S. (1983). Adjustment to threatening events: A theory of cognitive adaptation. *American Psychologist, 38*, 1161–1171.

Umbreit, M., & Coates, R. B. (2000). *Multicultural implications of restorative justice: Potential pitfalls and dangers*. St. Paul, MN: University of Minnesota, Center for Restorative Justice and Peace Making.

United Nations Office for Drug Control and Crime Prevention. (1999). *Handbook on justice for victims*. New York: Author.

U.S. Department of Justice. (2001). *Community Relations Service*. Retrieved September 28, 2008 from http:// www.usdoj.gov/crs/pubs/crs_pub_hate_crime_bulletin_ 1201.htm

Wallace, P. A. (1999, June). *Hate crimes: Legal issues* (Report for Congress No. RS20231). Washington, DC: Library of Congress Congressional Research Service.

Weinstein, N. D., & Lachendro, E. (1982). Egocentrismas a source of unrealistic optimism. *Personality and Social Psychology Bulletin, 8*, 195–200.

Wisconsin v. Mitchell, 113 S. Ct. 2194 (1993).

Wiseman, R. (1975). Crisis theory and the process of divorce. *Social Casework, 56*, 205–212.

Youngs, G. A., Jr. (1986). Patterns of threats and punishments in a conflict setting. *Journal of Personality and Social Psychology, 51*, 541–546.

CHAPTER 3

HOMOPHOBIC HATE CRIMES IN SWEDEN: QUESTIONS AND CONSEQUENCES

Eva Tiby

> Been at a party, RFSL club. About to go home. Someone comes up behind me, says "fucking queer" and knocks me to the ground. Glasses broken + cut on the forehead and sore down my left side, got kicked. (man, 49 years, no. 651)

The opening quotation is taken from a victim survey conducted among lesbian/gay/bisexual/transgender (LGBT) individuals in Sweden in 2004. This short narrative represents one of several different types of consequences following hate incidents. In this case, the focus is on physical injury, but many other narratives go beyond measurable bodily injury. Consequences such as avoiding certain locations, fleeing from one's home or hometown, or being excluded from one's religious community show that there is a need to discuss the consequences of homophobic hate crimes from both an individual and a structural perspective.

The various methods and types of data employed in criminological research are linked to different types of shortcomings, depending on one's view of what science and knowledge consist of. Official statistics are a result of human decisions and the human factor. They constitute a reflection of a decision-making process within and outside the justice system, rather than the actual distributions of crimes and offenders (Coleman & Moynihan, 2004). An incident must be detected, reported, registered, and cleared before it can find its way into the crime statistics.

The victim survey methodology was developed as a means of supplementing the picture provided by official statistics. It wasn't long before discussion began to focus on the *dark figure* associated with victim surveys themselves.

Victim surveys were found to include not only incidents that aren't reported to the police, but also reported incidents and incidents that are both reported and recorded. Moreover, they include those incidents that have been filtered through various actors: the perpetrator, the victim, and the police. They thus give rise to questions concerning why some become victimized and not others, and why some become *chronic* or *serial victims*, and perhaps most important, to questions relating to *the social meaning of criminal victimization* (Coleman & Moynihan, 2004). All this meant that the picture of perpetrators and victims could be revised. Different methods and measures give rise to different questions and different truths. It also became clear that the results of victim surveys did not describe the actual amount of crime, or the dark figure, but rather, the answers provided by certain individuals to certain questions in specific circumstances (Coleman & Moynihan, 2004).

RESEARCH QUESTIONS EXAMINED IN STUDIES OF HOMOPHOBIC HATE CRIMES

Hate crimes are a new construct in the Swedish legal arena. As with the offence of the violation of a woman's integrity, these offences constitute examples of what might be termed *motive criminality*. They are based on an intent to violate. Thus the acts themselves have long occurred, but the conceptualization is very modern. If someone commits an offence against another individual who is a member of a group specified in the legislation for increased sentence severity, and the motive was to violate the group member, the sanction may be stiffened. Since 1994, homosexuals have implicitly been "protected" by section 29:2:7 of the Swedish Penal Code, and since 2002, this has been expressed explicitly in the text of the legislation (in addition to the "genuine" hate crimes: agitation against a national or ethnic group, unlawful discrimination, and insulting behavior).

Internationally, a small number of isolated studies on crimes against homosexuals had been published prior to the 1980s (see, e.g., Sagarin & McNamara, 1975). With the trend toward what is often referred to as *gay liberation*, the number of studies has increased substantially. The earliest studies looked at the issue of whether there was victimization, and these were followed by studies of who was being victimized, where, when, and in what way, and possibly also by whom. Thereafter studies focused on legislation and its implementation. There was a period during which the research was dominated by issues relating to the types of consequence this type of victimization had for the victims and for society at large, with these issues often being linked to the question of the types of measure that might be introduced. Alongside these broad trends in the research, there are isolated studies/articles, often written from a legal studies perspective, that are critical of the practice of legislating against emotions (hate; see, in particular, Jacobs & Potter, 1997;

see also Dahl, 2005; Perry, 2003; Tiby, 1999, 2006; see Gårdfält, 2005, for a theological perspective on the hate crime complex). Some of the criminological research that proceeds from official statistics has argued that seven important questions need to be examined: What is the nature of the problem? How extensive is the problem? Who is involved/affected? Where does it occur? When does it occur? Why does it occur? What should be done? (Hall, 2005).

One overarching question, however, remains the same as it has always been: What are hate crimes? and consequently, How does the definitional process take place? How should hate crimes be defined, and by whom? and What are the consequences of this definitional process for statistics relating to hate crimes and for the measures introduced in response? (Hall, 2005).

SWEDISH STUDIES OF HOMOPHOBIC HATE CRIMES

The current author has been responsible for the majority of the criminological research into hate crimes against homosexuals that has been conducted in Sweden (see also Forum för Levande Historia, 2004). The field of occupational research has also made important contributions in relation to issues of discrimination, openness, and victimization due to sexual orientation (see Bildt, 2003; see also Forum för Levande Historia, 2006; Otterbeck & Bevelander, 2006; Sonnelind, 2006). A large number of research questions have been posed and in part answered in the context of a pilot study conducted in 1996, which resulted in the publication of a doctoral dissertation in 1999, a subsequent follow-up study, conducted in 2004, and a register study, conducted in 2006 (Tiby, 1996, 1999, 2005, 2006).

The 1996 Pilot Study

The initial study focused on questions of the prevalence, pattern, and consequences of threats and violence against homosexual women and men. The project was undertaken on the initiative of the Swedish National Institute of Public Health (Folkhälsoinstitutet). According to the then director general, the objective was to chart the nature of the situation to facilitate an assessment of the possible measures that could be introduced by state agencies and others that might produce improvements. A more detailed analysis of the study material would also hopefully provide a better basis for the work to combat the discrimination of homosexuals (Tiby, 1996).

The study was exploratory in character, and the research questions emerged in the context of an initial literature review, an interview study with key persons, and a pilot questionnaire study (Tiby, 1996). The subsequent questionnaire survey included items to collect data on classical criminological variables such as age, sex, nationality, location of residence, and occupation; detailed questions on the nature, location, time, and consequences of the victimization experienced; and questions about the perpetrator and on whether the incident had been reported to the police (Tiby, 1996; for a different system, see Lander, as cited in Tiby, 1996, pp. 104–106, where the research questions addressed in the analysis of the documentary material are presented in the introduction).

Less common questions were also included, relating to sexual identity, relational patterns (e.g., monogamy, casual sexual relations in public places), and knowledge of others' victimization (Tiby, 1996). The hate crime item (which is essential to the question of the study's validity) was operationalized as follows: "Have you ever been subjected to a crime because you are bi-/homosexual or lesbian, or because the perpetrator believed that you were?" The item was followed by a question asking, "What was it about the crime that indicated you were being victimized because of your sexual orientation?" (Tiby, 1996, p. 79).

The 1999 Hate Crime Study

The objectives of the 1999 study followed the design of the revised pilot study and were as follows:

- To produce a picture of people's perceptions of exposure to crime as a result of their being (or being perceived to be) homosexual, and of the consequences of this victimization.
- To examine which methods provide the most insight in relation to this type of crime.
- To examine what comparisons could be made with other vulnerable populations.

In addition, an important question relating to the issue of validity was also formulated: Can this victimization be characterized as hate crime?

The study employed an extensive triangulation in terms of both methods and data sources. In addition to the literature review, the study included two questionnaire surveys, one of approximately 2,800 individuals and the other of 28 organizations and their exposure to hate crimes. Since the personal questionnaire survey included an open-ended question that provided the respondents with the opportunity to freely describe what had happened to them and what they felt, a narrative study was also produced. In-depth interviews were also conducted with approximately 30 individuals, focusing on questions of what happened, how it felt, and later reactions. Two media analyses were also undertaken of how the gay press and the mainstream media depicted the phenomenon (Tiby, 1999).

The 2005 Follow-up Study

A grant from the Crime Victim Compensation and Support Authority (Brottsoffermyndigheten) made it possible to conduct a follow-up study. This study was much more limited in its scope than the hate crime study of 1999, however, and only certain elements could be replicated. These elements were the questions of victimization, the type of victimization, and the number of incidents of victimization. The object of the follow-up was to see if there had been any changes (Tiby, 2005)—and there had. First and foremost, it emerged that the proportion of respondents who perceived that they had been exposed to hate crime had increased from approximately 25 percent to approximately 50 percent. Whether this was due to an increase in the actual level of victimization or to methodological differences has been discussed elsewhere (Tiby, 2005). The response frequency was 67 percent in the original hate crime study, for example, and just under 50 percent in the follow-up study. In this context, it may be noted that the annual register study of homophobic hate crime conducted by the Swedish Security Police found a 75 percent increase in 2004, which was explained as being the result of changes in the methods used in the collection and handling of the police offense reports on which the study is based (Säkerhetspolisen, 2005).

The follow-up study placed a more concentrated focus on the victims' narratives. The questionnaire items took up a single page, and the reverse side was left blank for a narrative. The respondents were asked to write down what felt most important to them. The page began with an exemplification of what the narrative might be about: what happened, presence of feelings of fear, whether the incident had been reported to the police, and the consequences it had produced. The questionnaire was sent to just over 4,000 individuals, of whom slightly under 2,000 answered. Half of these respondents, approximately 1,000, answered that they had been exposed to an incident that they defined as a hate crime during the past eight years. Of these, approximately 500 had written a narrative of their own about the incident. In the case of these narratives, then, no concrete question had been posed, but they are rather the respondents' freely written descriptions. One of the aims of the use of this narrative initiative was to avoid directing the respondents too much, to avoid forcing their voices into a predetermined template; but it was also intended to collect material that would provide a basis for future research. The inspiration for this was a view of hate crimes and their consequences in terms of a process, rather than as individual incidents.

The 2006 Register Study

The Living History Forum is a state agency that also plays a role in the Swedish hate crime arena since the agency has the task of working to promote the equal value of all people through knowledge and culture. Among other things, the agency has published the report *Intolerance* (Forum för Levande Historia, 2004), which shows that youths who harbor negative opinions about a given group, for example, Jews, often have negative attitudes toward other groups, for example, homosexuals. The task to be undertaken in the register study was to examine hate crime incidents from police offence reports to court judgments. The research questions examined were as follows:

- Who are the suspected offenders, where do they commit the offences, and what is their relationship to the victims?
- What indicators of hate crime are presented?
- What happens to the police offence reports? Do they proceed to prosecution? Is anyone convicted? Are more severe sentences imposed? Are there any legal consequences?
- Are the legal tools intended to combat homophobic hate crime, such as the sentencing severity clause contained in 29:2:7 of the penal code, used in practice? (Tiby, 2006, p. 13)

The data comprised incidents reported to the police that included some kind of hate crime indicator relating to homophobia, records of how the investigation was concluded (thereby showing how the report has been assessed), information from the prosecutor on the assessment made in relation to the question of prosecution, and, where appropriate, court judgments (the project also includes an interview study conducted by Sörberg, 2006, in which in-depth interviews were conducted in connection with four of the cases). The results show that approximately 10 percent of the police offence reports led to a prosecution and a court conviction. This may be a result of the fact that the agencies that record the offence reports and those that prosecute and pass judgment on the offences appear to work with different definitions of what constitutes a hate crime (Tiby, 2006).

CONSEQUENCES OF HATE INCIDENTS AND HATE CRIMES

Swedish studies on the consequences of exposure to crime *in general* include physical, psychological, and economic consequences for the individual. These may in turn lead to negative social consequences such as the victim changing his or her behavior to avoid being victimized (Lindgren, 2001. It has been argued that the consequences of exposure to hate crime *in particular* are more severe than those of exposure to crime in general. This is due to the risks for self-blame on the part of the victim, to the questioning of one's own worth, to a high level of vulnerability, and to a lack of trust in the support provided by society to the members of the group to which one belongs (Tiby, 1999).

The 1999 study provides an example of the quantification of individual consequences, with between 66 and 76 percent of the victims stating that they were injured as a result of their victimization. Psychological injuries were the most frequent, at approximately 30 percent, with lasting fear being reported by between 17 and 49 percent, followed by bruising or bleeding wounds, at between 17 and 31 percent (Tiby, 1999).

The 1999 study showed substantial differences in levels of fear of "being exposed to crime as a result of one's homosexuality" between those who had been victimized and those with no experience of victimization. Generally speaking, levels of fear were twice as high among those who had been victimized. To take one example, 29 percent of those who answered that they had not been victimized reported fear of victimization, as compared with 60 percent of those who had been victimized (Tiby, 1999). It is unclear, of course, whether this difference in levels of fear already existed prior to the victimization. The respondents were therefore asked whether their victimization had led to an increase in their level of fear. Fifty-one percent of the female respondents and 57 percent of the males answered that it had (Tiby, 1999).

Thus the individual often feels afraid of (again) being exposed to a homosexual hate crime. This may lead him or her to start using avoidance strategies, which may in turn lead to meeting fewer open LGBT people, on one hand, and to meeting LGBT people who are "on their guard" and apparently at the ready to be attacked, on the other. Studies that attempt to quantify fear of crime are made more difficult by the fact that the phenomenon is difficult to define, to operationalize, and therefore also to measure (Heber, 2007), but these factors open up opportunities for a more qualitative research approach.

In the context of the 1999 study, in-depth interviews on inter alia fear were conducted with approximately 30 individuals. The interview data can be broken down on the basis of themes relating to fear *prior to, during*, and *subsequent to* the incident. The focus of the theme *prior to the incident* is specifically on fear of being subjected to crime. It also includes narratives on what may be referred to as supplementary fear, that is, a fear of being exposed as an LGBT individual if one were to be victimized (Tiby, 1999). The narratives relating to fear *during the incident* focus on what might happen, whether it might be even worse, and whether one will manage to cope. *Subsequent to the incident* are nightmares, discomfort, fear of going out, grief, avoidance, and flight behaviors (Tiby, 1999).

The fear of crime phenomenon may be said to constitute a bridge between the individual and the collective/societal consequence levels, first and foremost in the form of a public health problem. As such, it becomes defined as a problem that occurs more frequently in certain groups, that affects large numbers of people, and that may become more widespread (Tiby, 1999). In addition, a collective fear experienced by a certain minority group may create polarizations and conflicts within society. It may contribute to minority group members feeling isolated, abandoned, vulnerable, and unprotected by the justice system. It has also been argued that conflicts between groups may lead to special acts of vengeance or to people taking the law into their own hands (Kelly, Maghan, & Tennant, 1993). At the level of structural consequences, there is, of course, also a risk of the justice system facing problems of legitimacy both when hate crimes occur and when incidents that the public perceives as hate crimes are not prosecuted as such (Tiby, 2006).

The 2004 study included both a questionnaire section focused on what had happened to the victims and also a section set aside for the respondents to provide written narratives. In this latter section, respondents were asked to write freely about what they had been subjected to, for example, about possible fear and about other consequences of their victimization. The quotation presented at the beginning of this chapter constitutes an example of such a narrative. In texts of this particular type, the descriptions focused on physical and/or psychological individual consequences.

In the following sections, slightly edited narratives are presented that relate to the different levels of consequence experienced by victims as a result of their victimization. The presentation begins by focusing on physical and psychological consequences at the individual level. This is the level that usually constitutes the focus of victim surveys. Such surveys often include an indicator of the extent of the consequence in question. This might, for example, involve asking about the seriousness of the consequence: Did it require medical attention? Did it require sick leave? Thereafter, however, the narratives move on to consequences relating to other levels. These involve avoidance behaviors, lies, fear, flight, and being excluded from religious communities. The most far-reaching consequences relate to losing faith in one's fellow human beings, in public sector agencies, and in society at large.

Physical Consequences

Been at a party, RFSL club [RFSL is the Swedish Federation for Lesbian, Gay, Bisexual, and Transgender Rights]. About to go home. Someone comes up behind me, says "fucking queer" and knocks me to the ground. Glasses broken + cut on the forehead and sore down my left side, got kicked. (man, 49 years, no. 651)

In February 2003, I and two friends were on our way home from a gay bar in south Stockholm when I was attacked by a gang of immigrant youths. They screamed "fucking queer" and threw big chunks of ice at my head. I went into shock and started bleeding heavily. (man, 45 years, no. 518)

Was at a party at the local branch of the RFSL [in a small town]. A gang of teenage boys threw burning car tires into the building's stairwell.

We were on the third floor and had to go down ladders put up by the fire engines. Went to hospital with smoke-inhalation injuries. There were 10 of us that were taken to casualty. (man, 41 years, no. 698)

I was walking home from [gay club] with an acquaintance, my friend is a bit camp (it shows that he's gay). Then someone shouted queer and do you want some cock. Then he wiggled his arse and they threw bottles at us one hit my leg the other my friend's head. It was a long night at [the hospital]. (man, 23 years, no. 1790)

The above four narratives may be described as typical examples. They have several elements in common. The perpetrators are male, the victims are male, and the incidents occur in public places. The link between the victimization and the victims being LGBT individuals is found in the victims being near to a gay club or bar at the time, or in the attributes/mannerisms of the victims. And the consequences are first and foremost physical. In addition, the narratives in many cases provide not only information about the consequences of the victimization, but also about the context and about the actors involved in the conflict. This information may relate to the number of perpetrators, their ethnicity, the crime location, and what the victims were doing when the incident occurred. The range of narratives also, of course, includes cases that deviate from the typical, such as the following:

Was anally raped by 3 men during a trip to Dubai. Not injured but humiliating and very frightening. Not reported to the police. Distressing to be held down and afraid of possible infection. (man, 48 years, no. 1623)

Several of the respondents focus on both physical and psychological consequences. There are also narratives that focus more exclusively on the latter. These cases are dominated by narratives provided by women.

Psychological Consequences: Fear of Showing Oneself to Be a Lesbian/Gay/Bisexual/Transgender Person

On the boat from Stockholm to Turku, me and my then girlfriend were victimized by several guys who mocked us and tried to force their way between us when we were dancing cheek-to-cheek and who pushed, hit and kicked us on the dance floor. We were so frightened that we left the nightclub and went to our cabin. It was very distressing. (woman, 29 years, no. 924)

Feeling so vulnerable that one refrains from "showing oneself" to be an LGBT person constitutes one consequence of victimization, or of the perceived risk of being victimized. This may relate to specific occasions, such a holidays abroad, or more generally to one's everyday life, day in and day out.

Many of the narratives describe being on a constant state of alert that one may be victimized and developing strategies to avoid this victimization:

> In the summer of 2003 me and my boyfriend were in Crete. While we were there we were threatened twice. The first time we were walking hand in hand on the beach. When we passed a gang of youths having a party they stared at us. . . . Two individuals started running towards us. Luckily they were stopped by other members in the group. We experienced it as being very distressing and didn't dare openly show that we were a couple for the rest of the holiday. (man, 28 years, no. 1670)

> I think this is probably the toughest part, constantly being on your guard and "whether or not it's appropriate" to be open in the current situation. As regards verbal assaults, it's happened when me and my then girlfriend hugged each other during a walk together. (woman, 27 years, no. 211)

> I've been lucky and haven't been exposed to violence or threats of violence. On the other hand my experience is that discrimination is part of everyday life for homosexuals. In order to avoid this type of discrimination myself, either I *or* my partner usually deals with looking after the car and anything that involves workmen. Our experience of both of us having contact with the above mentioned has always been negative: discrimination in the form of inferior service and being treated badly are one part of it. (man, 34 years, no. 1450)

Behavioral Consequences: Moving, Flight, Exclusion, and Break-ups

There are also narratives that focus on what may broadly be referred to as the behavioral consequences of these incidents. These narratives involve no longer daring to live as one did before. It becomes too dangerous to go out to a certain place when one has been victimized outside the premises:

> I've been attacked by unknown men several times outside of the RFSL's party room—threatened but never hit. It was distressing and has led to me not wanting to go in and out by myself, I always go with my girlfriend, or with friends. (woman, 28 years, no. 1891)

> Me and my partner were on our way home after a party at around 2 in the morning. May 2002, people out walking. A man ran and caught up with us and shouted "fucking lesbian cunts" and started hitting us. Got my partner on the ground and was kicking and hitting her. I managed to pull him off and he just punched me again and again and again on my head and in my face. He then let go and ran away from the scene. The incident was reported to the police but no perpetrator could be identified. I had never been scared/worried about going home late before. I am now! My partner doesn't dare to go out alone at all when it's dark. This produced bigger/worse consequences than you'd dare to dream of, unfortunately. (woman, 38 years, no. 1591)

It is about no longer being able to live where you have been living. It is too dangerous to live near someone who subjects you to threats on a daily basis:

I moved to Stockholm from my apartment in Jönköping and it was because I had five Nazis living as neighbors and they weren't very pleasant. (man, 37 years, no. 841)

I was forced to sell my house and buy another in another part of town because of a neighbor. He'd somehow figured out what I am. He accused me of having repeatedly driven into his mailbox. He tried to scare me with his Doberman pinscher. He spat in my direction. I suspect it was he who stole my salary slip and threw it torn into small pieces into the garden of another neighbor. He got worse over time. His eyes actually radiated hatred. He started harassing my guests. "Are you as much of a lesbian as she is?" he said to a straight friend. He blocked in their cars. You could say that the threats escalated and I didn't dare do anything other than move. The day I moved he even tried to block the road for the moving van. It maybe doesn't sound so dangerous but I perceived it as extremely, palpably threatening. The escalation in particular concerned me. Who knows where this kind of thing might end? (woman, 59 years, no. 343)

It is about not being able to stay in the relationship you were in at the time of the victimization. When one's victimization is due to being in a relationship with someone, the victimization places too great a strain on the relationship:

My former partner and I were living under a death threat for a couple of months. Were forced to go "underground" and were given protection by police and security guards. It was colleagues of my ex who were behind it all. They thought there was something strange and disgusting about homos. My ex-partner reported it to the police and was given assistance by the RFSL. I was only indirectly involved and we broke up over it. (man, 29 years, no. 1893)

When my former girlfriend's parents confronted her about her relationship with me her father got a gun and said he'd shoot anyone who threatened to break up his family. Both I and my girlfriend perceived it as a threat directed at me. I got myself an unlisted telephone number but didn't report it to the police because she didn't want to. She is Greek and in the end she chose to obey her parents and stop seeing me. We met in secret for a while, but it became impossible and we broke up. (woman, 30 years, no. 598)

It is about consequences not only for yourself or your partner, but also for your children:

You could read about our case on the Internet Web site of the Swedish National Democratic Party in connection with the first "homo-adoptions."

They didn't publish our names, but it wasn't exactly a neutral news presentation. The worst thing about the "incident" is of course what violations of this kind "do" to our child. (woman, 34 years, no. 323)

Several times when I've shown myself in public with a partner, e.g., held hands, kissed, I/we've had insults shouted at us, including threats of violence. My daughter has been bullied in school and called lesbo and more besides because I am one. (woman, 41 years, no. 1878)

It's about not being able to live and work within the religious community you wish to because you are victimized there:

As a result of my orientation I was threatened with exclusion from the nonconformist church to which I belonged, and this also happened. The pastor and many of my "friends" threatened that God would leave me and that I would go to hell if I lived with another woman. It was terrible. (woman, 26 years, no. 1871)

I've been an active member of a fantastic, charismatic, Christian community where it was completely unthinkable for me as a girl to be together with another girl. I've been subjected to threats that God is going to leave me. Threatened with being excluded from the church. I've felt myself forced to give up the job I had within the church. Since I came out I've been frozen out and shut out by more or less my entire social network. I've been threatened that I'm going to go to hell. Accused of being unnatural, unhealthy, of going against the order of creation, of being abnormal and perverse. Because of my orientation and my choice of partner I've been indirectly accused of being part of the root of all evil in society. These accusations have been made as much through people's silence as through their words. I haven't reported anything to the police. (woman, 26 years, no. 578)

Consequences for the Victim's Working Life and Career

Many of the narratives relate to discrimination, bullying, harassment, or threats and violence in the workplace. One of the most common consequences of this is that one is always afraid of going to work. One may also feel excluded and unable to carry out one's work or make progress in one's career. In many cases, victims are forced to leave their jobs as a consequence:

At work I was often made to shut up, couldn't talk on the same level as my (female) workmates. I would hear that I was a disgusting gay, was often treated differently and not listened to. It was the younger people who treated me badly. (50+ treated me the same as they had before I came out as a gay.) Am in the process of changing occupation with the help of the Social Insurance Agency because I can never work in the care sector again/bullying and more. (man, 36 years, no. 341)

I've been discriminated against at my workplace, been more or less forced to move jobs because of my sexual orientation. When some of those at my employer's found out that I and my boyfriend had got engaged, demands were made that I should leave. I reported this to HomO [the Ombudsman against Discrimination on the Grounds of Sexual Orientation] and to my superiors, but was threatened with legal action by people at my employer's if I didn't retract my complaint. Despite written evidence, nothing could be done. I felt I'd been greatly violated and I felt terrible. One of those responsible is a lawyer in civilian life, and what do I have to counter such a person? I got very poor support from both the trade union and the employer. (man, 48 years, no. 7)

I've been recommended to resign from a job I've had for 8 years because the boss doesn't want to have anything to do with the "issue." I've moved jobs but demanded a year's salary, which I got. (man, 32 years, no. 534)

Consequences for Trust

A generalized lack of trust may emerge in response to hate crime victimization. This may relate to individuals in both the immediate environment and the wider environment around the victim:

In 2000 I'd been living for 11 years in a little village in rural Skåne. At the time I was in the middle of a deep depression following a divorce, which those around me knew about. When I took the rubbish out one evening the youths of the village (about 20 of them) stood by the road and shouted "fucking homo" as I came out. They stayed there and continued doing so for about two hours. I became very frightened and paralyzed. Spent the time on the floor in the hall and felt my life was under threat. The same children that I'd watched grow up, that I'd babysat, my friends' and neighbors' children were now standing outside my door and screaming. The whole thing was unreal. The worst part was that I couldn't see any possibility of getting help nearby. In the end it went quiet and then I crept into my bed, to wake the next day and pretend it hadn't happened. I think that was my only survival strategy. I didn't want it to have happened. It took over 1 year before I could talk about it. I was ashamed, which may seem completely absurd, but I was. (woman, 48 years, no. 973)

I was standing kissing my then girlfriend by the commuter train, central station in Stockholm. From a long distance away, a group of about five men aged 20–30 approached—speaking English (tourists?). They shout insults at us and when they pass we are rather brutally pushed into the wall. Extremely distressing. I've almost stopped listening to words, but physical violence. . . . Strong sense of powerlessness and not being able to defend oneself and one's partner and rage. Also fear when I later traveled home alone and found myself on the same train as my assailants—but wasn't recognized on my own. Nobody in the vicinity reacted—distressing. We could have been seriously assaulted. (woman, 20 years, no. 1441)

During a late-night walk in a suburb of Stockholm together with my husband, a car suddenly stopped. Someone opened the door and shouted at us and spat towards us, shouted that we were disgusting. We of course were shaken and frightened but nothing more happened. The car moved on straight away. After this happened we were more careful about holding hands in public. Our faith in Stockholm as an open and tolerant city was dented. (man, 46 years, no. 567)

At a town festival in Blekinge, both in the town, bars, and on the bus, I and my boyfriend were threatened, like "I'm going to kill you, you fucking queer." The most frightening was on the bus, which was packed and where you couldn't get away from the person who was making the threats. It was something I had nightmares about afterwards. Another thing that was very distressing was that not a one of all the other people who heard the threats said anything. We felt completely exposed. Since then I haven't been to anymore festivals out in the sticks. (man, 33 years, no. 1049)

Faith in the Justice System and Other Public Sector Agencies

A couple of quotations can illustrate the problems following disappointing treatment from authorities.

We in the RFSL association are often subjected to threats and vandalism both as a group and as individuals. Violence and threats that have been directed at me as a private individual haven't been reported to the police. On the other hand we've reported the threats and vandalism that have been directed at us as a group in the association several times. Feel that the police authority takes these reported offences lightly. Despite reporting them as hate crimes, they're most commonly recorded simply as vandalism. (woman, 51 years, no. 1960)

It wasn't an attack directly at me personally but it had a personal effect. One morning I walked past our local RFSL premises and they had been attacked during the night, I presume by Nazis. Swastikas had been painted with ketchup on all the windows, stickers with the same symbol and with Sweden Democrats. These hadn't been there the night before when I left the same building. We called the police and they came to the premises and we made a report, but then there was a conflict. The police just wanted to see it as an "ordinary" case of vandalism, whereas we wanted it to be recorded as a hate crime. I don't know what felt worse afterwards, not feeling safe around the building, or having to argue with state agencies. Not getting a sympathetic hearing from those who are there to help. Are they going to intervene when it comes to "worse things"? (woman, 23 years, no. 1254)

Resignation and Resistance

Some of the narratives include reflections that show the broad range of expectations and strategies that exist among the victims:

> As an open homosexual both privately and at work, there's only been one period (quite enough) when I've been subjected to direct harassment. Since I've been hired as a "professional homo" it's meant that I've been a public person and have met a lot of people. There was a period when neo-Nazis targeted homosexuals. The incidents of harassment, when you relate them, are both palpable but often subtle. My name and other personal information had been listed on a so-called death list. Neo-Nazis have also shown their hatred openly in their body language and words when I've met them about town. There's such an incredible amount of persecution and harassment, threats and violence, where do you draw the line? As a homosexual I think one has learned/got used to accepting a hell of a lot that the majority of people wouldn't accept. (woman, 34 years, no. 735)

> Most recently a group of 10 or so youths have thrown ice at my windows and shouted, I live isolated on the ground floor. They've also blocked my way home and been very threatening. It's always been dark so I don't know who they are—the police do nothing because "nothing's really happened." People laugh, point, shout, or insult me almost every day—mostly something about gender. "Are you a man or a woman!?" There are a lot of us in the suburb where I live who get harassed so we're in the process of building up a network, a homomilitia of our own. We do self-defense training and in the future we're going to talk to all the immigrant associations and schools, youth clubs. (man, 24 years, no. 834)

> Once I was out in a school class where some boys tried to harass me, but I put my foot down and had a go at them which the adults at the school hadn't done before. As a result I got their respect and they came to see me several times throughout their time in secondary school. I'm completely open, even at my schools, and I have to say it is going extremely well. (man, 45 years, no. 707)

CONCLUSIONS

What do the narratives tell us? The narratives tell us about consequences at the micro, meso, and macro levels for the individual victim and for society. They tell us about daily situations, about everyday situations, and about festive situations. Many, but not all, give a picture of constantly being on one's guard, being afraid, and being prepared to move away and flee.

Levels of Consequences Described in Narratives of Hate Crime

Are the narratives "true"? It is impossible to answer this question, and it is perhaps irrelevant to pose it. The people who have experienced these

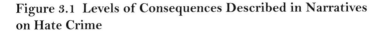

Figure 3.1 Levels of Consequences Described in Narratives on Hate Crime

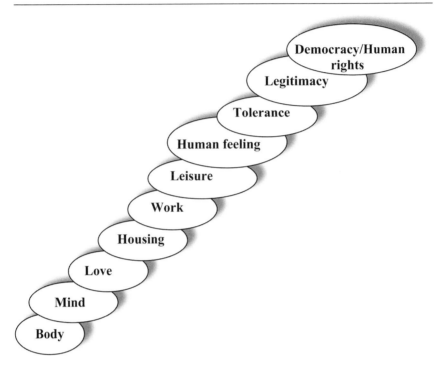

incidents perceive them to have occurred because the assailants had something against LGBT individuals and to have led to the consequences described in the narratives (see Figure 3.1).

Are the narratives of use? Yes, in that they may be viewed as indications of the consequences of homophobic hate crimes. Thus they provide information as to what we as researchers and people working with crime prevention issues should ask in the future. Focused questions in victim surveys may then result in more structured and quantifiable descriptions of consequences (see, e.g., Folkhälsoinstitutet, 2005; Ulstein Moseng, 2007). The different levels of consequences also show the necessity of seeing questions on (all types of) hate crime not as individual, but as structural problems. And it is thus on these levels that the solutions ought to be sought (Brottsförebyggande rådet, 2004).

REFERENCES

Bildt, C. (2003). *Diskriminering och trakasserier: Homo- och bisexuellas arbetsvillkor—en delrapport* [Discrimination and harassment: Working conditions for gays and bisexuals]. Stockholm: National Institute for Working Life.

Brottsförebyggande rådet. (2004). Brottsförebyggande arbete i praktiken [Crime prevention in practice]. In *Att förebygga hatbrott* [The prevention of hate crimes] Stockholm: Fritzes (pp. 51–64).

Coleman, C., & Moynihan, J. (2004). *Understanding crime data: Haunted by the dark figure.* Maidenhead, England: Open University Press.

Dahl, U. (2005). *En kunskapsinventering av forskning om homofobi och hetero-normativitet: "Det viktigaste är inte vad extremisterna tycker utan vad den stora majoriteten gör"* [Research on homophobia and heteronormativity: An inventory of knowledge: "The most important is not the thoughts of the extremists, but the actions of the majority"]. Stockholm: Living History Forum.

Folkhälsoinstitutet. (2005). *Hälsa på lika villkor? Hälsa och livsvillkor bland hbt-personer* [Public health on equal conditions? Health and living conditions among LGBT persons]. Stockholm: National Institute of Public Health.

Forum för Levande Historia. (2004). *Intolerans: Antisemitiska, homofobiska, islamofobiska och invandrarfientliga tendenser bland unga* [Intolerance: Anti-Semitic, homophobic, Islamophobic, and xenophobic tendencies among young people]. Stockholm: Living History Forum.

Forum för Levande Historia. (2006). *Antisemitiska attityder och föreställningar i Sverige* [Anti-Semitic attitudes and conceptions in Sweden]. Stockholm: Living History Forum.

Gårdfält, L. (2005). *Hatar Gud bögar?* [Does God hate queers?]. Stockholm: Normal.

Hall, N. (2005). *Hate crime.* Devon, England: Willan.

Heber, A. (2007). *Var rädd om dig! Rädsla för brott enligt forskning, intervjupersoner och dagspress* [Be cautious! Fear of crime according to research, informants and media]. Unpublished doctoral dissertation, Department of Criminology, University of Stockholm.

Jacobs, J., & Potter, H. (1997). Hate crimes: A critical perspective. In M. Tonry (Ed.), *Crime and justice: A review of research* (Vol. 22, pp. 1–50). Chicago: University of Chicago Press.

Kelly, R., Maghan, J., & Tennant, W. (1993). Hate crimes: Victimizing the stigmatized. In R. Kelly (Ed.), *Bias crime: American law enforcement and legal responses* (pp. 23–47). Chicago: Office of International Criminal Justice, University of Illinois.

Lindgren, M., Pettersson, K. Å., Hägglund, B. (2001). Brottsoffer. Från teori till praktik [*Crime victims, from theory to practice*]. Stockholm: Jure, CLN AB.

Otterbeck, J., & Bevelander, P. (2006). *Islamofobi* [Islamophobia]. Stockholm: Living History Forum.

Perry, B. (Ed.). (2003). *Hate and bias crime: A reader.* New York: Routledge.

Sagarin, E., & McNamara, D. E. J. (1975). The homosexual as a crime victim. *International Journal of Criminology and Penology, 3,* 13–25.

Säkerhetspolisen. (2005). *Brottslighet kopplad till rikets inre säkerhet 2004* [Crimes toward internal security] (Report No. 2005:4). Stockholm: Author.

Sonnelind, E. (2006). *"Don't bitch med mig liksom": En undersökning om anmälningsbenägenhet hos HBT-personer i Stockholmsområdet* ["Don't bitch with me, sort of": A study on propensity to report victimization concerning hate crimes in a Stockholm population of gays, lesbians, and transgendered persons]. Unpublished doctoral dissertation, Department of Criminology, University of Stockholm.

Sörberg, A. M. (2006). Intervjuer [Interviews]. In E. Tiby (Ed.), *En studie av homofoba hatbrott i Sverige* [A study on homophobic hate crimes in Sweden] (pp. 33–44). Stockholm: Living History Forum.

Tiby, E. (1996). *Hat, hot, våld—utsatta homosexuella kvinnor och män* [Hate, threats, and violence—victimized women and men]. Stockholm: National Institute of Public Health.

Tiby, E. (1999). *Hatbrott? Homosexuella kvinnors och mäns berättelser om utsatthet för brott* [Hate crimes? Gays' and lesbians' narratives on victimization]. Unpublished doctoral dissertation, Department of Criminology, University of Stockholm.

Tiby, E. (2005). Vem vinner och vem försvinner? Från händelse till hatbrott [Who does, who does not count? From episode to hate crime]. In M. Seppänen (Ed.), *Kärlekens pris: En antologi om homofobi och heteronormativitet* (pp. 42–57). Stockholm: Atlas.

Tiby, E. (2006). *En studie av homofoba hatbrott i Sverige* [A study on homophobic hate crimes in Sweden]. Stockholm: Living History Forum.

Ulstein Moseng, B. (2007). *Vold mot lesbiske og homofile tenåringer: En representativ undersökelse av omfang, risiko og beskyttelse* [Violence against gay and lesbian teenagers: A representative study on extent, risk, and protection] (NOVA Report No. 19/2007). Oslo: NOVA.

CHAPTER 4

BODY MAPS: ENVISAGING HOMOPHOBIA, VIOLENCE, AND SAFETY

Gail Mason

Several years ago, a paper was presented at an international victimology conference held in Adelaide, Australia.[1] This paper was part of a session on hostility against members of the gay and lesbian communities. Prior to the presentations, a signed letter of complaint was submitted to the conference administration. The author of the letter objected to the inclusion of the gay and lesbian session in the program. Expressing both anger and disappointment at the presence of the session, which she described as an "advertisement" for a "deviant pressure group," she asserted, "If gays and lesbians give public witness to their sexual preferences their 'acts' are no longer in private, and cannot be said to have a private connotation any longer." Although the session proceeded unimpeded, I was struck at the time by the particulars of this grievance. The writer seemed less concerned with gay and lesbian sexualities per se and more concerned with the public witness of such sexualities. The open admission of a (presumed) preference for certain sexual acts appeared to arouse her anger rather than the acts themselves. Ironically, her certainty that this breakdown of privatized homosexuality provided a legitimate ground for complaint seemed to find some fuel in the right to privacy arguments that have marked many claims by the gay and lesbian movement for social and legal reform.

The emergence of one complaint within the context of a large and diverse international conference is hardly significant in itself. Nor is disdain for the public acknowledgment of gay and lesbian sexualities in any way peculiar to this complainant. What is of interest, however, is the framing of these sentiments within a trope of visibility, that is, the way in which heteronormative attitudes are articulated as a question of the degree to which we can "see" same-sex sexualities. This trope is the crystallization of assumptions that circulate in contemporary Western nations regarding the appropriateness, or otherwise, of expressions and representations of homosexuality.

We need look no further than the popular and long-standing refrain against those who "flaunt" their homosexuality to realize that the very suggestion that homosexuality can be flaunted is itself the product of the social and political hush that has historically enveloped the subject of same-sex sexuality. While the cultural mandate to conceal one's homosexuality may have waned, the knowledge that it is possible to do so continues to serve as the favored benchmark against which all representations of homosexuality are measured.

In this chapter, the unspoken question that this letter of complaint posed for those of us at the victimology conference who sought to highlight the problem of homophobic hostility and violence is picked up: how is this hostility marked by notions of visibility and invisibility that circulate within contemporary discourses of sexuality, and homosexuality in particular? Specifically, how are the implications (or effects, if you like) of hostility and violence configured by the trope of visibility?

In many Western nations, there is now an important body of literature on what has become known as homophobic violence, a concept that seeks to capture hostile, aggressive, and violent behaviors that are motivated by an antagonism toward same-sex sexualities. The results from research, particularly large victimization surveys, in the United States, Australia, New Zealand, and the United Kingdom all point to disturbingly high rates of verbal abuse, harassment, threats of violence, and physical violence as well as incidents of homicide directed toward men and women who are assumed to be gay, lesbian, or in some way "queer" (Berrill, 1990; Gay Men and Lesbians against Discrimination [GLAD], 1994; Gay Task Force, 1985; A. Mason & Palmer, 1996; Tomsen, 1997). The effects of homophobic hostility on the individual are a source of ongoing concern. For many lesbians and gay men, these include not only the emotional and physical pain of the immediate incident, but also long-term psychological distress and trauma (Garnets, Herek, & Levy, 1990; Hunter, 1990; Ryan & Futterman, 1998; van den Boogaard, 1989).

Without wishing to downplay the harm that homophobic violence inflicts on those who are personally targeted, the purpose here is to explore the implications of homophobic hostility as they are amplified beyond the question of individual injury. Feminism has shown us that gendered violence has the capacity to affect the lives of women, irrespective of whether they have direct and personal experience of it. This chapter is premised on the idea that violence does not have to be experienced to have repercussions. To understand the cultural, or collective, implications of homophobic hostility, it is necessary to position this hostility in the wider context of discursive statements of sexual visibility, that is, to see how homophobic violence functions through the relation between homosexuality and visibility. The collective implications of violence can be understood as a question of knowledge. What does it mean for lesbians and gay men to know, whether through individual experience or not, about the risks and possibilities of homophobic hostility and violence? One answer to this question is found in the specific techniques that lesbians and gay men use to negotiate a sense of safety from interpersonal violence. By looking at the contribution that lesbian and gay knowledge of homophobic violence makes to the construction of these "safety maps," we hope to be able to say something about the significance of the homosexuality-visibility nexus to the capacity of violence to infiltrate the lives of lesbians and gay men.

To consider these issues, an empirical study is drawn on that was conducted into homophobia-related hostility and violence in Australia. This qualitative research (involving individual and group interviews) focused on aggression, negativity, hostility, and violence in the lives of 75 women who identified as lesbian, gay, or queer. In conducting this research, not only experiences of hostility were drawn out, but also perceptions and opinions about the ways in which the knowledge of such hostility functions in the everyday lives of lesbian women. The women who participated in this study were diverse in terms of age, lifestyle, education, ethnicity, socioeconomic background, employment, area of residence, and parental status.[2] Focus is not so much on the details of their actual encounters with hostility, but more on their responses to the possibility of a hostile or violent reaction to their sexuality. The epistemological approach to these interview narratives seeks to recognize that experiential accounts of the material world, like theoretical accounts, are always an interpretation of events. In positioning experience somewhere in the middle of what Haraway (1991) calls the "slippery pole of objectivity," we draw on it not as a raw or unmediated form of evidence, but rather, as the product of an interaction between material and discursive fields of meaning (Gavey, 1993; Grosz, 1993; Scott, 1991). This relay between practice and theory (Foucault & Deleuze, 1977) means that interview accounts of experience provide an informed commentary, or springboard, for thinking about the ways in which notions of sexual visibility permeate the violent practices of homophobia.

One of the significant issues to emerge from this empirical research has been the central role that gendered power relations play in the enactment and experience of violence that is commonly characterized as homophobic (G. Mason, 1997a, 1997b). It is crucial to recognize that systems of gender and sexuality interact to produce differences between the violence that is committed against lesbians and the violence that is committed against gay men. However, for the moment, the motivation is to look at the congruence, rather than the variance, between antilesbian and antigay violence.[3] The relation between homosexuality and visibility marks all forms of violence where homophobia comes into play. The specificities of how it does this are, of course, configured through innumerable interacting variables, not just of gender, but also of race, ethnicity, class, age, and the like.

THE TROPE OF VISIBILITY

There is a vexed relationship between discourses of sexuality and notions of visibility. Historically, the obligation to confess one's sexual desire as a means of revealing the inner truth about oneself lies side by side with the imposition of silences and secrecies about all forms of sexual behavior. In Western cultures, this tension between the obligation to tell the truth and the cultural convention of verbal prohibition continues to engender a bifurcated understanding of sexual desire as both a means for deciphering who one is and the source of an imperative toward hiding what one does (Foucault, 1988). The historical classification of sexual desires and practices into observable categories of sexual identity thus represents a technology through which one comes to know and speak of oneself as a certain type of sexual being, for example, as heterosexual or homosexual. At the same time, however, the production of these visible identities also functions as a trap (Foucault, 1977).[4] In providing us with the means to recognize ourselves, and others, as certain types of subjects, sexual identities prompt us to assume responsibility for curtailing, confessing, and regulating our own behavior so as to conform to the expectations attached to these particular subject positions. While all sexual subject positions are vulnerable to the sense of personal and social scrutiny that prompts us to monitor our own behavior in this way, the extent to which we feel the need to hide what we do will be shaped, in part, by the uneven implications of being visible as a specific type of sexual person. Despite the recent recognition of heterosexuality as an identity in itself—most likely bringing with it new constraints as well as freedoms—the historical privilege accorded to monogamous heterosexual marriage means that heteroerotic desires continue to be seen as unremarkable and unproblematic expressions of sexuality. While the very normativity of the institution of heterosexuality inevitably constrains the sexual subjectivities of those who choose it as a lifestyle, the negative implications of openly identifying as heterosexual remain minimal. In contrast, visibility can operate to trap the many women and men whose sexual desires and practices deviate from this benchmark (e.g., gay men and lesbians, sex workers, or those who engage in sadomasochistic sexualities), not only because it restricts their sense of sexual subjectivity, but also because it brings with it the threat of social or legal sanctions, including discrimination, incarceration, violence, or personal rejection.

Sedgwick (1990) captures the importance of the trope of visibility to the particular politics of homosexuality when she argues that the privacy of the "closet," and the demarcation between being in or out of the closet, is the defining structure for lesbian and gay oppression in the twentieth century. The very idea that "coming out" is a possible moment for any lesbian or gay man exemplifies her point well.[5] Although Western nations are currently witnessing the burgeoning emergence of an undisguised and unapologetic homosexuality into the public domains of law, media, culture, and politics, the legacy of a history of disapprobation and pathologization is found in the continued heteronormative predilection for censoring certain expressions of same-sex sexual desire. This permeates the everyday lives of lesbians and gay men in routine yet heterogenous ways. Surveys, interviews, fiction, and personal anecdotes all reveal pervasive and complex pictures of veiled, sometimes secreted, homosexualities, including the refusal of some (certainly not all) heterosexual women and men to legitimate, or even acknowledge, the homosexuality of others; the perception among gay men and lesbians that they need to masquerade, or "pass," as heterosexual in situations of work, family, or even friendship; the tendency to ignore or trivialize the act of coming out; and the recent promotion of acceptable expressions of monogamous or "vanilla" homosexualities at the expense of less "respectable" homoerotic practices (Eliason, Donelan, & Randall, 1992; GLAD, 1994; G. Mason, 1995; McGregor, 1996). Cumulatively, these kinds of engagement with homosexuality produce not so much a ubiquitous or universal exclusion as a pervasive atmosphere of inarticulation or silence (to momentarily invoke a different metaphor), a veil that is only broken by repeated representations of gay and lesbian ontologies.[6] This means that the decision to come out to others frequently involves a careful (although sometimes spontaneous) weighing of the likely rewards and possible repercussions. Many ingredients go into this somewhat unpredictable process, for example, personal experience, individual ideology, and the sociopolitical atmosphere at the time. On a more fundamental level, the act of coming out is deeply shaped by specificities of identity and corporeality such as gender, age, and ethnicity. These variables do not just influence the actual decision to disclose one's homosexuality; they literally mold the meaning of visibility. For example, certain acts, such as walking arm in arm, may be a greater signifier of homosexuality for men than for women, or more acceptable in some ethnic communities than in others. In turn, the age of the individuals involved affects the extent to which others even recognize that they are sexual beings with preferences and desires.

While the everyday silences of lesbians and gay men may contribute to the wider social and political opaqueness of homosexuality, such practices cannot be altogether portrayed as the oppressive product of a homophobic culture. The sexual privacy afforded by the closet also proffers a strategic means of control over the extent to which one is subjected to the undesirable implications of being marked as gay or lesbian in everyday life such as disparagement, discrimination, and hostility. Furthermore, the hesitation to publicly identify as gay or lesbian does not only stem from the desire to avoid the more obvious forms of intolerance and inequity. It may also reflect an individual's belief that the very act of coming out entails an inevitable, even if unintended, disavowal of competing or contradictory aspects of identity, not to mention an invest- ment in fixed and essential notions of sexuality. Once an individual makes a declaration of homosexuality, there is no means to control or redress the ways in which that knowledge is interpreted by others and little opportunity to challenge the standpoints through which it will be digested (Cohen, 1991). In particular, the political imperative to stand up and be counted may be out- weighed by the risk that other facets of one's self, such as ethnic or racial identities, will be subsumed or "whitewashed" in the process (Omosupe, 1991; Walker, 1993). Quite simply, the rush to declare who we are can bring with it an unintended series of assumptions about who we are not. This is not to say that the shortage of unsullied public representations of homosexuality is not a prime mechanism in the processes of subjugation, but rather, to take seriously the idea that resistance is integral (rather than external or oppositional) to any given power relation (Foucault, 1978). In this sense, the closet represents both a technique of self-surveillance and a strategy for resisting the surveil- lance of others; or, as Bordo (1989) suggests, "the very same gesture that expresses protest . . . can also signal retreat" (p. 21). This vacillation between the closet as an oppressive place of enforced secrecy and a place from which to refuse the subjugatory implications of visible homosexuality (by encourag- ing the misrecognition of one's sexuality) should remind us that "silence and secrecy are a shelter for power, anchoring its prohibitions" at the same time that they "loosen its holds and provide for relatively obscure areas of toler- ance" (Foucault, 1978, p. 101).

In short, the closet is a rather contradictory and unstable place. Not only is it necessary to continually repeat the act of coming out to actually be out, but, as Butler (1991) notes, what it means to be out at any given moment is inevitably dependent on what it means to be closeted. Hence one can never be completely in or completely out of the closet. If we add to this discursive ambiguity the more personalized tension between the desire for recognition and the desire not to be recognized—to borrow from Skeggs's (1997) in- sights into identity among working-class women—the distinction between visibility and invisibility begins to look somewhat equivocal. The open secret of homosexuality, the reality of living in and out of the closet at the same time, denotes a shifting, context-dependent, and disputed line of demarcation between what it means to be visible in social and political terms and what it means not to be visible. It is doubtful that homosexuality can be, unequivo- cally, one or the other.

BODY MAPS

Vision has long been a metaphor for knowledge. In Foucauldian terms, things made visible are things that are shown to knowledge, or, as Rajchman

(1988) puts it, "to see is always to think . . . and to think is always to see" (p. 92). In other words, how we see and how we know are inextricable from each other. It is not, therefore, surprising that visibility is one of the tropes through which we come to know homosexuality. Indeed, the construction of homosexuality as a discrete sexual preference that is capable of being concealed or exposed means that same-sex desire is always troubled by the ever present possibilities of being visible or not visible, of being closeted or out, of speaking up or remaining silent, of being known or not known. If homosexuality is constructed in part through this trope of visibility, then what might this mean, in turn, for violence that is motivated by hostility toward this same sexuality? One suggestion is that the escalating visibility of lesbians and gay men in contemporary Western culture has led to a rise in the prevalence of homophobic violence (Dean, Wu, & Martin, 1992). Although this is an intriguing argument, the approach put forth in this chapter does not follow this teleological route. Instead, we are interested in exploring how the question of visibility might be entangled in the implications of violence. Indeed, if we were to take momentarily the risk of representing the relation between violence and visibility in linear terms, we might say that our interest lies at the other end of the cause-and-effect equation, that is, in considering how the trope of visibility shapes the effects of violence, rather than the causes.[7] To come to terms with the implications of violence in any collective sense, it is necessary to consider what it means for lesbians and gay men to know that homophobic violence is a tangible, if not always immediate, threat to their personal safety. In other words, if we accept that knowledge itself is the product of a *mutual presupposition* (Deleuze, 1988) between materiality, on one hand, and language and discourse, on the other—that is, of the way in which they inform each other—then the knowledge that lesbians and gay men have of homophobic violence (as a material practice) is inevitably "inscribed in a series of statements" (Kendall & Wickham, 1999, p. 42) about visibility. The significance of this inscription becomes apparent if we take a closer look at the capacity of homophobic violence, as a knowledge, to mold lesbian and gay perceptions of personal safety.

Concerns about crime and violence in contemporary Western societies, especially in urban regions, lead most people, and seemingly women in particular, to assess the danger to personal safety posed by particular spaces, situations, and individuals (Pain, 1997; Stanko, 1993; Valentine, 1992). These assessments become the basis for the construction of what have been called *safety maps* (von Schulthess, 1992). A safety map is an ever changing, personalized, yet shared matrix of attributes and relations that individuals employ to make their way in public and private spaces. In constructing these maps, individuals draw on their knowledge of the ways in which specific variables render them vulnerable to personal danger. This conjunction of personal, spatial, and temporal variables is likely to include previous experience of violence; the degree to which an individual feels more or less vulnerable to violence because of his or her age, gender, ethnicity, and the like; understandings of the risks associated with particular areas; the time of day; perceptions about the type of people likely to be encountered in particular areas or within particular social situations; popular discourse around violence and risk; the purpose an individual has for being at a particular place or with a particular group of people; perceptions about physical appearance and gesture; and so on.[8] While the adoption of some form of safety map into our daily lives is so commonplace that most of us treat it as second nature, the actual ways in which we choose to map our safety are the product, in part, of the types of violence to which we believe we are vulnerable.

Like other forms of hate crime, an act of homophobic violence is symbolic (Cunneen, Fraser, & Tomsen, 1997; Whillock & Slayden, 1995). It stands as a sign of the potential danger for all individuals who identify with the same target group(s) as the victim. This argument has been well made in the context of gendered violence, where feminist research has demonstrated that many women interpret a seemingly "minor" or "everyday" form of unwanted sexualized attention or aggression within the context of other, more serious possibilities. For example, encounters with flashing or obscene phone calls can generate concerns not only about the incident itself, but also about what might happen next (Kelly, 1988). In particular, women's awareness of their vulnerability to certain types of violence, such as rape and sexual assault, shape their perceptions of, and practices around, personal safety.[9] A similar process is evident in relation to homophobic hostility. Seemingly small incidents (such as homophobic remarks, name-calling, or verbal abuse) can transform the generic hazards of heteronormativity into the tangible threat of more severe hostility. Although minor incidents (which are disturbingly common, according to the survey research cited previously) are generally experienced as violating in themselves, their effects are magnified if individuals view them as part of a continuum (Kelly, 1988) that links supposedly lesser incidents with those that are of greater concern. Like sexual violence and racially motivated violence, the symbolism of homophobic violence is therefore contingent on the extent to which an individual first recognizes his or her own vulnerability in the victimization of others with similar identities or lifestyles and, second, interprets abusive, hostile, and violent acts within a continuum of possible interconnected dangers.

Hence the implications of symbolic crimes are not confined to those individuals who experience the violence itself. For many lesbians and gay men, the knowledge that they may be targeted for homophobic violence (or, indeed, anyone who thinks they may be) becomes a variable in the mapping of safety, whether they have directly encountered violence or not. Like all other variables, such knowledge makes its own particular contribution to the spatialization of personal safety. To think about this contribution in empirical terms, and particularly the ways in which visibility configures gay and lesbian safety maps, four excerpts are introduced here, drawn from interviews with women who participated in the research project described earlier. In these excerpts, each woman responds to a question about the ways in which she goes about maximizing personal safety in her daily life, specifically, safety from hostility or violence that is likely to be related to homophobia. Although the remarks are made by four different women, they are treated as an aggregate form of commentary by discussing them collectively, rather than taking each one in turn. Although each has a unique narrative, the accounts they provide are typical of research participants' understandings of the risk that homosexuality poses to personal safety. In other words, the material specificities they discuss vary greatly, but they are all linked by a common thread:

Kim, 34-Year-Old Anglo Australian Mother of Two and Recipient of Government Welfare Payments

You just do little precautionary things. . . . The kind of strategies that you might employ when you know that you might be gonna cop a stone through the window. . . . Well, I took the bumper sticker off my car that said something about "gay love rights." . . . We stopped holding hands at the shops. . . . For a while I even drove the long way home so they [a group of young men at the local shops] wouldn't know where I lived.

Jennifer, 18-Year-Old Anglo Australian Student

Before I come home from a dyke bar I sometimes take off my jacket or brush my hair forward, depending on what I look like. I don't worry about how much flesh I'm showing. When I go home I'm only worried about how much I look like a dyke. It freaks me out that my old man might be waiting for me. He suspects, but I don't want to give him the proof he needs to justify his own aggression.

Rose, 27-Year-Old Chinese Australian Doctor

Sure sometimes you make big conscious decisions, like, saying to yourself, "No. I'd never ever hold hands in that part of town or in that racist, homophobic crowd." . . . But really it's the little things that you do to yourself every day, that you've gotten so used to doing that you barely realize. Its about not being too blatant. A little bit is okay.

Mel, 45-Year-Old Anglo Australian Postal Worker

I used to get hassled a lot because I looked like a dyke. Now I look straight it's a completely different thing. . . . Well, monitoring your clothes in the morning. If I wear this jacket with this butch haircut and those boots will everyone at work just find it too much? . . . Should I wear earrings to my sister's wedding to tone it down a bit and my god, what about a dress? . . . Setting up two bedrooms in your house, so your parents or, more importantly, friends of your kids won't realize you sleep together. That's a popular one.

Each of these women recounts a series of daily, localized practices designed to monitor, and often minimize, visible manifestations of her sexuality. Each situation calls for different precautionary responses to the conundrum of being "too blatant." These behaviors include removing overt political paraphernalia; toning down the degree to which they look too much like a "dyke"; not expressing intimate affection with a girlfriend or partner in front of others; not going to certain parts of town because they feel unsafe; going out of their way to ensure that people they don't trust won't find out where they live; and hiding the fact that they sleep together in their own house. Certainly not all of these practices are a direct response to the presumed risk of violence. Most, however, are. While the behaviors themselves are often about what the women do with objects as diverse as cars, bedrooms, and clothes, it is significant that the overall purpose of all of the strategies they describe is to reduce the degree to which they themselves are visible as lesbians, whether that visibility be in terms of personal demeanor, the places they go, or the daily details of their domestic lives. It is important to remember that many factors go into the construction of gay and lesbian safety maps overall. However, the prevalence of these strategies among lesbians and gay men suggests that homophobic violence, as a form of knowledge, engenders a distinct tendency to monitor one's own body for signs of homosexuality. Given the centrality of the body to the processes of self-surveillance via which human subjects are subjugated, it is hardly unusual for individuals to adopt a plethora of bodily images, gestures, and movements in response to the threat of violence. What is notable in this instance is that safety from homophobic violence is conceptualized primarily (albeit not solely) as a question of the extent to which one is visible as a certain type of sexual subject in the eyes of others, as a homosexual in the eyes of the homophobe. If visibility is a key to safety from the hostility of homophobia, then it is unavoidable that in mapping safety, lesbians and gay men will be mapping their own bodies for manifestations of sexuality. Hence we might usefully acknowledge the primacy of the body to the negotiation of safety from the specific problem of homophobic violence by thinking of this process as a form of body map in itself: a cartographic matrix of practices for surveying, screening, and supervising the times, places, and ways in which one is manifest as a homosexual.

There is, of course, no such thing as a lesbian or gay body map. Practices for monitoring the visibility of one's homosexuality are refracted not only by the shifting dynamics of the situation at hand, but also by relations of ethnicity, gender, class, and so on. As I mentioned earlier, these variables mediate the very meanings of visibility. However, they also fashion the components that go into gay and lesbian body maps, sometimes in contradictory ways. For example, during the course of my interview with Rose, she suggested that, among the non-Asian population, extreme racism and homophobia often go hand in hand. This allows her to use what she calls her "antenna for racism" to determine whether a group of people are likely not just to be racist, but also homophobic. Yet the very same ethnocentric assumptions that fuel the threat of racism can sometimes operate to obscure what might otherwise be a visible expression of homosexuality. Rose puts it like this: "Anglos are often so naive about other cultures that they think there's no such thing as Asian lesbians. . . . I can hold hands with my girlfriend as much as I like in some places and they just think we're 'nice Asian girls.'" Not surprisingly, Rose is only too happy to "exploit" these kinds of cultural assumptions when mapping her own safety. The realities of socioeconomic difference also shape the extent to which different groups of lesbians and gay men feel the need to monitor their own visibility. Quite simply, the more money you have, the more options you have for choosing where you live, how you travel in your daily life, and where, and with whom, you spend your leisure time. While the signifiers of homosexuality may vary across different class contexts, the bottom line is that it is a lot easier to look "blatant" when you are able to live and socialize in areas known as "gay-friendly" or when the luxury of owning your own car allows you to avoid the everyday contingencies of public transport. Similarly, it is important to recognize that gender also frames the practices through which lesbians and gay men monitor their appearance and behavior for visible expressions of sexuality. Given the prevalence of sexual violence against women, and the possibility of antihomosexual sentiment leading to such violence, lesbians (like heterosexual women) have more reason than gay men to pay attention to the ways in which their physical appearance will be sexualized by heterosexual men. Yet, as with ethnicity and class, the interaction between gender and sexuality is unlikely to follow a straightforward formula. For example, while it is not unreasonable to expect that women's (supposed) greater fear of violence will produce more extensive practices of self-surveillance among lesbians than among gay men, other factors, such as gay men's apparent greater vulnerability to random homophobic assaults, may counter this. Although the details of such scenarios remain to be explored in any comprehensive manner, there is little doubt that the notion of visibility itself, and the practices through which it is charted, are the product not simply of homosexuality as an isolated identity, but of the ways in which it is refracted by these (and other) subjectivities.

Stanko and Curry (1997) have demonstrated how a "climate of unsafety" encourages gay men and lesbians to take responsibility for personal safety by self-policing their own behavior. They suggest that homophobic violence "leads to a continuum of self-regulation, whereby the physically threatening behaviour of the homophobe is intertwined with self-imposed regulation of self in heterosexual space" (p. 525). I wish to pick up on the importance of this point by suggesting that the discursive tension between homosexuality and visibility represents interacting axes on which the specificities of various practices of self-regulation pivot. In other words, safety from the hostility of homophobia may be negotiated in a multitude of ways, but each negotiation inevitably turns on the question of visibility. The implications of knowing (and, of course, believing) that one may be subjected to physical violence or verbal hostility are found in the construction of body maps that incorporate an understanding of the hostile contingencies of displays of homosexuality; that is, body maps are the specific product of the integration of the trope of visibility into the broader safety maps that lesbians and gay men construct. If the corporeal practices that lesbians and gay men engage in to attain a sense of safety from homophobic violence are an effect of their knowledge of this hostility, then, in an epistemological sense, it is possible that homophobic violence is always inscribed in—but never confined by—a series of statements about visibility.[10] Or, to relate this to our overall concern with the collective effects of homophobic violence, the negotiation of visibility through the construction of lesbian and gay body maps may be an inevitable material implication of homophobic hostility, one that is not bound by the immediate and personal injuries inflicted by the act of violence itself.

FLOUTING DANGER

Like the woman at the International Victimology Conference who was resistant to the public witness of homosexuality, the perpetrators of homophobic violence (who appear to be primarily, but not exclusively, male) often seem to be more antagonistic toward unabashed and unashamed representations of gay and lesbian sexualities than they are toward homosexuality itself. It is therefore not surprising that homophobic violence generates a tendency among lesbians and gay men to construct safety from homophobia in terms that are in some way framed by the question of visibility. The centrality of visibility to the body maps that lesbians and gay men create in the pursuit of safety suggests that it is not possible to formulate the full social implications of homophobic violence in isolation from statements of sexual visibility. Nonetheless, this is not the same as saying that violence gives rise to a monolithic form of social invisibility.

Let us explore the significance of this distinction by considering what can be called the "holding hands" example. Among all the questions that were put to the women interviewed, the one that received the most consistent response was a direct question about whether or not they tended to hold hands, or otherwise express intimacy, such as kissing, with a partner or girlfriend when they were in predominantly heterosexual spaces. Taking into account individual preferences around the public display of affection, and the fact that concerns about hostility and violence are just one aspect of broader concerns about disapproval and discrimination, the overwhelming response from this group of women was that "it depends": it depends on the atmosphere and terrain of each and every situation as it arises; it depends on the gender and ethnicity of the people likely to be encountered; it depends on the possible repercussions; it depends on the short- and long-term significance of any negative responses; it depends on staying attuned to any changes in the situation; and so on. No one said, "I always feel safe enough to display such affection." No one said, "I never feel safe enough to display such affection." The decision to hold hands or kiss was always a question of weighing up the risks and rewards. Even those women who saw themselves as "blatant" about their sexuality exercised caution about the contexts within which they were so: "I reckon I'm as out as anyone can be. But, yeah, I'm still careful about when I can afford to flaunt it. I'm not stupid, you know." On the other hand, women who saw themselves as being relatively closeted also monitored and assessed situations for the degree of security they were likely to provide: "Sometimes when I'm feeling really brave and things looks okay I'll grab my girlfriend's hand. It never lasts. But, hey, I did it!"

The correlation between the risk of hostility and the decision not to disclose one's sexuality—which can also be read as a correlation between being "blatant" and being "stupid"—is not a simple linear one. Danger does not necessarily signify a return to the closet. Many lesbians and gay men derive pleasure from being blatant about their sexuality and, moreover, from deliberately creating a bit of a spectacle. Russo has suggested that to make a sexual spectacle of oneself is a particularly feminine danger that invites one to be read as grotesque. It seems, however, that sexualized displays of homosexuality in men and women transgress the boundaries of decorum in ways that attract similar condemnation: to borrow from Russo (1986), "certain bodies, in certain public framings, in certain public spaces, are always already transgressive—dangerous and in danger" (p. 217). In different ways, and to different degrees, lesbians and gay men may actively court this danger (and blame) to experience "the pleasure of showing off, scandalizing, or resisting" (Foucault, 1978, p. 45). For example, Helen, one of the women interviewed, described one of her favorite pastimes in these terms. In particular, Helen likes to shock groups of young men who cross her path. Pulling up in her car at a traffic light often provides a perfect opportunity to do this: "If there's a bunch of yahoos pulling up at the side, I can get quite bold and start passionately kissing my lover in the car. They'll wind down the window and say, 'Dirty lesos! Lesos! . . . You just can't get a man.'" Helen then takes great "'delight as she 'leaves them for dead'" by speeding off when the light changes to green. Sometimes they follow, sometimes they don't. For Helen, the thrill and amusement of this experience is the product not only of the sense of travesty that an open display of lesbian passion engenders, but, more specifically, of evading the danger that the young men embody for her. By mocking their heterosexist insults, she is able to trivialize and express contempt for the potential of homophobic hostility to injure her. Just as attempts to camouflage homosexuality represent both an oppressive silencing and a resistance to the trap of visibility, so, too, does this act of "flaunting" homosexuality expose one to the possibility of homophobic repercussions at the same time that it challenges the very ability of these repercussions to cause harm.

It is important to recognize that the pleasure of "flaunting" one's sexuality may derive its effect in part from flouting, perhaps flirting with, danger. However, it is equally important to recognize, as suggested previously, that blatancy is not the same as stupidity. Helen is always careful to stage her performances so that the risks to her safety do not outweigh the rewards. If her experience is in any way representative, such acts of deliberate affront are most likely to take place in situations where lesbians and gay men already feel safe enough to flirt with danger because they can control the outcome of the risks they take, for example, driving in their cars with their lovers; walking with a group of leather men; coming out to a violent father surrounded by friends; or dancing with thousands of other queers in a Mardi Gras parade, wearing nothing but body paint. Personal safety is a perception as well as an embodied material condition. It cannot be procured or guaranteed once and for all. It is always a process of negotiation. To negotiate safety, lesbians and gay men (like everyone else) must find ways to continually reinforce and reproduce their own sense of it. It is possible that the integration into one's own body maps of controlled engagements with what it means to be unsafe is one method of doing this.

MANAGING SAFETY

In their work on the policing of "the responsible" homosexual, Stanko and Curry (1997) suggest that the risk of violence is intertwined with the risk of self-exposure. Violence prevention strategies that pressure gay men and lesbians to "pass" as heterosexual engender a form of self-regulation that supposedly allows individuals to manage potential harm. I am drawn to Stanko and Curry's use of the concept of management in this context. If the body maps that flow from gay and lesbian knowledge of homophobic violence are constituted by acts that seek both to avoid and to flout the danger of a visible homosexuality, then does the concept of management, especially self-management, offer a useful theoretical and linguistic tool for articulating these complexities? Might it be helpful to try to capture gay and lesbian attempts to corporeally map personal safety through the idea that visibility is managed, rather than, say, regulated?

In Foucauldian terms, the broad concept of regulation (in departure from but subsuming, the notion of repression) captures most effectively the "process of subjection" that "activates or forms the subject" (Butler, 1995, p. 230). In particular, the inscription of systems of knowledge (such as the classification of sexual desire into categories of homosexual and heterosexual) on "wayward populations" allows dysfunctional personalities and behavioral deficiencies to be understood as essential or self-evident properties of individuals (Rajchman, 1988). This process of reducing and containing human multiplicities to a tight space (the category of homosexuality) facilitates the imposition of a "particular conduct on a particular human multiplicity" (Deleuze, 1988, p. 34).[11] This means that the choice to act in certain ways is shaped by the way in which subjects see themselves and others as certain types of individuals: "'seeing' in this sense is part of doing" (Rajchman, 1988, p. 94). In other words, once subjects are seen, and see themselves, in a particular light, their choices, decisions, and actions are all affected by the parameters of these identity categories. They adapt to the cultural expectations attached to specific identities and restrict their behavior accordingly. As we have already witnessed, it is not only formal systems of knowledge (such as sexology and psychology) that are deployed in the regulation of human multiplicities. Informal systems of knowledge (such as the exchange of anecdotes about homophobic hostility, rumors about unsafe spaces, and so on) are also crucial to the ways in which particular actions are taken up by subjects (Hunt & Wickham, 1994). It is this merger of formal and informal knowledge systems that allows gay men and lesbians to know that they might be the object of someone else's homophobic hostility, irrespective of whether they have encountered that hostility directly themselves, and to employ this knowledge in the construction of their own maps for the pursuit of safety. It is via this imperative to normative obedience that subjects are regulated.

Certainly the daily, localized decisions and embodied actions in which lesbians and gay men engage to negotiate safety can be well articulated as practices of self-surveillance in the wider regulatory processes of disciplinarity. We know, however, that subjects simultaneously defy this process. For example, the interview excerpts quoted previously suggest to me that a safety map is not a blueprint for a secreted homosexuality; violence does not just function to coerce lesbians and gay men to stay in the closet (indeed, any such function will always be disrupted by the very instability of the closet itself). Safety is never a static condition, but rather, it is a context-dependent form of negotiation. In particular, safety from homophobia involves a continual process of monitoring and balancing the potential risks of disclosure with the potential rewards—assessments that, as I have suggested previously, are always made through the conjunction of homophobia with other specificities. In any given situation, the way in which an individual has mapped out the meaning of safety may guide him or her toward a series of corporeal practices that effectively confine, conceal, or exclude expressions of homosexuality. This much is clear. However, the imperative to map one's own safety is not only a matter of bridling, moderating, or restricting bodily representations of homosexuality to "make regular." It is also an imperative toward "looking after" these representations by controlling and taking charge of them: practices that might involve not only regulating one's self-representations to conform, but also refusing to regulate them in this way (a form of resistance in itself).

The collective implications of homophobic violence need to be formulated so as to account for these cartographical practices of compliance and defiance. This is where the concept of management might be useful. In a literal sense, the notion of management denotes the organizing and handling of things, taking charge of situations and people. This involves strategies of self-regulation—moderation, correction, and restriction—as well as a sense of command, stewardship, and the manipulation of events that comes with being in a position that demands, and allows, this kind of control. Although the relation between Foucauldian notions of management, regulation, discipline, and governance is somewhat slippery and far from incontrovertible, we can briefly traverse some of this ground with the specific purpose of positioning the terms *management* and *self-management*. The purpose in seeking to flesh out these notions is not to make a pedantic point about the importance of semantic distinctions between concepts that are, to be honest, closely entwined with each other. More simply, it is to suggest that the dictionary-type description of management provided previously hints at a more theoretical meaning of the concept, especially as it relates to the self, that might prove useful in the analysis of homophobic violence.

Management makes a brief appearance in Foucault's (1977) initial account of the disciplinary society (or, at least, in English translations of it). Specifically, the kinds of self-monitoring practices depicted previously are, for Foucault, techniques that render the unpredictable, confusing multiplicities of human populations more manageable (Foucault, 1977). While Prado (1995) suggests that the disciplines can therefore be glossed as techniques for managing people, a more precise interpretation of management really only becomes apparent within the context of Foucault's later work on governmentality.[12] If government is understood as a broad regulatory strategy for the "conduct of conduct" (Rose, 1996, p. 134), particularly as it relates to populations and nation-states, then the notion of management most commonly signifies the techniques through which knowledge systems are brought to bear on particular objects to achieve the overall objectives of government. Although governmentality has many components, one of the ways in which the "collective mass" of human phenomena is controlled and managed is via the very depths and details of individual practices of self-surveillance (Foucault, 1991). In other words, the government of populations is not just a matter of the "calculated management" of others, but also of the small, everyday "technologies of the self" through which subjects "experience, understand, judge and conduct themselves" and which are so often implemented through the body (Rose, 1996, p. 135). Hunt and Wickham (1994) pick up on Foucault's use of management by referring to these more micro elements of government as "self-management" (or self-government). It is significant that this managerialization of identity and personal relations is not experienced exclusively as the imposition of a set of rules that serve the interests of others. Indeed, the very capacity of knowledge systems to engender an imperative to self-management is determined by the extent to which this imperative is understood as a question of "caring" for one's self (Gordon, 1991).

The danger that homophobic violence, like other forms of violence, poses to one's physical and psychological integrity means that the safety practices in which lesbians and gay men engage are a matter of both regulating the ways in which oneself is vulnerable to violence and of caring for the safety and security of that self. If we understand homosexuality as an object or thing to be governed in the pursuit of personal safety, then certainly lesbians and gay men do chart their bodies for visible manifestations of homosexuality in ways that can only be described as an undesirable adaptation to the requirements of homophobic sentiment. But in constantly mapping their bodies for signs of homosexuality, lesbians and gay men are also able to exercise a form of control. They cope with the knowledge of violence by organizing their bodies and optimizing the ways in which others react to them. It seems to the author that the concept of self-management may offer a fruitful formulation for recognizing that this response to violence encompasses both the imperative to moderate and restrict the ways in which one is visibly homosexual and the desire to carefully handle one's homosexuality as a means of looking after and caring for one's personal security and integrity. Self-management hints at the agency of subjects who do not just control themselves (or are controlled) in the face of danger but who also "take control" of certain situations, that is, subjects who literally subject things to their control. Gay men and lesbians may rarely be in a position to take charge of the hostility that is committed directly against them, but as the managers of their own visibility, many are able to take charge of the contexts that feed into and flow from their knowledge of such hostility.

CONCLUSION: MANAGING THE UNMANAGEABLE

In avoiding or flouting danger, in negotiating safety, in hiding or flaunting sexuality, lesbians and gay men are involved in the complex daily management of a plethora of choices around the relation between homosexuality and visibility. As the corporeal spatialization of these negotiations—what Foucault (1977) might call a diagram of "the location of bodies in space" (p. 205)—body maps resonate with panoptic principles of vision and visibility. They represent the collective implications of the knowledge that homophobia brings to the broader construction of a sense of personal safety. This includes, but is never confined to, a plethora of options for managing the ways in which one's homosexuality is recognizable, or visible, to audiences who may pose a threat. Irrespective of how a given individual experiences and responds to the question of personal safety, the knowledge of violence means that lesbians and gay men must grapple (whether regularly or irregularly) with the specter of the closet; the kinds of management practices that are described previously are only possible because visibility fashions our understandings of homosexuality and the choices available for negotiating safety. In short, it is suggested that no matter how gay men and lesbians deal with the risks that homophobia poses to their safety, they are invariably drawn into an imperative to manage self-representations of their sexuality toward desirable ends. If managing homophobic violence means managing one's homosexuality, then the risk of homophobic violence does not simply lie side by side with the risks associated with coming out. As Stanko and Curry (1997) suggest, the two are intertwined. The imperative to manage the visible representations of one's homosexuality suggests that the specifics of this entanglement lie in the fact that lesbian and gay knowledge of homophobic hostility is always infused with the homosexuality-visibility nexus.

The very fact that at any given moment, it might be possible to be anything less than "blatant" about one's homosexuality inscribes the choices one has for negotiating safety. In this way, homophobic hostility, and the body maps it engenders, is inescapably configured by the "trap of visibility." Quite simply, it may be that to know of homophobic hostility is to manage visibility.

What, then, of the ambiguity of the trope of visibility? While it is commonplace to represent the question of sexual visibility in dichotomous terms (visible-invisible, public-private, in-out, inside-outside, closet-freedom), as argued previously, the meanings attached to being in or out of the closet are neither singular nor universal. To be closeted about one's sexuality can be both a form of acquiescence and a form of control. Similarly, the decision to come out may be an act of resistance at the same time that it feeds into the "trap" of visible sexualities. If, therefore, it is never possible to be completely closeted, it is likely that it is never possible to be completely safe from homophobic violence.[13] Furthermore, even if it were possible, the equivocal nature of the closet means that every time lesbians and gay men grapple with the question of visibility, they must grapple with the uncertainty and duplicity of the options available to them. Every small act of self-management, every body map, then, is a part not just of a larger diagram of the connection between homosexuality and visibility, but, more specifically, of the flux and ambiguity of this relation. This means that the collective legacy of homophobic violence is found not only in the harm and injury it inflicts on many individuals, nor in the personal and social veiling of a "wayward" or "unruly" population, but, moreover, in the capacity to incite this population to manage the equivocal and contested nexus between homosexuality and visibility, when the very troubled nature of that nexus is itself the source of much uncertainty and tension. The imperative to manage one's homosexuality is, in this instance, an imperative to manage the unmanageable.

NOTES

Reproduced in a slightly different form with permission of Sage Publications Ltd. from Gail Mason, "Body Maps: Envisaging Homophobia, Violence and Safety," *Social and Legal Studies: An International Journal*, Volume 10, no.Number 1, March (2001):, pp. 23–44, (© 2001 by Sage Publications Ltd., 2001), by permission of Sage Publications Ltd.

1.   The Eighth International Symposium on Victimology, "Victimisation and Violence: Strategies for Survival," August 1994, Adelaide, Australia.

2.   This research provided an empirical basis for much of the author's doctoral thesis. However, several interviews were conducted at a later date and are not included in the thesis (see G. Mason, 2002).

3.   This chapter primarily relies on the terms *gay* and *lesbian* to denote same-sex desires and lifestyles among men and women. However, as queer politics and theory have shown us, such terminology is deeply problematic and should not be taken to signify fixed identities or subjectivities (Butler, 1990, 1991). Also, the word *homosexuality* is used. Although homosexuality has virtually no currency as a contemporary identity, and mindful of the many criticisms of it, *homosexuality* can be strategically employed as a linguistic tool for denoting a cultural construction (neither an identity nor a universal subjectivity) that has emerged from modern discourses of sexuality that classify sexual desire in dichotomous terms.

4.   Although Foucault may suggest to us that power in contemporary Western societies is better understood through relations of disciplinary surveillance, rather than the spectacle of force and punishment, the way in which these mechanisms are themselves dependent on visible sexual categories—which, in their less legitimate forms, represent a spectacle of their own—suggests that it might be more helpful to think of different forms of social spectacle as elements of, rather than oppositions to, surveillance. Indeed, as a model for the disciplinary society, the panoptic metaphor itself only functions as a form of surveillance through the production of visible types of subjects. In this sense, the relation between spectacle and surveillance is not so much a question of "incompatibility" as of "difference" (Foucault, 1977).

5.   The term *coming out* refers to those times when individuals deliberately say or do something to indicate to others that they are gay or lesbian. An alternative, broader use of *coming out* refers more to the self-recognition of one's homoerotic desires.

6.   Butler (1991) has suggested that, in some contrast to gay men, the exclusion of the lesbian subject from Western discourse itself is a form of violence that refuses her a site of prohibition from which to resist her own subjugation. Thus the lesbian is only thinkable and imaginable as an "abiding falsehood." Given the prominence of the lesbian subject in some contexts, such as the pornographic genre (Roof, 1991), it is perhaps more helpful to characterize this as an exclusion from mainstream or legitimate discourse.

7.   Although it is believed that violence does have effects, we remain cognizant of the Foucauldian point that in moving away from determinist assumptions, such effects might be more appropriately understood as contingencies (Kendall & Wickham, 1999).

8.   Although personal safety concerns may be projected onto the figure of the "unpredictable stranger" (Lupton, 1999), Stanko (1993) nonetheless reminds us that women's "precautionary behavior occurs in public and private, [and is] aimed to minimize violence from strangers as well as loved ones" (p. 160).

9.   Research on violence against women has often highlighted women's "fear" of violence. I have chosen not to use the notion of fear because, at least in the context of homophobic

violence, l believe it has a tendency to overstate and overdetermine the problem. For a discussion of the rhetoric of fear in classic feminist texts on violence, see Burton (1998).

10.   A careful distinction must be noted here. Practices of self-surveillance are in no way determined only by the threat of hostility and violence. As some of the women quoted previously suggest, the concerns that prompt the self-regulation of visible representations of one's homosexuality exceed questions of violence or direct hostility. My suggestion that the knowledge of violence is inscribed in statements of visibility should not be taken to imply that the negotiation of visibility can be reduced to the negotiation of personal safety. Violence is never the sole factor in the decision not to disclose one's sexuality.

11.   The imposition of conduct on subjects in turn allows for the "ordering" of these multiplicities (Foucault, 1977).

12.   Just as the disciplinary society does not replace sovereignty, neither does governmentality replace the disciplines. Instead, sovereignty, discipline, and government function as a "triangle," with "its primary target the population" (Foucault, 1991, p. 102).

13.   As one interviewee put it, "You can't totally avoid it. Unless you're gonna be totally insulated from the rough, the straight, the homophobic society, you know. You have to get in a leso taxi, you have to go to a leso bar, you have to go to a leso house . . . there is nowhere that you can go that [you] are guaranteed not to get homophobia."

REFERENCES

Berrill, K. (1990). Anti-gay violence and victimization in the United States: An overview. *Journal of Interpersonal Violence, 5*, 274–294.

Bordo, S. (1989). The body and the reproduction of femininity: A feminist appropriation of Foucault. In A. Jaggar & S. Bordo (Eds.), *Gender/body/knowledge: Feminist reconstructions of being and knowing* (pp. 13–33). New Brunswick, NJ: Rutgers University Press.

Burton, N. (1998). Resistance to prevention: Reconsidering feminist antiviolence rhetoric. In S. French, W. Teays, & L. Purdy (Eds.), *Violence against women: Philosophical perspectives* (pp. 182–200). Ithaca, NY: Cornell University Press.

Butler, J. (1990). *Gender trouble: Feminism and the subversion of identity.* New York: Routledge.

Butler, J. (1991). Imitation and gender insubordination. In D. Fuss (Ed.), *Inside/out: Lesbian theories, gay theories* (pp. 13–31). New York: Routledge.

Butler, J. (1995). Subjection, resistance, resignification: Between Freud and Foucault. In J. Rajchman (Ed.), *The identity in question* (pp. 229–249). New York: Routledge.

Cohen, E. (1991). Who are "we"? Gay "identity" as political emotion (a theoretical rumination). In D. Fuss (Ed.), *Inside/out: Lesbian theories, gay theories* (pp. 71–92). New York: Routledge.

Cunneen, C., Fraser, D., & Tomsen, S. (Eds.). (1997). *Faces of hate: Hate crime in Australia.* Sydney, NSW: Hawkins (Federation) Press.

Dean, L., Wu, S., & Martin, J. (1992). Trends in violence and discrimination against gay men in New York City: 1984 to 1990. In G. Herek & K. Berrill (Eds.), *Hate crimes: Confronting violence against lesbians and gay men* (pp. 46–62). Newbury Park, CA: Sage.

Deleuze, G. (1988). *Foucault.* London: Athlone Press.

Eliason, M., Donelan, C., & Randall, C. (1992). Lesbian stereotypes. *Health Care for Women International, 13,* 131–143.

Foucault, M. (1977). *Discipline and punish: The birth of the prison.* Harmondsworth, England: Penguin.

Foucault, M. (1978). *The history of sexuality: An introduction.* Harmondsworth, England: Penguin.

Foucault, M. (1988). Technologies of the self. In L. Martin, H. Gutman, & P. Hutton (Eds.), *Technologies of the self: A seminar with Michel Foucault* (pp. 18–49). Amherst: University of Massachusetts Press.

Foucault, M. (1991). Governmentality. In G. Burchell, C. Gordon, & P. Miller (Eds.), *The Foucault effect: Studies in governmentality* (pp. 87–104). Chicago: University of Chicago Press.

Foucault, M., & Deleuze, G. (1977). Intellectuals and power. In D. Bouchard (Ed.), *Language, counter-memory, practice* (pp. 205–217). Ithaca, NY: Cornell University Press.

Garnets, L., Herek, G., & Levy, B. (1990). Violence and victimization of lesbians and gay men: Mental health consequences. *Journal of Interpersonal Violence, 5,* 366–383.

Gavey, N. (1993). Feminist poststructuralism and discourse analysis. *Psychology of Women Quarterly, 13,* 459–475.

Gay Men and Lesbians against Discrimination. (1994). *Not a day goes by: Report on the GLAD survey into discrimination and violence against lesbians and gay men in Victoria.* Melbourne, VIC: Author.

Gay Task Force. (1985). *Survey on anti-gay/lesbian violence.* Wellington, New Zealand: Author.

Gordon, C. (1991). Governmental rationality: An introduction. In G. Burchell, C. Gordon, & P. Miller (Eds.), *The Foucault effect: Studies in governmentality* (pp. 1–51). Chicago: University of Chicago Press.

Grosz, E. (1993). Bodies and knowledges: Feminism and the crisis of reason. In L. Alcoff & E. Potter (Eds.), *Feminist epistemologies* (pp. 187–215). New York: Routledge.

Haraway, D. (1991). *Simians, cyborgs and women: The reinvention of nature.* New York: Routledge.

Hunt, A., & Wickham, G. (1994). *Foucault and law: Towards a sociology of law as governance.* London: Pluto.

Hunter, J. (1990). Violence against lesbians and gay male youths. *Journal of Interpersonal Violence, 5,* 295–300.

Kelly, L. (1988). *Surviving sexual violence.* Cambridge: Polity Press.

Kendall, G., & Wickham, G. (1999). *Using Foucault's methods.* London: Sage.

Lupton, D. (1999). Dangerous places and the unpredictable stranger: Constructions of the fear of crime. *Australian and New Zealand Journal of Criminology, 32,* 1–15.

Mason, A., & Palmer, A. (1996). *Queer bashing: A national survey of hate crimes against lesbians and gay men.* London: Stonewall.

Mason, G. (1995). (Out)laws: Acts of proscription in the sexual order. In M. Thornton (Ed.), *Public and private: Feminist legal debates* (pp. 66–88). Melbourne, VIC: Oxford University Press.

Mason, G. (1997a). (Hetero)sexed hostility and violence toward lesbians. In S. Cook & J. Bessant (Eds.), *Women's encounters with violence: Australian experiences* (pp. 55–70). Thousand Oaks, CA: Sage.

Mason, G. (1997b). Sexuality and violence: Questions of difference. In C. Cunneen, D. Fraser, & S. Tomsen (Eds.), *Faces of hate: Hate crime in Australia* (pp. 115–136). Sydney,, NSW: Hawkins (Federation) Press.

Mason, G. (2002). *The spectacle of violence: Homophobia, Gender and Knowledge.* London: Routledge.

McGregor, F. (1996). I am not a lesbian. *Meanjin, 55*(1), 31–46.

Omosupe, E. (1991). Lesbian/bulldagger. *Differences: A Journal of Feminist Cultural Studies, 3*, 101–111.

Pain, R. (1997). Social geographies of women's fear of crime. *Transactions of the Institute of British Geographers, 22*, 231–244.

Prado, C. (1995). *Starting with Foucault: An introduction to genealogy.* Boulder, CO: Westview Press.

Rajchman, J. (1988). Foucault's art of seeing. *Spring*, October, 89–117.

Roof, J. (1991). *A lure of knowledge: Lesbian sexuality and theory.* New York: Columbia University Press.

Rose, N. (1996). Identity, genealogy, history. In S. Hall & P. Du Gay (Eds.), *Questions of cultural identity* (pp. 128–150). London: Sage.

Russo, M. (1986). Female grotesques: Carnival and theory. In T. de Lauretis (Ed.), *Feminist studies/critical studies* (pp. 213–229). Bloomington: Indiana University Press.

Ryan, C., & Futterman, D. (1998). *Lesbian and gay youth: Care and counseling.* New York: Columbia University Press.

Scott, J. (1991). The evidence of experience. *Critical Inquiry, 17*, 773–799.

Sedgwick, E. K. (1990). *Epistemology of the closet.* Berkeley: University of California Press.

Skeggs, B. (1997). *Formations of class and gender.* London: Sage.

Stanko, E. (1993). Ordinary fear: Women, violence, and personal safety. In P. Bart & E. Moran (Eds.), *Violence against women: The bloody footprints* (pp. 155–164). Newbury Park: Sage.

Stanko, E., & Curry, P. (1997). Homophobic violence and the self "at risk": Interrogating the boundaries. *Social and Legal Studies, 6*, 513–532.

Tomsen, S. (1997). Sexual identity and victimhood in gay-hate murder trials. In C. Cunneen, D. Fraser, & S. Tomsen (Eds.), *Faces of hate: Hate crime in Australia* (pp. 97–114). Sydney, NSW: Hawkins (Federation) Press.

Valentine, G. (1992). Images of danger: Women's sources of information about the spatial distribution of male violence. *Area, 24*, 22–29.

van den Boogaard, H. (1989). Blood furious underneath the skins . . . On antihomosexual violence: Its nature and the needs of the victims. In D. Altman (Ed.), *Homosexuality, which homosexuality? Essays for the International Scientific Conference on Lesbian and Gay Studies* (pp. 49–60). London: GMP.

von Schulthess, B. (1992). Violence in the streets: Anti-lesbian assault and harassment in San Francisco. In G. Herek & K. Berrill (Eds.), *Hate crimes: Confronting violence against lesbians and gay men* (pp. 65–74). Newbury Park, CA: Sage.

Walker, L. (1993). How to recognize a lesbian: The cultural politics of looking like what you are. *Signs: Journal of Women in Culture and Society, 18*, 866–890.

Whillock, R. K., & Slayden, D. (1995). *Hate speech.* Thousand Oaks, CA: Sage.

CHAPTER 5

THE PSYCHOLOGICAL AND SOCIAL EFFECTS OF ANTIBISEXUAL, ANTIGAY, AND ANTILESBIAN VIOLENCE AND HARASSMENT

Monique Noelle

Mark, a 38-year-old, white, single, gay-identified man, had just dropped off a friend in a borough of New York City and was driving home alone late at night in an area unfamiliar to him, when four young men in an SUV with the window down pulled next to his moving car. Mark thought they were trying to ask him for directions, so he had lowered his window and was addressing them politely, when he heard the word *faggot*. At that, he raised his window and drove on, but the next thing he knew, the back window of his car was shattered by a full beer bottle. Before long, the SUV had maneuvered in such a way as to force Mark, in his small sports car, onto the median. At least three of the men exited their vehicle, opened the doors of Mark's car, and began punching him in the face. When he was later diagnosed with a broken rib, Mark realized that they must have been kicking him as well. While observing his own blood on his clothes and inside the car, Mark tried to talk down the assailants, saying, "OK, guys, you've made your point, you've hurt me." Mark didn't know why the attackers stopped and left suddenly until he saw the blue and red flashing lights of a police vehicle that was responding to another incident.

Ted, a 46-year-old, white, gay-identified man, was walking home late at night with his partner, Kurtis, through the downtown of their small city, which was generally considered gay-friendly. Ted, who, twice in the past, had vehicles try to run him down as a pedestrian because he was perceived as gay, let go of Kurtis's hand when they approached a main intersection. This sparked the recurrence of a disagreement about the safety of their showing affection in public. A short time later, just a few blocks from the local police station, a car with four men inside appeared, and the couple heard antigay

slurs and obscenities. Incensed at this and at all the antigay harassment to
which they'd ever been subjected, Ted and Kurtis yelled one brief obscenity
back. Soon, the car had circled back around to obstruct the crosswalk they
were in, the four passengers still shouting antigay obscenities. Concerned
because he was separated from Kurtis, who was frozen in fear near the front
of the car, Ted slapped the side of the car in an attempt to take control of the
situation. Just as Kurtis began to move away, two of the men got out of the
car and began kicking Ted and hitting him in the head, still yelling epithets,
and continued when he fell to the ground. Fortunately, a police cruiser came
on the scene shortly. Disoriented and angry, Ted was nonetheless able to
communicate clearly to the officers that he and Kurtis were being assaulted
based on their sexual orientation.

Mark and Ted shared these two stories in interviews for a qualitative study
of the psychological effects of hate crime victimization based on sexual orientation bias (Noelle, 2003). Previous research has documented the prevalence
of antibisexual, antigay, and antilesbian (anti-BGL) hate crimes and the nature
and severity of their effects. Psychological consequences have been shown to
be more severe for victims of anti-BGL hate crimes than for bisexual, gay,
and lesbian (BGL) victims of nonhate crimes (Herek, Gillis, & Cogan, 1999).
Qualitative studies like the present one add to the predominantly quantitative
body of research on this topic by detailing the significant ways in which anti-
BGL hate crime victimization fits into and shapes the lives of BGL victims.
The case studies presented in this chapter represent 10 bisexual-, gay-, or
lesbian-identified participants in New England who self-reported a range of
violent and nonviolent hate crimes, harassment, and/or homophobia to the
researcher. They all shared details about their emotional and cognitive reactions as well as effects on coming out (BGL identity development and related
behavior), their social worlds, and their view of the world generally. The
qualitative analysis of these effects allowed them to be richly contextualized
within interviewees' own histories and prior experiences of homophobia and
heterosexism.[1] Discussion of psychological and social effects of hate crime
victimization is organized by topic area, including issues of prevalence, incidence, and reporting as well as effects on identity, various forms of social
support, and worldview. Case studies are provided as illustration, and when
each participant's story is first introduced, a general overview is provided.[2] A
summary of relevant aspects of each participant's demographics and history,
for reference during reading, is presented in Table 5.1.

PREVALENCE, INCIDENCE, AND DESCRIPTION
OF ANTI-BGL HATE CRIMES

Over the last two decades, researchers have documented that hate crime
victimization based on sexual orientation (SO) represents a commonplace

Table 5.1   Overview of 10 Interview Participants

Pseudonym	Sex	Age	SO	LGBT activism	Race/ ethnicity	Outness inventory score[a]	Main type of crime
Mark	M	39	Gay	No	White	3.0	Assault
Ted	M	50	Gay	Yes	White	7.0	Assault
Kris	F	43	Lesbian	Yes (past)	White	3.8	Neighbor-hood harassment
Pam	F	37	Lesbian	Yes (past)	White	3.0	Sexual assault
Dani	F	37	Bisexual	Yes	White	6.0	Work harassment
Meera	F	26	Bisexual	No	South Asian American	6.2	Various harassment
Michael	M	42	Gay	Yes (past)	White	5.0	Various harassment
Gillian	F	20	Lesbian	Yes	White	5.4	School harassment
Charles	M	37	Gay	No	White	5.7	Harassment, intimidation
Katina	F	47	Lesbian	Yes (past)	White	6.5	Neighbor-hood harassment

Note: LGBT; lesbian/gay/bisexual/transgender; SO, sexual orientation.

[a]On an anchored scale ranging from 1 to 7, asking how open the participant is about sexual orientation with 10 categories of people in her or his life, then averaged (Mohr & Fassinger, 2000).

threat to the physical and psychological safety and well-being of BGL people, showing that the rate of violent victimization for lesbians and gay men surpasses that of the general population (Comstock, 1991). Lifetime prevalence of hate crime victimization against person or property, reported from 1991 to 1999, ranged from 25 percent of men and 20 percent of women of sexual minority status (Herek et al., 1999) to about 50 percent of BGL people (Comstock, 1991; Herek, Gillis, Cogan, & Glunt, 1997; Peel, 1999). Seventy-three percent of those surveyed in a more recent study reported having been the target of at least one homophobic incident (Rose & Mechanic, 2002). Many of the prevalence studies provide more detailed data on types of crimes experienced, including physical violence, being chased, being threatened, and vandalism (Comstock, 1991; D'Augelli, 1992; D'Augelli, Pilkington, & Hershberger, 2002; Herek et al., 1999; Herek et al., 1997; Otis & Skinner, 1996; Pilkington & D'Augelli, 1995; Rose & Mechanic, 2002).

The severity of hate crimes based on SO bias may be greater than hate crimes based on other biases (Dunbar, 2006). The crime features most typical of anti-BGL bias crimes are those associated in previous literature with more negative psychological outcomes and less help-seeking: these include known perpetrators, multiple perpetrators, and repeated victimization (Rose & Mechanic, 2002). Generally, victims of crime based on bias (racial, ethnic, SO, and religious) have been found to experience significantly longer duration of distress than victims of nonbias crime, in areas such as nervousness, depression, difficulty concentrating at work, and unbidden vengeful and suicidal thoughts (Garcia, McDevitt, Gu, & Balboni, 1999, 2000).

Antigay and antilesbian violence is common in rural and suburban areas as well as urban; a smaller number of lesbians than gay men experience victimization; and a higher percentage of middle-income people than high- or low-income people experience victimization (Comstock, 1991). Although results of a review were mixed as to whether white people or people of color experienced more victimization, one national survey indicated higher levels of victimization for lesbians and gay men of color (Comstock, 1991).[3] In one northeastern U.S. city, Latino bisexual, gay, lesbian, and transgender (BGLT) people were shown to be likely to experience more serious personal offenses than African Americans, whites, and other races, and Latinos also were less likely to report the crimes (Kuehnle & Sullivan, 2001). Men's and women's experiences may have different characteristics, with one study showing that the majority of women victims had been attacked by someone they knew (77%) and in a private setting (62%), while men tended to have been attacked by one or more strangers (58%) and in a public setting (75%; Herek et al., 1997). Men and transgender victims may be more likely to have experienced violent attacks, women are more likely to have been victims of harassment or attempted assault, and transgender individuals the most likely to be victimized in private residences and also to be killed (22% compared to 2% of lesbians and no gay men; Kuehnle & Sullivan, 2001).[4]

Bias victimization, including verbal abuse, physical assault, and sexual assault, appears to start early in the lives of many BGL individuals (D'Augelli, 1992; D'Augelli et al., 2002). Twenty percent of BGL high school students reported having been threatened with disclosure of their sexual orientation (D'Augelli et al., 2002). Youths who came out earlier were more likely to have been victimized, as were those who reported themselves to be more "obviously" lesbian or gay, or more gender atypical (D'Augelli et al., 2002; Pilkington & D'Augelli, 1995). In one sample of youths less than 20 years old, over 83 percent had experienced at least one form of victimization, and respondents had experienced three forms of victimization on average (Pilkington & D'Augelli, 1995). In the same sample, young men were more likely to have encountered verbal insults, but young women were just as likely as young men to have experienced other types of victimization. Young people of color and whites were found equally likely to have been victimized, but whites tended to report to police and authorities slightly more often. Demonstrating a climate of homophobia, 99 percent of a college sample said they had overheard derogatory antigay or antilesbian comments, and 67 percent said often (D'Augelli, 1992).

Incidence Reporting

The Federal Bureau of Investigation (FBI) has been collecting data on hate crime incidents since 1991, following from the Hate Crimes Statistics Act of 1990. The FBI relies on locally trained law enforcement agents to determine whether an "offender's actions were motivated, in whole or in part, by bias" (Federal Bureau of Investigation [FBI], 2001, p. 1), and therefore whether an incident is classified as a hate crime. Participation of local law enforcement agencies is voluntary (National Coalition of Anti-Violence Programs [NCAVP], 2006). For the year 2005, a total of 7,163 hate crime incidents were reported in the United States through these channels, and 1,171 (14.0%) of these were based on SO,[5] which comprised the third most frequent bias motivation after race and religion. The 1,171 hate crimes reported included no murders, one rape, 510 assaults, 301 incidents of intimidation, 30 robberies, 10 burglaries, 29 thefts, and 275 incidents of destruction or vandalism. The greatest number of reported anti-BGL crimes (328) took place in residences/homes, followed by highway/road/alley/street (254) and school/college (123; FBI, 2006).

The National Coalition of Anti-Violence Projects (NCAVP) consists of 26 agencies covering cities and states around the United States. This coalition collects reports of anti-BGLT hate crime incidents directly from victims and others in the community. NCAVP defines hate crimes as "all crimes and offenses in which victims are chosen by offenders wholly or in part because of the former's actual or presumed sexual/affectional orientation and/or gender identity" (NCAVP, 2000, p. 7). NCAVP's list of incidents that fall under their broader definition include preying on BGLT people as easier targets for crimes such as robbery, and unsolved murders in which certain characteristics of hate crimes, such as excessive mutilation or torture, are evident in the absence of other motivations. NCAVP's classification of hate crimes, for the most part, relies on the report of the victim, rather than a law enforcement agent. Note also the explicit inclusion of crimes against transgender individuals.

With only 12 of the 26 affiliated agencies contributing data to their 2006 report, NCAVP documented 1,339 bias-related incidents in 2005 (compared to the FBI's 1,171). These included 11 murders, 551 assaults or attempted assaults, 63 sexual assaults, 737 incidents of intimidation, and 115 incidents of vandalism, with the first four of these five categories being notably higher than the FBI's statistics, despite the much smaller geographical area of coverage. The discrepancy between FBI and NCAVP figures has been consistent over the years of data collection and has been taken by activists to suggest that FBI data vastly underrepresent the incidence of anti-BGLT crimes (National Gay and Lesbian Task Force, 2001).

Victim Reporting and Secondary Victimization

Underreporting of anti-BGL hate crimes by victims has been well established. According to the NCAVP, only 37 percent of the incidents reported to them in 2005 were also reported to the police at the time the NCAVP agency was contacted. One study conducted in the United Kingdom found that only 18 percent of BGL people who had experienced anti-BGL violence had reported it to the police (Peel, 1999). Of hate crimes committed in Los Angeles in 1994–1995, 72 percent of SO hate crimes were reported by victims, compared to over 90 percent of hate crimes based on race/ethnicity and religion (Dunbar, 2006). In a study of anti-BGLT crimes reported to a victim agency in a northeastern U.S. city between 1995 and 1998, 77 percent had reported to police (Kuehnle & Sullivan, 2001). Moreover, BGL crime victims are less likely to have reported a hate crime to the police than a nonhate crime (Herek et al., 1999),[6] and more severe SO hate crimes may be less likely to be reported (Dunbar, 2006). Among youths, 79 to 88 percent who have been the targets of harassment, threats, or violence based on SO said they did not report at least one of the incidents they had experienced (D'Augelli, 1992; Pilkington & D'Augelli, 1995). In addition, gay men and lesbians of color have been found less likely to report SO hate crime victimization than gay men and lesbians who are white (Dunbar, 2006).[7]

An investigation of reasons for underreporting showed that "concerns about police prejudice" and not wanting to disclose SO were significantly more likely to play a role when BGL people did not report bias crimes, compared to when BGL people did not report nonbias crimes (Herek, Cogan, & Gillis, 2002). Reasons for nonreporting include fear of consequences (Dunbar, 2006; Peel, 1999), not feeling safe to report, feeling partly to blame for the attack, the assumption and fear of police homophobia (Peel, 1999), embarrassment, feelings of helplessness, expectations of no help, and not knowing how or where to report (Dunbar, 2006). On the other hand, reasons that some victims did report were that otherwise, the attacker would have "won," that the victim was angry, and that the victim believed that police are effective (Peel, 1999).

A Case of Nonreporting

Kris, a woman whose family experienced homophobic harassment by another family in the neighborhood (further detailed later), explained that she never called the police because of her belief that due to racism (her family was biracial) and homophobia, "sometimes people ask for help [from the police] and they don't really get it." She also found it more difficult to consider involving authorities because the perpetrators were people she knew and saw daily, versus strangers.

All crime victims may weigh the pros and cons of reporting to police, for example, the comfort of knowing justice may be done versus the discomfort of encountering potentially unsympathetic justice personnel and attorneys (Greenberg & Ruback, 1992). BGL victims face the added fear of encountering further homophobia, which may result in being treated unfairly or further abused by those who are supposed to help, for example, police and the judicial system. When others respond to victims negatively after the crime, due to SO bias, this is known as *secondary victimization* (Berrill & Herek, 1992). In fact, of NCAVP hate crime reporters who had also reported to the police in 2005, 11 percent said that police were verbally abusive, and 6 percent said that police were physically abusive (NCAVP, 2006).

Perceived Secondary Victimization

The following case illustrates the salience and vulnerability that can develop following a crime perceived to be motivated by SO bias. Pam, a 37-year-old, white, lesbian-identified woman, was sexually assaulted 10 years prior to her interview by two young men who fraudulently pulled over her friend's car with a flashing light on their dashboard. Pam's friend was physically assaulted, and one of the perpetrators forced his tongue into Pam's mouth and reached down her shirt. Although no antigay slurs occurred until Pam encountered the perpetrators later in the police station, the crime had occurred after she and a friend had left the parking lot of a gay bar, and the perpetrators had a history of victimizing others in the same circumstances.

Pam wondered in the aftermath of the crime how much her SO affected treatment she received from others in support roles. Pam complained that the victim advocate assigned to her case didn't return phone calls and that she "made it seem like the most important thing she could do was get my [stolen] 60 dollars back, and to me that was the last thing that was important." Pam was more concerned about her future safety from the perpetrators, as her name and address had been published in the local paper. She wondered whether the lack of sympathy she felt from the victim-witness assistant was due to "maybe because of *her* biases, because we were victimized after leaving the [gay] bar." Similarly, Pam wondered whether the long wait she and her friend experienced in the emergency room that night had to do with their SO. She said, "I didn't question bias at *that* time, but later on I did, simply because there wasn't a whole lot of people in the emergency room and it was taking forever . . . so I was like, 'Why is it taking so long?'" On a more positive note, Pam said that "the state police I felt were very supportive," although they did not at any point acknowledge the issue of targeting based on SO.

Influence of Justice Personnel

Further details of the cases of Mark and Ted (introduced at the opening of this chapter) illustrate the substantial influence the responses of law enforcement, justice personnel, and others who are involved from hate crime incident through trial can have on the overall experience of a violent hate crime. Ted reported that when two of his four assailants were prosecuted, their defense attorney argued for a conceptual reversal of charges; the attorney claimed that "there were four innocent men, boys, minding their own business at the red light when [Ted] decided to attack them in order to become a victim to further the cause of gay rights, special rights for gay people," and that Ted had "violated their heterosexual rights and attacked them because they were heterosexuals." Looking back, Ted said, "In some respects the trial [was] almost more damaging than the actual attack, because it was smart, educated, articulate people *slowly* twisting the truth," which he said led to strong feelings of "helplessness" and anger. Furthermore, at times, the events of the trial caused him to question his own knowledge of the hate crime experience. The jury acquitted the defendants based on the defense attorney's version of events, which left Ted feeling isolated and unprotected: "We can have all the [hate crime] laws we want, but unless there's people to enforce them, those laws won't do any good."

In contrast, on the night of his assault, Mark generally felt that police and others were supportive and sympathetic. Mark perceived one of the paramedics who arrived on the scene to be possibly a lesbian and told her about being called "faggot"; her immediate response was to say he hadn't deserved this, that she was so sorry, and to inform him that the borough they were in had a zero-tolerance policy for hate crimes. Mark was taken immediately to the emergency room, and the police held the assailants overnight on the justification of not yet knowing the extent of Mark's injuries and therefore the degree of the charges. While at the hospital, Mark was interviewed by a detective, who immediately and nonjudgmentally addressed the hate crime aspect of the incident: "The first words out of his mouth when he came in [were] 'I do not care what your sexual orientation is, . . . no one should be subjected to the type of crime that you were a victim of this evening.'" Mark elected not to file charges himself or to be present at the trial, largely because he did not want his sexual orientation to be made public; he explained that he was not out to his parents and others in his life, and he was concerned that the case would be covered in the media. Nonetheless, the perpetrators were prosecuted by the state and convicted with the maximum allowable sentence for the charges filed (30 days in jail).

PSYCHOLOGICAL EFFECTS OF ANTI-BGL HATE CRIME VICTIMIZATION

When BGL individuals who were victims of anti-BGL hate crimes[8] were compared with those who were victims of non-hate-based person and property crimes of similar severity, hate crime victims showed greater psychological distress on measures of depression, traumatic stress, anxiety, and anger (Herek et al., 1999). In addition, anti-BGL hate crime victims were more likely to see the world and people as less benevolent than non-hate-crime victims and more likely to attribute negative life events and setbacks to homophobia or heterosexism.[9] It appears that "experiencing a hate crime links the victim's post-crime feelings of vulnerability and powerlessness with her or his sexual orientation and personal identity" (Herek et al., 1999, p. 949–950). One study, focused on mostly gay male youths, suggested that hate crime victimization (ranging from insults and threats to assault) leads to higher levels of psychological distress, specifically through its effect on self-esteem (Waldo, Hesson-McInnis, & D'Augelli, 1998). Another examining lesbians' recent experiences of SO hate crime victimization as well as sexist events showed that these correlate with psychological distress both independently and in combination with one another (Szymanski, 2005).

Literature and cases presented subsequently will detail some of the factors that may be unique to hate crime victimization based on SO bias and may contribute to their observed greater impact. These include effects on identity development and social relationships, the availability of social support, and the sociopolitical and personal context of these events. In addition, some cases illustrate the differences between victimization based on SO and that based on more visible minority identities such as race.

The Backdrop of Anti-BGL Victimization

The antigay or antilesbian attack is never an isolated occurrence, as it takes place against a backdrop of societal heterosexism (Stermac & Sheridan, 1993), prior experience with victimization (Barnes & Ephross, 1994), and knowledge of other BGL people who have been victimized. The latter may be through personal acquaintances or incidents that were widely covered in the media such as the hate crime murder of Matthew Shepard in Wyoming in 1998 (see Noelle, 2000, 2002, for illustration of the effects of this incident on other members of the BGL community). Anti-BGL hate crime victims may be reminded, for example, of national coverage of picketers at Shepard's funeral holding signs reading "God Hates Fags."

Idiographic Nature of Violent Victimization

Further review of the cases of Mark's and Ted's violent crimes demonstrates the idiographic nature of victimization experiences. There were a number of notable differences between their cases. For example, Ted had a prior history of harassment and of witnessing an antigay assault as an adult, while Mark's history of homophobic harassment had been in the form of bullying as a child. Mark was attacked alone. Although Ted and his partner were victimized together, they were never able to process the crime together in a meaningful way, and Ted felt that this had weakened their relationship and contributed to their breakup. The aftereffects of Ted's injuries (headaches) were also more persistent than Mark's. Mark had rated himself as being less out than Ted (Mark at 3 on an anchored scale ranging from 1 to 7, compared to Ted at 7).[10] It is worth noting, in the context of these factors and also of their contrasting experiences with law enforcement and the judicial system (presented previously), that Ted scored much higher on a retrospective measure of trauma symptomatology[11] and remained hypervigilant even four years later. He described:

> I'm *very* aware of who's coming towards me, who is walking away, who's coming from this direction, who is driving by, how many people in the car, if there's yelling, who are they yelling at? Can I use my peripheral vision? I'll look, I'll do things, I'll stop to tie my [shoe]. I'll do whatever I need to do to assess the situation.

He said he carried pepper spray for two years in an attempt to feel safer. In his interview, Ted talked about an emotional aftermath that consisted primarily of fear, sadness, and depression (no longer enjoying activities, socially isolating, feeling hopeless, and experiencing a sense of his life contracting).

Both Ted and Mark had grown up in highly homophobic environments: Ted in a Calvinistic religious culture in the Midwestern United States, with parents who tried to have him psychiatrically hospitalized when they learned he was gay, and Mark in a Baptist family in the southern United States. It was Mark, though, whose reaction appeared to be most related to internalized homophobia and early coming-out history. The strongest emotional themes he related to the hate crime were shame, self-blame, and even guilt for the fate of his perpetrators, although he was able to take a rational perspective and challenge each of these feelings. When asked, Mark said he believed he would have felt less ashamed and more free to share his experience if it had been "a random crime" rather than "targeted" against him as a gay man. While Ted was generally angry that the effects of the event had been so lasting and pervasive for him, Mark expressed anger at concrete aspects such as the degree of violence and the unfairness of being outnumbered by his attackers. Mark was also easily able to articulate that something positive had come of the experience: that he was a stronger, more complex person for having survived it. As a result of participating in the study, Mark told his current partner about the assault for the first time. For Ted, the positives he could name involved receiving support from some people from whom he had not expected it and being spurred to deal with other past traumas in the psychotherapy he began after the assault.

Psychological Effects of Anti-BGL Harassment

The manifest severity of a hate crime may not always dictate the severity of psychological impact. A range of psychological reactions, independent of severity of crime, is to be expected, given theory about the role of individuals' experiences and interpretations in trauma reactions (Janoff-Bulman, 1989; Root, 1992; Saakvitne, Tennen, & Affleck, 1998) and research about the cumulative nature of lifetime trauma experiences (Nishith, Mechanic, & Resick, 2000; Winkel, Blaauw, Sheridan, & Baldry, 2003). Levels of posttraumatic stress and other symptoms can be just as high for threats of violence or other bias-related acts as for actual acts of violence (Kilpatrick et al., 1989; Meyer, 1995; Rose & Mechanic, 2002). This can be attributed to the power of the perception of threat, especially in the context of widespread SO bias and prior personal victimization. Among youth reporting anti-BGL victimization in high school, those who had greater internalized homophobia as well as those who had experienced more verbal abuse showed more severe trauma-related symptomatology (D'Augelli et al., 2002). Herek and colleagues (2002) captured this quality of amplification of hate crime experiences by both prior history and societal context:

> The ubiquity of hate crimes might make even minor instances of harassment more frightening for the victim. . . . A gay or bisexual person who encounters an expression of hostility because of her or his sexual orientation does not know in advance how the incident will end. She or he may be attacked with words, a raw egg, . . . or a deadly weapon. Consequently, an incident that appears minor in retrospect might nevertheless have considerable psychological impact on the victim. (p. 336)

Anti-BGL discrimination and harassment—including job discrimination, social hostility, such as being forced out of a neighborhood, and being called names or threatened—have been shown to raise levels of depression, anxiety, and substance abuse (Mays & Cochran, 2001). Hateful words may be an integral ingredient of harm in any anti-BGL attack: "Verbal abuse that accompanies physical attacks is particularly injurious to a survivor's sense of self, as it provokes feelings of self-hatred and self-loathing that may have been previously resolved" (Stermac & Sheridan, 1993, p. 37). When faced with hate speech, individuals who are members of the target group tend to believe the speaker's motive is either ignorance or repressed hostility, that is, fixed, dispositional motives (rather than situational) that might engender feelings of hopelessness in regard to the prejudice (Leets, 2002).

Harassment: The Importance of Prior History and Context

Kris, a 43-year-old, white, lesbian-identified woman is the single mother of two biracial boys. Her case of protracted harassment in her neighborhood exemplifies the inextricability of a single incident from prior history, as well as the importance of context. The harassment began after her young son revealed to a friend that he was conceived by alternative insemination and had two mothers, and it included the friend's mother and other members of her family yelling homophobic and other slurs and obscenities as they passed by Kris's house. Also, they threw trash and, once, a dead possum in Kris's yard, and the other mother forbid her children to play with Kris's children. Kris's son also began to receive notes at school saying things like, "Your mom is a *fucking* lesbian." The harassment continued for 11 months, until Kris decided to sell her home and move her family out of the neighborhood.

Kris's most severe prior hate crime experience had taken place within her family of origin. When she was around age 19, Kris came out to her father, a conservative Christian pastor, when he confronted her about her SO; his response was to tell her she was "damned to hell" and to hold her arm to a hot stove burner. Another incident occurred when she was in her twenties and babysat frequently for the child of friends; she came out to a mutual friend, and "the next time I came to their house to do my regular babysitting, [the child's] father met me at the door with a gun and put it right to my forehead and told me to leave and never ever come back to his house," citing his dislike of "queers." Kris expressed her amazement that this could occur with someone she had known fairly well: "We had been friends. We had gone hiking together several times, and how somebody's feelings can change that quickly, that intensely with that information just blows my mind, because I was the *same* person I had been all along." Such incidents of having people one is so close to suddenly turn abusive or violent arise as a result of the coming-out process, intentional or unintentional, that accompanies BGL identity.

When asked to compare and contrast having the gun held to her head with the harassment in her neighborhood, Kris highlighted the context of family and neighborhood: she said, "the first thing that came to my mind when you asked that question was the second one involved my children" and explained that "my children were at risk, I felt, when they were outside in their yard playing, or even at school." The situation felt pervasive and unavoid-able to her: "This was someone who lived at the end of our same street, that we saw *every* day," including when the two mothers were picking up their children from school. One study of victims of bias crime assaults found that "victimiza-tion in locations usually deemed safe by the victim (e.g., home, school, work-place) may generate more consequences" (Garcia et al., 1999, p. 79), and we can assume that they leave victims more fearful in the face of similar situations in the future.

Harassment and Identity Development

Dani, a 37-year-old, white, divorced, bisexual-identified woman, had ex-perienced a period of homophobic workplace harassment about six years earlier, when she was dating a woman for the first time, who was also the manager of another department at work. Secrecy developed around Dani's relationship because neither she nor her partner wanted to be out in that setting. For her part, Dani attributed this to internalized homophobia at the time, and also to a sense that the environment was generally homophobic. Thus, when confronted by a supervisor who said she didn't think the rumors of Dani's dating the coworker were true because the supervisor didn't think Dani was gay, Dani denied the relationship. Other coworkers began to fol-low Dani and her partner when they were together, taking notes, and Dani was confronted by another supervisor. At this point, she said,

> I thought, Oh my god, it was so *bad!* You know, I really bought into this whole, like, "I'm a pervert, because I like, looked at her in a loving way, while I was at work. I should have never done that on company time." I mean, I was freaking out.

Next, coworkers reported dishonestly that Dani and her partner had been having sex in the workplace. Dani felt clear throughout that none of this would have occurred had she been dating a male coworker; in fact, it was not happening to opposite-sex couples there. The worse the accusations became, the less Dani felt safe to be out in the workplace, and the more entrenched she became in deception and shame. While there was no outright homopho-bic verbal abuse, Dani said that coworkers "would say things like, 'I know what they say about you,' you know, and kind of roll their eyes."

At the time of the interview, about six years later, Dani described the ex-perience as "one of the worst years of my life, still, and . . . what made it even harder, was living this *closeted* life." During this time, she experienced depres-sion and isolated herself from social supports, and she also had a brief, intense crisis in her coming out. She said that she considered only dating men in the future, thinking, "I was just going to shut that door, [because being bisexual was] way more painful than I ever thought it would be. I can't do it."

EFFECTS OF VICTIMIZATION ON BGL
IDENTITY DEVELOPMENT

Because of the nature of sexual identity, anti-BGL hate crime victimization has the potential to affect victims in some ways that are unique from hate crimes based on race, ethnicity, or religion. As with those identities, SO is generally experienced to be a fundamental, relatively unchanging aspect of identity, but is not necessarily visible or shared with family. For many BGL people, sexual identity develops over time, through the process known as coming out. Anti-BGL hate crime victimization can disrupt this process and leave victims isolated from their nonfamily in-group—an important source of social support. In addition, damage to this aspect of the self inherently disturbs intimate partnerships and/or one's vision of them.

In anti-BGL hate crimes, "the victim's homosexuality may become directly linked to the heightened sense of vulnerability" (Garnets, Herek, & Levy, 1992, pp. 208–209), resulting in characterological self-blame, which is thought to be more detrimental than situational self-blame, in which one feels there is something they could do differently if faced with a similar situation again (Janoff-Bulman, 1992). Furthermore, according to Garnets and colleagues (1992),

> one's homosexual orientation . . . may be experienced as a source of pain and punishment rather than of intimacy, love, and community. Internalized homophobia may reappear or be intensified. Attempts to make sense of the attack, coupled with the common need to perceive the world as a just place, may lead to feelings that one has been justifiably punished for being gay. (p. 209)

In addition to the ordinary psychological aftermath of victimization, anti-BGL hate crime victims may feel compelled to suppress or hide BGL identity. Any event that causes BGL people to be closeted will likely have a negative impact on their overall mental health (Garnets et al., 1992; Meyer, 1995; Morris, Waldo, & Rothblum, 2001; Schmitt & Kurdek, 1987). Kitzinger (1994) summarized the effects of forces that discourage nondisclosure of SO:

> In an oppressive heterosexist society it is not necessary, most of the time, to beat up lesbians, or to murder or torture us in order to ensure our silence and invisibility. Instead, a climate of terror is created in which lesbians "voluntarily," and of our own free will, "choose" to stay silent and invisible. (p. 127)

Among the 10 case studies of anti-BGL hate crime and homophobia victims, effects on identity and coming out were highly variable and individualized. Some found that their self-concepts as bisexual, gay, or lesbian people were affected, while others railed against such effects.

Coming Out: Behavior Changes

Mark (whose case of violent crime was discussed previously) found that internalized homophobia was activated and that he made certain behavior changes. He had "debated for a long time" whether to put a subtle rainbow sticker (symbol of gay pride) on the bumper of his car, weighing the pros of an added sense of "comradery" and community against the perceived cons of increased visibility at work. The day after he was attacked in his car, while cleaning the blood stains and removing the broken glass, he also removed the sticker because, he explained, it had "led to my worst fears coming true, in a sense." Having had a conservative, Baptist upbringing, Mark found that in making sense of the crime initially,

> I actually thought, "You know, I'm getting what I deserved because of [being gay]." Part of me thought that God was giving me a little wake-up call, because I'm also taught as part of my religion . . . that you can only keep committing a sin or doing something wrong for so long before it's going to come back to you.

While he did not believe he could change his being a gay man, he thought perhaps he "should not be too involved in the whole gay lifestyle."

Ted echoed this sense of being punished, although not by a higher power. He articulated that the assault he and Kurtis experienced "had *everything* to do with who we were and who [the assailants] perceived us to be" and said that this led to his questioning his own sexual identity. At the time of the interview, Ted had recently put a BGLT-themed bumper sticker on his car and said, "Everyday I think when someone's behind me, . . . I look in the mirror, I'm conscious of that fact that I'm going, 'Are they reading that? Should I take that off?' I never used to do that." After the crime, he had also quit a theater troupe, partly because of depression, and also because

> I don't want to be in the *gay men's* theater troupe. I don't want to have to walk in or leave. And I was also just not feeling proud, you know, proud, I didn't *feel* that way. I was feeling more devastated.

Despite having been out for 30 years, he became less willing to be visible as a gay man, in various ways that constricted his life.

Coming Out Stronger

In contrast to those who were inclined to be more secretive about SO following victimization, some reported that their victimization led them to come out more strongly in some settings, but typically not all. After leaving the job where she had been harassed, Dani adopted a policy of immediately coming out in future workplaces: "I have found that I'm a much more likely victim if I'm closeted, because others have more power over me if I'm hiding something or fearing something. Being out is actually a safety mechanism for me. It gives me strength, and people notice it." At the same time, she continued to hide her sexual orientation from anyone associated with the former workplace, and for a period of years, if she even thought she saw someone she knew from that time, her heart would race and she would want to get away; she seriously considered moving out of the area for this reason.

Meera, a 26-year-old, South Asian American, bisexual-identified woman, whose gender identity fluctuated between *butch* (a masculine woman) and transgender, described two incidents of harassment. In the most recent, a woman in a passing minivan had yelled, "How does it feel to suck pussy?" at Meera and her girlfriend, Ellen, who were walking home holding hands. About two years earlier, Meera had been on a road trip and a man in the parking lot of a convenience store, who had presumably mistaken her for a man, approached her and "probably a foot and a half from my face started yelling at me about my earrings and how I was [a] 'faggot.'" Meera was determined not to let such incidents affect her being out and her related psychological well-being:

> I'm not ever going to not hold [Ellen's] hand. . . . I'm not ever going to go back in the closet for anybody. Even if it means somebody's going to pick on me, they're going to have to pick on me because I would feel so wrong afterwards that that would be worse than somebody taking a swing at me.

She also said she would not change any behaviors or limit where she went. She was aware that being more out might bring more harassment, but these risks were politically and personally meaningful to her:

> The more openly I'm gay wherever I go, the more change I can help along just by my presence. And so even if people pick on me, in general I'm doing more good by living what I think is the right thing to do. . . . All those people in the [19]50s who had a really hard time *really* did a lot to make life what it's like for me now. So if I do the right thing now, then maybe in 20 years when *my* kids are 20 or 30, they won't even know what homophobia is. I mean, I don't know, probably they will but, you know.

Michael was a 42-year-old, single, white, gay-identified man. He generally discussed a number of homophobic incidents over the past 30 years (but had never been physically assaulted), and he was remarkable for having developed the coping style of confronting perpetrators, either directly or through reporting to authorities, and holding them "accountable" for their words and acts. For example, in a New England city about a year earlier, Michael was threatened by a teenager on a bicycle, who said, "I'm going to kick the shit out of you. I'm going to kick your ass, you faggot." Michael replied provocatively: "'Why don't you try it?' I said, 'Why don't you come over here and try it?' I said, 'Because I will *knock* your *fucking* head off, you asshole.'" Michael then took down the address of the apartment that the young man entered and called the police; he requested that they arrange a meeting between the young man and Michael, at which Michael presented his family photo album and said to the boy,

> I just wanted to tell you a little bit about who I am. . . . So the next time you see somebody that you think might be gay, remember that they also have a brother, or a sibling, and parents, and family, and so, I'm a whole human being.

During his interview, Michael offered a rallying plea that more victims of homophobia take his accountability stance:

> A lot of [social] progress has been made, but there's still far too many attacks against gay or lesbian people. But people also have to start fighting back. People are going to keep seeing us as targets unless we fight back, whether it be physically or in the courts. . . . People need to somehow process their shame, and say either, "I'm this, or I'm not" . . . but if you don't sort of stand up, then people are going to keep thinking that that's license for them to keep doing it.

Michael had always tried to be as out as possible, including in environments such as living and working in a conservative, southern U.S. city in the 1970s. He explained,

> I can't not be who I am to accommodate somebody else. . . . That's crazy to live [in the closet]. . . . The emotional stress of that seems even more challenging than just simply ridicule. The pressure that that creates to lie and deceive, it goes to the core of your existence.

Despite this stance, Michael also related that since an incident in which he was chased in his car by a driver who tried to force him off the road, he had stopped putting all but one small gay-themed sticker on his car. He explained his thought process:

> I thought, OK, I've had stickers on for years, I don't need to keep cluttering the thing up. I know what I believe. I don't hide it. I don't need to advertise it to other people to feed into their pathology. . . . All it'll do is just encourage their pathology and then, you know, [I'll have to] go through the criminal justice system and then I'll be exhausted from that process.

He also described that "I think I monitor my mannerisms a little more [as I'm getting older]. I don't know if it's directly as a result of [homophobic incidents]."

INTERACTION OF COMING OUT AND COPING

Coping with a hate crime likely interacts with the victim's stage in the coming out process, with BGL individuals who are further along in their sexual identity development having greater access to internal and external resources to cope with victimization (Dunbar, 2006; Garnets et al., 1992), while those in early stages may experience more harm (Stermac & Sheridan, 1993). Those who are more out may have more practiced coping resources, access to greater community support, and a store of positive experiences associated with being gay. Victims who are not out in all areas of their lives may be less likely to report hate crime victimization for fear of exposure and therefore less likely to obtain support and care (Garnets et al., 1992). On the other hand, being more out may also make one more visible and therefore more vulnerable to anti-BGL sentiment and attack (Herek & Berrill, 1992). And in some cases, as in Pam's, where she may have been victimized due to being seen leaving a gay bar, or in the case of those who present a stereotypically gay or lesbian appearance, who knows or thinks they know about one's SO may not be a matter of choice.

Harassment Early in the Coming Out Process

Gillian, a 20-year-old, white, lesbian-identified college student, had experienced homophobic harassment continuously for her last two years of high school in a small town. At that time, she said, she was not out to herself or to others, despite growing up in a "gay-positive" environment, including her family, the school she attended prior to high school, and the Unitarian Universalist church to which her family belonged. During high school, she said, "I thought of myself as asexual, as just sort of this *weird* sexual freak.... I just knew I was just radically different, but I didn't . . . classify myself correctly." As a result, the whole experience of being targeted was very difficult for her to process and to understand coherently.

At the beginning of her high school experience, Gillian was very aware of homophobic slurs not directed at her: "[I] could not walk down the hall without hearing 20 anti-gay slurs. . . . They were just like 'fag this' whatever." She began to be more directly targeted during her second year, and this worsened gradually over the next two years, until she arranged to graduate a year early because of it. She felt she was targeted despite not being out because she was a vocal supporter of gay rights and would confront other students about their use of slurs, a stance she attributed to "the values I was raised with." Generally, Gillian experienced other students avoiding her in the hallways and "a lot of talking and looking and smiling, like, 'We're talking about *you*.'" More specifically, she once spoke up for gay rights during a class discussion, which then "escalated to the point where [another student] was just screaming, 'You fucking,' you know, 'queer.' [He] was like, 'Are you? You are?' Like, 'Are you? Are you gay?'" She also told of a locker room incident in which another girl accused Gillian of staring at her. Gillian summarized her experiences over these years:

> There was no overwhelming moment when I was afraid for my life, or really afraid. But just going to school for three years and having people not talk to [me] and just *hate* [me] all the time, that made a big effect. It wore [me] down gradually.

Gillian felt that her situation was particularly complicated due to being a less visible minority (compared to racial, for example), as she was able to remain in denial of her own identity. She highlighted the dilemma that if she had been more out, the harassment might have been worse, but at the same time, "it was really damaging to live like I wasn't who I was."

Overall, Gillian felt that her coming out process was arrested for two years, but that this had been psychologically "very smart" and self-protective. Instead of coming out, she said, "I was sort of packing these things up inside of me, and just waiting for the right spot where I could sit down and slowly go through what was going on in my head, have some kind of support," which she found in her college environment. Even since coming out in a safer environment, though, she tended to interpret positive experiences related to her identity to be situational only, not generalizing them to other settings. In her words,

> I think all these good experiences I've had just being gay [and out have led to] now I'm pretty open. People [at college] know that I'm gay pretty soon after meeting me. But when I'm in another town or something . . . I don't really tell that many people, not for a long time until I know I'm safe.

Gillian related that she was planning her future career so as not to have to live in a small town again, and that she sometimes took concrete steps to conceal her SO:

> I think I'm self-conscious, like some situations I just check myself, "Do I have any signs of being gay?" And . . . [I] put the [BGLT-themed] necklace underneath, take the [BGLT] pins off the bag. . . . If I go back to my town I'll like take [off] all the new signs [that] identify me because I'm just like, "This is an unsafe environment."

Research suggests that Gillian's high school environment was not a unique one. For example, anti-BGL derogatory remarks may go unchallenged when parallel racist remarks would not (O'Conor, 1994). BGL students are less likely to find adult role models within the school because such individuals may be closeted in that setting. High school students have reported hearing peers use derogatory anti-BGL words on average once per day, and hearing derogatory words has been shown to be related to negative feelings (Jordan, Vaughan, & Woodworth, 1997). While a majority of BGL students report finding at least one person at school supportive of their SO, less than half say that BGL issues have been addressed in the classroom, and few that BGL-related books are available in the library (Jordan et al., 1997). Truancy, dropping out, and failing a grade have been documented as prevalent in this group, and sometimes as being due to harassment by peers (Savin-Williams, 1994). Concluding a qualitative study of the common use of homophobic pejoratives in the school environment in England and Wales, Thurlow (2001) comments,

> Sticks and stones may be more likely to break their bones but the relentless, careless use of homophobic pejoratives will most certainly continue to compromise the psychological health of young homosexual and bisexual people by insidiously constructing their sexuality as something wrong, dangerous or shameworthy. (p. 36)

Another interviewee's experience illustrated both the vulnerability inherent in not being out and the powerful impact that harassment can have. Charles, a 37-year-old, single, white, gay-identified man, experienced several years of perceived targeted homophobia consisting of verbal harassment, threats, and vandalism in his New England hometown. In stark contrast to Michael (in the preceding discussion), Charles felt unable to defend himself or to seek any support, due to being closeted. Charles described incidents such as someone throwing pebbles at the roof and windows of his home at 3:00 A.M. and messages left on his answering machines at home and at his business saying things such as, "Charles is dead," or sexual comments and put-downs. Also, several times, windows at his business were broken in a manner that he said appeared to be due to vandalism, rather than burglary. The perpetrator was never identified, although Charles suspected one individual whom he knew to be spreading rumors that he was gay. The harassment went on until Charles sold his business and took an extended international trip.

Charles said that although he'd never feared for his physical safety, he felt that "this kind of psychological [attack], it was *far* more damaging, and *far* more painful than any kind of actual physical attack actually would have [been]." A small business owner and a coach at the high school, Charles emphasized that he "absolutely believed that [being outed] would ruin [him], completely." Charles reported that he had been suicidal for a period of this time, and when asked what effect he thought it would have had if, for example, the vandalism had been more openly antigay, he said, "At the time, it would have been *absolutely*, utterly devastating, and I'm sure I would have committed suicide, if it had become *that* explicit."

One victim may survive an assault with feelings of anger and little question about his or her sexual identity, while another may be temporarily "devastated" by far more subtle perceived homophobic harassment, depending on factors such as context, individual history, personality, and interpretations of events.

EFFECTS ON SOCIAL SUPPORT AND RELATIONSHIPS

Preventing further victimization can be a major motivation for not disclosing SO, avoiding other BGL people or places where they gather, and trying to pass as heterosexual (D'Augelli, 1992; Pilkington & D'Augelli, 1995). Such behavior might reduce access to social support, which ordinarily serves as protection against crime- and hate crime–induced symptomatology (Green & Diaz, 2007; Kaniasty & Norris, 1992; Waldo et al., 1998).

Fear of Bisexual/Gay/Lesbian/Transgender Events

Pam (whose case was introduced previously) recalled during her interview that she had been afraid of attending the first BGLT activist March on Washington, D.C., a very large gathering that occurred a few years after she was sexually assaulted in her friend's car, because she thought that "if people wanted to take out a bunch of gays and lesbians this would be the perfect opportunity." As for attending smaller-scale gay pride events, or going to gay bars, Pam said that she became hesitant to do so alone: "I would only go with other friends." She described,

> I was *very* apprehensive going out by myself, to a bar by myself. It had nothing to do with just being there, it was like *going* there, it was like it was a safety thing getting from the car into the bar. . . . I was more inclined to go for happy hours, you know, it was daylight, and lots of people on the streets.

Family Relationships

Hate crime victims who indicate that family was unsupportive or unavailable after the crime—a circumstance that may be more likely in the case of BGL victims due to SO nondisclosure or to homophobia or biphobia in the family—report significantly higher levels of certain symptoms such as withdrawal, sleep problems, and difficulty   centrating at work (Garcia et al., 1999, 2000). BGL victims, unlike most other minority group members, most likely do not share their stigmatized identity with their family of origin. One study has suggested that BGL people are more likely to perceive emotional support from friends than from family (Kurdek & Schmitt, 1987). Although the 10 interviewees were all out to at least some members of their families, 7 of them had unambiguous histories of negative, hostile, or even violent interactions with their parents at the time of coming out as bisexual, gay, or lesbian (as in the cases of Kris's father assaulting her and Ted's parents attempting to hospitalize him psychiatrically based on his SO). One study of BGL youths from community centers around the country found that family support following anti-BGL victimization was associated with greater self-acceptance (Hershberger & D'Augelli, 1995). The barriers to BGL victims receiving family support may be a factor in the observed increased impact of hate-motivated crimes.

Responses of Family

Some interviewees had turned to their families for support when victimized, and others had not. Ted felt only fresh rejection from his family in response. He said, "They believe all the [antigay] stereotypes. I'm sure they believe that *I* must have done something that brought it on myself," and also that "they don't want to be reminded that I'm gay, they spend their entire life trying to *not* know that." Pam, on the other hand, received support, but with no recognition of her sense that she had been targeted as a lesbian. Charles was the only one who had told his parents, much later, after having fled his hometown and having come out as a gay man, and conveyed that their response was, overall, positive.

Those Who Did Not Tell Family

Mark, Meera, Kris, and Gillian chose not to share their homophobic experiences with their parents. Mark and Meera both felt that they were cut off from support from which they would otherwise have benefited, as they felt they would have told their families had the incidents not involved their identities as gay and lesbian. Both also yearned to know whether their parents would have been supportive or blaming but were unable to take the risk to find out. Meera noted that it was difficult to talk to her parents about anything gay-related in her life:

It's hard enough to just say "I'm gay" every once in a while. That's very difficult. Most of the time it's like, "Well you *know* I'm in a relationship with Ellen, and you *know* it's very serious." So there's almost like no room and no vocabulary to be able to have a conversation that has the word *gay* in it more that once. So I don't even know how I would bring up something like [the harassment she experienced].

Kris, given the history of violence from her father, didn't even consider telling her parents an option, despite their being somewhat supportive in other areas of her life.

Gillian had been raised in a BGL-positive family and environment. In some ways, that appeared to have made the contrast of the homophobic school environment more distressing, but it also lent her strength. Although Gillian had always perceived her parents as BGL-friendly, she still did not tell them about the harassment at school because she was not out to herself or to others at the time.

Romantic Relationships

By the nature of BGL identity, anti-BGL sentiment and events impact not only BGL people's feelings about who they are, but also about who they are in relationships. Individuals who have experienced anti-BGL hate crime, and especially same-sex couples who have been targeted for displaying affection, can become inhibited from doing so, both in public and in private (Wertheimer, 1992). Whether they are victimized alone or with their partner, intimate relationships can be impacted in various immediate or long-lasting ways.

Victimization with a Partner

Ted and Meera, who were with their partners when assaulted and harassed, respectively, both spoke about the ways that the anti-BGL event interfered with or created distance in their relationships. In Ted's case, it appeared that this contributed significantly to his losing his partner. He described that tension was created when friends asked how Ted was, but not his partner, Kurtis (who did not sustain physical injury), and that Kurtis felt a sort of survivor's guilt. Generally, Ted said, "It was blame, it was guilt, it was uncertainty, it brought our other issues that we hadn't dealt with to the fore." In the trial, Ted felt that things he had done to try to protect Kurtis were twisted to make him look like an aggressor. Communication broke down around the incident: "It was always something that was unspoken between us, we *never* talked about it," except "to the extent of trial strategy." This in turn contributed to a breakdown of physical intimacy.

Meera related that one of the most upsetting aspects of the drive-by harassment was how it had affected her and Ellen as a couple. Although they initially laughed awkwardly together about it, they did not talk to one another about the distressing aspects of the experience, and Meera felt that this silence and the feeling of distance it created in their relationship was more damaging than the actual slur that had been made. As a butch-appearing lesbian, Meera also worried that she introduced danger into Ellen's life that Ellen would otherwise not have encountered. She felt protective about this and also wondered a little whether it could affect Ellen's willingness to be in the relationship.

The case of Katina and her partner, Mary, provides a contrast to those of Ted and Meera. Katina was a 47-year-old, white, lesbian-identified woman. She and Mary had been harassed in the neighborhood in her hometown in the southern United States when they returned there to care for ailing elderly family members. The harassment included rude sexual gestures and indirectly threatening interactions with a next-door neighbor, in what felt to them like a prying neighborhood where they already felt very out of place and were not out due to perceived conservatism. Katina explained that she and her partner, Mary, were "very good at communicating" and had not avoided talking about what was going on. Overall, Katina felt that the most salient effect on their relationship was positive: "We've been through a tremendous amount in a short period of time together, and I think it's just made us have a very deep and strong relationship."

Effects on Current Relationships

Two other participants noted how their histories of victimization affected their ways of being in current relationships. Mark became aware that he had viewed his assault as emotional "baggage" and had felt for some time that he needed to hide it from his current partner. Similarly, Pam recognized that her "apprehensiveness to be affectionate in public" was a long-lasting aftereffect of her victimization 10 years earlier and that this had created tension in her current relationship, without her ever having thought to disclose the reasons for her caution to her partner.

BGL Community: Positives and Negatives

Given that BGL individuals' romantic and family supports may not be available in an uncomplicated way following a hate crime, it is also of interest to examine how they turn to BGL and non-BGL friends and community and what they find there.

Positive BGL Support

Mark stated the most clearly of all the participants how BGL friends were particularly valuable to his recovery process, as "they had all at some time in their lives" experienced something similar to what he had gone through. Mark also said that straight friends were empathic and supportive. Pam reported that she had been more likely to talk about bias experiences with BGL friends, as she held an expectation that straight people would not understand. Dani felt, in retrospect, that she would have benefited from more BGL community, specifically from talking to people who she felt would have been more familiar with the experience of internalized homophobia than her straight friends were; in fact, shortly after she left the workplace where she was harassed, she began to seek more BGL community. Katina talked about the unique support that was available from one lesbian friend who had previously been shot in an antilesbian attack, although knowing about this person's experience also heightened her own fear during her harassment.

Lack of BGL Support

Not all participants experienced positive support from the BGL community. Ted was sorely disappointed that more gay friends had not approached him to offer support. He interpreted that what had happened to him might have been too painful and potentially personal for them to bear. In contrast to Mark, Katina found that none of her immediate BGL friends had been through, or could empathize with, what was happening to her. She found it "shocking" that most of them minimized the harassment and intimidation she experienced.

Complications of BGL Support

Kris related that when she turned to lesbian friends for support, "they were angrier than I was" and wanted to take action such as go to the police or "stage a big full rally and go to the papers." Despite a history of BGL activism, Kris was not comfortable with this:

> I didn't really want that attention, maybe there was some internalized homophobia there, but I just didn't want—as radical as I can be about other people's plights, it's really hard for me to call attention to myself. I'm actually pretty shy.

She also felt that it could escalate the situation and cause more danger. As a result, she withdrew from that community, which likely impeded her ability to recover from these experiences and their sequelae of anxiety and fear (Kaniasty & Norris, 1992; Waldo et al., 1998). She felt that this cycle would not have occurred with a more random crime that was not targeted due to SO.

Salience of Sexual Orientation of Others

Overall, issues of sexual identity, not only the victims' but that of others around them, were infused through participants' experiences of victimization and recovery. Many had learned or speculated as to the SO of potential allies or helpers, and even perpetrators. Ted's narrative included the SO of both lawyers in his case and how he felt this affected the strategy and outcome of the trial. On the night of his assault, Mark automatically made guesses about the SO of the EMT and the police detective. Charles believed that his harasser was an older, closeted gay man whom he had looked up to when he was growing up. Katina was alert to the SO of not only other neighbors, but the main perpetrator, who appeared behaviorally to be a gay man. And Kris looked to lesbian neighbors to find out whether they also were being harassed. This may also be more characteristic of experiences based on SO bias than other identities, such as race, which would be more visible to all.

Non-BGL Support People

Gillian experienced the school administration as being insensitive to the level of homophobia in her school, particularly around a "poster war" that occurred when a student group put up gay-positive posters and, the next day, they were outnumbered by posters with antigay obscenities and accusations that gay people were child molesters. The administration "let it go on for a few days" and then responded by removing both the positive and the negative posters, and then banning BGLT "safe zone" signs because they implied that the rest of the school was not safe, something Gillian found particularly ironic. She also felt that this stood in stark contrast to the administration's appropriately more swift and thorough response to a prior anti-Semitic vandalism incident. Her strongest feelings of anger about the whole situation were directed at the administration "because they *required* me to go to school, they *required* that I be there, and then they let this stuff happen."

FEELINGS OF ANGER AND EFFECTS ON WORLDVIEW

Anger is a common response to hate crime victimization in general (Barnes & Ephross, 1994) and for anti-BGL hate crime victims specifically (Herek et al., 1999; Herek et al., 1997). While a victim of any crime may experience anger, in the case of a hate crime, anger may be more diffuse, rather than being directed at the perpetrator (Noelle, 2000). Perhaps "the ultimate enemy—the conditions and institutions that breed the isms in society—seems undefeatable" (Weiss & Ephross, 1986, p. 134) to victims of hate crimes; such a sense of hopelessness could contribute to the measurable differences in symptomatology and beliefs.

Anger at Homophobia and Heterosexism

Michael, who described himself as "furious" and "outraged," said that this was most often directed (very openly) at the specific perpetrators. At the same time, though, he felt that each incident represented the degree of heterosexism or homophobia in society: "People obviously say these things because they feel it's acceptable, and they feel it's tacitly condoned, and they feel it's OK, and they have license to do that, they're licensed to do all that." Meera echoed this:

> Some of [the experience of] a hate crime is knowing that [the perpetrator] speaks for a number of other people in the world, and they are just vocalizing the hatred that other people maybe don't have the guts to say, but think all the time.

When asked about her emotional response to her belief that she was targeted for leaving a gay bar, Pam replied that she was "very angry, angry, helpless." She, too, cited her awareness of living in a heterosexist society:

> It was a *generalized* anger that we live in the state that we do. You hear so much about how gays and lesbians have more rights than we ever have [before], or it's safer now than it was, but in many ways it doesn't feel that way. So, things can happen all the time, it's just a matter of what we hear about and what we don't. And maybe we hear more about it *because* we subscribe to . . . the gay magazines and belong to different groups.

Pam added, "I remember being younger, but I hoped things would change by the time I was the age I am now, I had hoped that we would be a lot further along." Kris also described a sense of generalized anger, rather than anger at the members of the family that had harassed her, and she saw this as being a defensive tactic at times:

> I think the safest thing for me sometimes is to direct it at the culture. This is a misogynist, homophobic, racist, in some ways really disgusting, unsafe culture. And sometimes if I feel that, I don't have to feel the individual, the personal, as much. So, yeah, I get angry, I get angry that these hate crimes happen, more than specifically at this woman [whose family harassed me], who I think has a lot of real personal issues.

Herek and colleagues (1999) suggested that one essential recovery task for survivors of a hate crime may be "regaining a balanced world view that allows them to recognize the objective dangers posed by society's prejudice while not being overwhelmed by a sense of personal vulnerability and powerlessness" (p. 950).

Increased Awareness of Danger

Kris spoke directly of becoming aware of such objective dangers: "to have a gun in your face . . . you *know* without any uncertainty that this world is dangerous and hostile towards gays and lesbians. That's *useful* information and I can make a lot of decisions now based on that information." Of the cumulative impact of homophobic events, she commented, "It affects not only how I feel about myself and how I fit in with other people who walk on this planet, but my behavior." She also highlighted how meaningful context and cumulative events were to her:

> I don't want it to be like, [you] interviewed this person and this one thing happened to her, . . . because it's *so* hard to pull out an incident and give it a lot of attention when it's just part of a lifetime. "How do you cope with that?" And, "Is this a result of that?" Well, I don't know, it could be a result of that and the five things that happened before that, or it could be just how I've learned to *cope.*

In Contrast

Mark was the only participant who made sense of his experience in a strictly positive manner: he said, "I'm a more strong individual than some people who've just led these perfect lives."

SOCIOPOLITICAL CONTEXT

The preceding sentiments highlight the sociopolitical context within which hate crimes occur. Living in a heterosexist society results in cumulative "insidious trauma" (Root, 1992). Knowledge of others' victimization creates a "ripple effect" of vicarious traumatization (Noelle, 2002). The effect of political heterosexism on the psychological well-being of BGL people has been illustrated in a study of the 1992 campaign and voter approval for a Colorado constitutional amendment that would have "removed any legal recourse for [BGL] people who encountered discrimination" based on SO (Russell & Bohan, 1999, p. 406). In the study, individual BGL participants overall reported increased psychological distress (depression, trauma symptomatology, anxiety, and indices of fear) in relation to this political event. At the same time, some study respondents also reported that they became more out and had an increased sense of having sympathetic heterosexual allies (Russell, 2000).

CONCLUSION

Previous research has shed some light on what might cause hate crimes to have a greater psychological impact than nonhate crimes of similar severity, pointing to differences such as the greater likelihood of known perpetrators, multiple perpetrators, and repeated victimization (Rose & Mechanic, 2002). The case studies presented in this chapter suggest additional factors for further investigation, including secondary victimization; disruption to one's expression of identity, one's identity development, and one's access to BGL community; lesser availability of family support; intrusion into the realm of romantic relationships; a diffuse sense of anger about the victimization; and lowered expectations of how one will be viewed and treated as a BGL person in the world. Qualitative investigation allowed for the elucidation of these factors as well as a rich view of the context provided by each individual's history and personality, and by sociopolitical factors. This method is a helpful augmentation to quantitative methods and brings much to bear within the field of trauma research due to the idiographic nature of trauma responses (Janoff-Bulman, 1992; Saakvitne et al., 1998).

These case studies offer some direction for intervention and amelioration of the effects of hate crimes, as well. Psychotherapists should keep in mind that for BGLT clients, hate crimes and homophobia may have had significant impact on their lives, whether they are a focus of therapy or not; in fact, some interviewees had never brought this up on their own with therapists they had seen. Given the variability in available support seen across these cases, it would seem that the more widespread development of support groups for victims of anti-BGL hate crimes and harassment would also be helpful. Last, it is helpful to victims when homophobia, heterosexism, and hate crimes are spoken of, both within the BGL community and by heterosexual allies, especially those in positions of authority such as school leaders and law enforcement agents. This was evident in the appreciation of the study expressed by many of the interviewees and by their willingness to share their stories even at significant emotional cost to themselves.

NOTES

1. The term *homophobia* refers throughout to anti-BGL sentiments, attitudes, and behaviors at the level of the individual. The term *heterosexism* refers to anti-BGL or heterosexual-centric practices, institutions, and attitudes at the societal level as well as the advantages and privileges conferred to heterosexual people.

2. All participants are given pseudonyms, and, when necessary, possibly identifying information is changed in ways intended to be neutral to results and interpretation. For more complete case study details and formulations, the reader is referred to the entire dissertation produced (Noelle, 2003).

3. It is important to note the deficiency of research adequately addressing the experiences of BGL people of color. Samples in studies reviewed here, for example, have been 93 percent white (Otis & Skinner, 1996), 78 percent white (D'Augelli et al., 2002), and 66 percent white (Pilkington & D'Augelli, 1995). Qualitative results reported here (Noelle, 2003) are based on interviews with 10 individuals, 9 of whom were white.

4. Only very recently have the hate crime experiences of transgender individuals been examined, and research is lacking in this area. The study from which case examples are taken (Noelle, 2003) included one transgender-identified individual, who was the victim of antilesbian harassment. Victims of antitransgender hate crimes were not recruited in that study due to the paucity of prior literature on transgender identity.

5. Note that 2 percent of the SO-based crimes were listed as being due to "antiheterosexual bias."

6. For lesbians, 35 percent of bias crimes compared to 68 percent of nonbias crimes; for gay men, 46 percent compared to 72 percent; for bisexual women, 35 percent

compared to 62 percent; and for bisexual men, 24 percent compared to 61 percent (Herek et al., 1999).

7.   Eighty-one percent of gay white men, 71 percent of white lesbians, 66 percent of gay men of color, and 52 percent of lesbians of color reported.

8.   Sexual orientation bias is typically identified by victims based on factors including antigay slurs; location of the crime, such as a gay bar; recency of identifying behavior, such as same-sex affection; or inferences based on timing (e.g., the day of a BGLT pride parade) or perceived recognition as bisexual, gay, or lesbian (Herek et al., 2002; Herek et al., 1997).

9.   These differences were found for gay men and lesbians, but not for bisexual people; the authors caution that this may have been due to the small number of bisexual participants. The SO bias hate crime literature to date generally neglects the experiences of bisexual-identified individuals or does not address them separately.

10.   The Outness Inventory (Mohr & Fassinger, 2000).

11.   The Impact of Event Scale–Revised (Briere & Elliott, 1998). On Intrusive, Avoidant, and Hypervigilant subscales, Mark scored 1.1 (70th–74th percentile), 2.4 (85th–89th percentile), and 0.3, respectively, while Ted scored 2.5 (90th–94th percentile), 2.6 (85th–89th percentile), and 2.8.

REFERENCES

Barnes, A., & Ephross, P. H. (1994). The impact of hate violence on victims: Emotional and behavioral responses to attacks. *Social Work, 39*, 247–251.

Berrill, K. T., & Herek, G. M. (1992). Primary and secondary victimization in antigay hate crimes: Official response and public policy. In G. M. Herek & K. T. Berrill (Eds.), *Hate crimes: Confronting violence against lesbians and gay men* (pp. 289–305). Newbury Park, CA: Sage.

Briere, J., & Elliott, D. M. (1998). Clinical utility of the Impact of Event Scale: Psychometrics in the general population. *Assessment, 5*, 171–180.

Comstock, G. D. (1991). *Violence against lesbians and gay men.* New York: Columbia University Press.

D'Augelli, A. R. (1992). Lesbian and gay male undergraduates' experiences of harassment and fear on campus. *Journal of Interpersonal Violence, 7*, 383–395.

D'Augelli, A. R., Pilkington, N. W., & Hershberger, S. L. (2002). Incidence and mental health impact of sexual orientation victimization of lesbian, gay, and bisexual youths in high school. *School Psychology Quarterly, 17*, 148–167.

Dunbar, E. (2006). Race, gender, and sexual orientation in hate crime victimization: Identity politics or identity risk? *Violence and Victims, 21*, 323–337.

Federal Bureau of Investigation. (2001). *2000 uniform crime reports for the United States.* Washington, DC: U.S. Government Printing Office.

Federal Bureau of Investigation. (2006). *Uniform crime report: Hate crime statistics, 2005.* Washington, DC: U.S. Government Printing Office.

Garcia, L., McDevitt, J., Gu, J., & Balboni, J. (1999). *Final report on the psychological and behavioral effects of bias- and non bias-motivated assault.* National Institute of Justice and City of Boston Police Department.

Garcia, L., McDevitt, J., Gu, J., & Balboni, J. (2000). *Summary report on the psychological and behavioral effects of bias- and non bias-motivated assault: Implications for criminal justice practitioners.* National Institute of Justice and City of Boston Police Department.

Garnets, L., Herek, G. M., & Levy, B. (1992). Violence and victimization of lesbians and gay men: Mental health consequences. In G. M. Herek & K. T. Berrill (Eds.), *Hate crimes: Confronting violence against lesbians and gay men* (pp. 207–226). Newbury Park, CA: Sage.

Green, D. L., & Diaz, N. (2007). Predictors of emotional stress in crime victims: Implications for treatment. *Brief Treatment of Crisis Intervention, 7,* 194–205.

Greenberg, M. S., & Ruback, R. B. (1992). *After the crime: Victim decision making.* New York: Plenum.

Herek, G. M., & Berrill, K. T. (Eds.). (1992). *Hate crimes: Confronting violence against lesbians and gay men.* Newbury Park, CA: Sage.

Herek, G. M., Cogan, J. C., & Gillis, R. J. (2002). Victim experiences in hate crimes based on sexual orientation. *Journal of Social Issues, 58,* 319–339.

Herek, G. M., Gillis, J. R, & Cogan, J. C. (1999). Psychological sequelae of hate crime victimization among lesbian, gay, and bisexual adults. *Journal of Consulting and Clinical Psychology, 67,* 945–951.

Herek, G. M., Gillis, J. R., Cogan, J. C., & Glunt, E. K. (1997). Hate crime victimization among lesbian, gay, and bisexual adults: Prevalence, psychological correlates, and methodological issues. *Journal of Interpersonal Violence, 12,* 195–215.

Hershberger, S. L., & D'Augelli, A. R. (1995). The impact of victimization on the mental health and suicidality of lesbian, gay, and bisexual youths. *Developmental Psychology, 31,* 65–74.

Janoff-Bulman, R. (1989). Assumptive worlds and the stress of traumatic events: Applications of the schema construct. *Social Cognition, 7,* 113–136.

Janoff-Bulman, R. (1992). *Shattered assumptions.* New York: Free Press.

Jordan, K. M., Vaughan, J. S., & Woodworth, K. J. (1997). I will survive: Lesbian gay, and bisexual youths' experience of high school. *Journal of Gay and Lesbian Social Services, 7,* 17–33.

Kaniasty, K., & Norris, F. H. (1992). Social support and victims of crime: Matching event, support, and outcome. *American Journal of Community Psychology, 20,* 211–241.

Kilpatrick, D. G., Saunders, B. E., Amick-McMullan, A., Best, C. L., Veronen, L. J., & Resnick, H. S. (1989). Victim and crime factors associated with the development of crime-related post-traumatic stress disorder. *Behavior Therapy, 20,* 199–214.

Kitzinger, C. (1994). Anti-lesbian harassment. In C. Brant & Y. L. Too (Eds.), *Rethinking sexual harassment* (pp. 125–147). London: Pluto Press.

Kuehnle, K., & Sullivan, A. (2001). Patterns of anti-gay violence: An analysis of incident characteristics and victim reporting. *Journal of Interpersonal Violence, 16,* 928–943.

Kurdek, L. A., & Schmitt, J. P. (1987). Perceived emotional support from family and friends in members of homosexual, married, and heterosexual cohabiting couples. *Journal of Homosexuality, 14*(3/4), 57–68.

Leets, L. (2002). Experiencing hate speech: Perceptions and responses to anti-Semitism and antigay speech. *Journal of Social Issues, 58,* 341–361.

Mays, V. M., & Cochran, S. D. (2001). Mental health correlates of perceived discrimination among lesbian, gay, and bisexual adults in the United States. *American Journal of Public Health, 91,* 1869–1876.

Meyer, I. H. (1995). Minority stress and mental health in gay men. *Journal of Health and Social Behavior, 36*, 38–56.

Mohr, J. J., & Fassinger, R. E. (2000). Measuring dimensions of lesbian and gay male experience. *Measurement and Evaluation in Counseling and Development, 33*(2), 66–90.

Morris, J. F., Waldo, C. R., & Rothblum, E. D. (2001). A model of predictors and outcomes of outness among lesbian and bisexual women. *American Journal of Orthopsychiatry, 71*(1), 61–71.

National Coalition of Anti-Violence Programs. (2000). *Anti-lesbian, gay, transgender, and bisexual violence in 1999: A report of the National Coalition of Anti-Violence Programs.* New York: Author.

National Coalition of Anti-Violence Programs. (2006). *Anti-lesbian, gay, transgender, and bisexual violence in 2005: A report of the National Coalition of Anti-Violence Programs.* New York: Author.

National Gay and Lesbian Task Force. (2001). *FBI hate crimes data woefully under-reports crimes against GLBT people.* Retrieved in 2001 from http://www.ngltf.org/news/release.cfm?releaseID=368

Nishith, P., Mechanic, M. B., &. Resick, P. A. (2000). Prior interpersonal trauma: The contribution to current PTSD symptoms in female rape victims. *Journal of Abnormal Psychology, 109*, 20–25.

Noelle, M. (2000). *The ripple effect of a sexual orientation hate crime: The psychological impact of the murder of Matthew Shepard on non-heterosexual people.* Unpublished master's thesis, University of Massachusetts, Amherst.

Noelle, M. (2002). The ripple effect of the Matthew Shepard murder: Impact on the assumptive worlds of members of the targeted group. *American Behavioral Scientist, 46*, 27–50.

Noelle, M. (2003). *The psychological effects of hate-crime victimization based on sexual orientation bias: Ten case studies.* Unpublished doctoral dissertation, University of Massachusetts, Amherst.

O'Conor, A. (1994). Who gets called queer in school? Lesbian, gay and bisexual teenagers, homophobia, and high school. *High School Journal, 77* , 7–12.

Otis, M. D., & Skinner, W. F. (1996). The prevalence of victimization and its effect on mental well-being among lesbian and gay people. *Journal of Homosexuality, 30* , 93–121.

Peel, E. (1999). Violence against lesbians and gay men: Decision-making in reporting and not reporting crime. *Feminism and Psychology, 9*, 161–167.

Pilkington, N. W., & D'Augelli, A. R. (1995). Victimization of lesbian, gay, and bisexual youth in community settings. *Journal of Community Psychology, 23*, 34–56.

Root, M. P. (1992). Reconstructing the impact of trauma on personality. In L. S. Brown & M. Ballou (Eds.), *Personality and psychopathology: Feminist reappraisals* (pp. 229–265). New York: Guilford Press.

Rose, S. M., & Mechanic, M. B. (2002). Psychological distress, crime features, and help-seeking behaviors related to homophobic bias incidents. *American Behavioral Scientist, 46*, 14–26.

Russell, G. M. (2000). *Voted out: The consequences of anti-gay politics.* New York: New York University Press.

Russell, G. M., & Bohan, J. S. (1999). Hearing voices: The uses of research and the politics of change. *Psychology of Women Quarterly, 23*, 403–418.

Saakvitne, K. W., Tennen, H., & Affleck, G. (1998). Exploring thriving in the context of clinical trauma theory: Constructivist self development theory. *Journal of Social Issues, 54*, 279–299.

Savin-Williams, R. C. (1994). Verbal and physical abuse as stressors in the lives of lesbian, gay male, and bisexual youth: Associations with school problems, running away, substance abuse, prostitution, and suicide. *Journal of Consulting and Clinical Psychology, 62*, 261–269.

Schmitt, J. P., & Kurdek, L. A. (1987). Personality correlates of positive identity and relationship involvement in gay men. *Journal of Homosexuality, 13*(4), 101–109.

Stermac, L.E., & Sheridan, P.M. (1993). Anti-gay/lesbian violence: Treatment Issues. *The Canadian Journal of Human Sexuality, 2*(1), 33–38.

Szymanski, D. M. (2005). Heterosexism and sexism as correlates of psychological distress in lesbians. *Journal of Counseling and Development, 83*, 355–360.

Thurlow, C. (2001). Naming the "outsider within": Homophobic pejoratives and the verbal abuse of lesbian, gay and bisexual high-school pupils. *Journal of Adolescence, 24*(1), 25–38.

Waldo, C. R., Hesson-McInnis, M. S., & D'Augelli, A. R. (1998). Antecedents and consequences of victimization of lesbian, gay, and bisexual young people: A structural model comparing rural university and urban samples. *American Journal of Community Psychology, 26*, 307–334.

Weiss, J. C., & Ephross, P. H. (1986). Group work approaches to "hate violence" incidents. *Social Work, 31*, 132–136.

Wertheimer, D. M. (1992). Treatment and service interventions for lesbian and gay male crime victims. In G. M. Herek & K. T. Berrill (Eds.), *Hate crimes: Confronting violence against lesbians and gay men* (pp. 227–240). Newbury Park, CA: Sage.

Winkel, F. W., Blaauw, E., Sheridan, L., & Baldry, A. C. (2003). Repeat criminal victimization and vulnerability for coping failure: A prospective examination of a potential risk factor. *Psychology, Crime, & Law, 9*, 87–95.

CHAPTER 6

BEYOND THE IMMEDIATE VICTIM: UNDERSTANDING HATE CRIMES AS MESSAGE CRIMES

Helen Ahn Lim

In 1990, Congress passed the Hate Crime Statistics Act, which authorized the U.S. attorney general to collect data from state and local law enforcement agencies. The U.S. attorney general assigned this responsibility to the Federal Bureau of Investigation's (FBI's) Uniform Crime Reporting (UCR) program. Since its inception, the FBI has been collecting hate crime statistics reported to the agency by local and state law enforcement departments. Initially, these reports focused on "criminal offenses motivated by the victim's race, ethnicity/national origin, religion, or sexual orientation" (Federal Bureau of Investigation [FBI], 2006). Since 1997, the FBI has been collecting statistics on bias crimes against persons with disabilities (FBI 2006). Law enforcement agencies also report hate crime data to the FBI's National Incident-Based Reporting System (NIBRS). NIBRS is a more comprehensive crime reporting system capable of capturing a wide range of information on specific incidents.

Although these data are useful in identifying reporting trends and the kinds of hate crimes that are reported,[1] they tell us nothing about the impact of hate crime on targeted communities. Since the specific person is immaterial to the perpetrator in a hate crime offense, victims are interchangeable so long as they are members of the targeted community. Indeed, victims of hate crime are attacked not as individuals, but as symbols. They are attacked to send a message to the rest of their community (Hwang, 2001). Hate crimes are attacks not only against the direct individual, but against the entire targeted community.

Through Asian American narratives, this chapter demonstrates that the harm of hate crime extends beyond the immediate victim and to the entire targeted community. In effect, every hate crime incident harms the entire targeted victim group. The chapter begins by introducing the author's research and the Asian American narratives. The next sections illustrate how hate crimes function as message crimes. For Asian Americans, the message is, "You are a foreigner; you do not belong." These narratives also plainly reveal how hate crimes terrorize targeted populations. The fact that Asian Americans adjust their lives to the "threat of hate crime" demonstrates that this threat is real, dangerous, and costly. The chapter concludes with some final thoughts on how these narratives enhance our understanding of racial victimization and on the collective impacts of hate crime.

ASIAN AMERICAN RESPONDENTS AND NARRATIVE RESEARCH

The narratives in this chapter are based on 45 in-depth interviews with Asian Americans in 2002–2003. Relying on the snowball method, respondents were interviewed who represented various ethnic backgrounds: Chinese, Korean, Japanese, East Asian Indian, Vietnamese, Chinese Indonesian, Chinese Filipino, Chinese Malaysian, Japanese Caucasian, and Korean Caucasian. Since snowball sampling begins with contacts known to the researcher, nearly all of the interviewees lived near my own place of residence, in New Jersey, and New York. There were a few exceptions. Five of the interviewees resided in California, Texas, and Indiana. I interviewed these Asian Americans based upon travel convenience and the belief that they had important stories to share.

Twenty-three of the respondents are women and 22 are men. As far as their resident status, they are legal permanent residents or naturalized and natural-born U.S. citizens. Each interviewee was assigned a pseudonym to protect his or her identity. The respondents were asked to answer questions related to the problem of racial bigotry and hate crime.

What is persistent throughout these interviews is the pervasive role of whites as offenders. Although racially motivated bias crimes include aggressions between minorities (Abelmann & Lie, 1995; Kim, 2000; Levin & McDevitt, 2002; Min, 1999), this research centers on what is overwhelmingly reflected in the narratives: hate crimes against Asian Americans committed by the racial majority, herein also referred to as whites. The narratives in this chapter overwhelmingly reflect the views of Asian Americans on how they perceive and experience hate crimes committed by the white majority.

A pattern of responses began to materialize from these interviews. By examining how Asian Americans respond to the threat of hate crime, the narratives in this chapter explicitly demonstrate how the harm of hate crime extends beyond the direct victim to the targeted population. From the perspectives of Asian Americans, theses narratives demonstrate how hate crimes intimidate and shed fear on the entire targeted community.

TARGETING ASIAN AMERICANS: TARGETING "FOREIGNERS" WHO ARE NONWHITE

Although hate crimes tend to be random events, victims of hate crimes are not attacked for random reasons. The presumed racial distinction of Asian Americans as nonwhite and the meaning of Asian Americans as nonwhite serve as a source of their racial victimization.[2] The "perpetual foreigner" image underlies hostile treatment against Asian Americans. Although stereotypes and popular images do not cause bias incidents or bias crimes, they can be used to justify harm against targeted groups, including serious forms of violence (Kang, 1993):

> [Hate crime is] a crime where it's not about the personal experience or personal feelings that initiate the crime . . . but, like in New Jersey, when the white community members were attacking Indians, even when they didn't know them personally. That's a hate crime and it doesn't have to do with the person specifically . . . like with the Dotbusters in the late 1980s. (interview with Mary, first-generation East Asian Indian American, Parsippany, New Jersey)

In 1987, the violence associated with New Jersey's "Dotbusters," an insensitive reference to the *bindi* (cosmetic mark) some Indian women wear on their foreheads as a symbol of sanctity, demonstrated strong resistance to the presence of Pakistan and Indian residents in the Jersey City area (home of approximately 15,000 Asian Indians). A hate letter published in a local New Jersey newspaper exemplifies the threat the Dotbusters felt to be posed by the presence of "foreigners": "We will go to any extreme to get Indians to move out of Jersey City. If I'm walking down the street and I see a Hindu and the setting is right, I will just hit him or her. We plan some of our more extreme attacks such as breaking windows, breaking car windows and crashing family parties. We use the phone book and look up the name Patel. Have you seen how many there are?" (cited in Takaki, 1998 p. 482). Dozens of attacks actually occurred, ranging from verbal harassment to serious beatings. Outside a Jersey City area restaurant on September 27, 1987, a gang of youths chanting "Hindu, Hindu" beat Navroz Mody to death and permanently maimed Kaushal Sharan. A grand jury indicted four teenagers for the murder (Takaki, 1998). In Boston, Massachusetts, when a housing inspector came to inspect the home of an Asian American woman, her white neighbors yelled, "Get rid of the Chinese" to the housing inspector. This incident occurred in an area where white residents have resented the increase of Asian immigrants moving to the area (National Asian Pacific Legal Consortium

[NAPLC], 1997). The Asian American resident was an unwelcome resident who came to "invade the white people's turf." Protecting racial purity is an all too common justification for hostility toward Asian Americans, who come to "contaminate" the white community (see Kang, 1993).

Regardless of how long Asian American families have lived in America, an individual of Asian descent is often assumed to be a foreigner. The construction of race and the treatment of Asian Americans as "perpetual foreigners" have long been a source of racial discrimination and continuing potential for abuse (see Fong, 2000; Takaki, 1998 Tuan, 1998). The foreigner image can also creep up in the most unexpected ways. When MSNBC announced the gold medal winner of the 1998 Olympic Games in women's figure skating, the headline read, "AMERICAN BEATS KWAN . . . AMERICAN FINISHES STRONG TO OVERTAKE KWAN, WHO TAKES THE SILVER," despite the fact that both Tara Lipinski and Michelle Kwan are Americans. In fact, Michelle Kwan was the U.S. national favorite to win the Olympic gold medal. Tuan (1998) argues that although this unconscious slip reflects poorly on the writer, it is important to understand the social context in which this could occur. The mistake may be excused as petty, but the impact is far reaching when Asian Americans are deprived of their American identity and citizenship (Tuan, 1998):

> I have to admit that sometimes I get intimidated by certain Caucasians because they think that I don't have the same rights as them. . . . You can just feel that Caucasians feel that way about us sometimes. I'm very aware that I look different. I know there were specific situations that they were being racists. When they are doing that I feel like saying, "Look, just because I look different I still have just as many rights as you do." . . . You feel like they feel like you don't belong here and don't have the same rights as them because we just look different. There are certain people that are very ignorant and they think we can't speak English and live a normal life. This is something I worry about. . . . If you live here for six generations you still will look different even though you are every bit of American and still be treated differently. (interview with Young, second-generation Korean American, Bridgewater, New Jersey)

The respondent believes that Caucasians see her as unlike them and therefore as someone who doesn't belong in America or who is not deserving of the full rights of an American. Even though U.S. citizenship status grants all people constitutionally protected rights, the respondent is troubled by the treatment of Asian Americans as foreigners who are inferior and feels pessimistic that these conditions will improve over time. Her response draws attention to the significance of race and notions of belonging.

What may intensify the reaction against Asian Americans is the large influx of immigrants and refuges from Asia. Between 1980 and 1990, the Asian population grew from 1.5 to 2.9 percent (U.S. Commission on Civil Rights,

1992). By 2000, the Asian American population increased to 4 million (4.2%; U.S. Census Bureau, 2002.

Though it may be realistic to think that racial attacks on minorities will occur more frequently where their numbers increase, what is significant is the speed of growth and the racial context in which it occurs (Green, Strolovitch, & Wong, 1998). Although the number of Asian Americans is very small compared to the rest of the population, since Asian Americans tend to concentrate in certain geographical areas, the population increase is much more dramatic in some communities. According to the 2000 census, the largest concentrations of Asians tended to be found in coastal and/or urban counties, while smaller percentages resided throughout an array of counties. The majority of counties with Asian populations more than twice the national average were found in suburbs of large metropolitan areas such as Seattle, Los Angeles, the San Francisco Bay area, New York City, Newark, Washington, D.C., Chicago, Houston, and the Minneapolis–St. Paul metropolitan area. A large number of Asians residing outside the suburbs of large metropolitan areas were typically located near colleges or universities. Among cities with a population of 100,000 or more, New York had the largest Asian population, with 872,777, followed by Los Angeles, with 407,000. This large influx of Asian Americans, or "foreigner presence," may aggravate existing anti-Asian sentiments experienced by earlier immigrants (see Takaki, 1998). The "perpetual foreigner" not only distinguishes Asian Americans from white Americans as the "outside Other," but also underlies the racial antagonism that is expressed as bias incidents and bias crimes (see Fong, 2000, 2002; Hwang, 2001; Takaki, 1998).

UNDERSTANDING THE IMPACT OF HATE CRIMES AS MESSAGE CRIMES

The respondent quoted in the following extract views hate crimes as message crimes intended to intimidate the targeted victim group:

> Hate crimes are acts of violence to others based on racism; based on the sense of superiority over the other . . . as violence as injustice that might seem justifiable to them . . . kind of an "us and them" mentality. . . . The people who are engaging in hate crimes believe that their collective whole, whether it's the KKK or skinheads, they are fighting against outsiders who don't share their values, who are a threat to their freedom, their rights . . . so they feel the need to send the message out there through violence. (interview with Jamie, second-generation Korean American, Bound Brook, New Jersey)

The preceding respondent's definition of hate crime is multifaceted. The respondent's comprehension of hate crime as acts committed against "outsiders" addresses the human propensity to classify and categorize groups of people and to treat these groups as different Others, or nonequals (see Baird & Rosenbaum, 1992). Moreover, it speaks to how hate crimes can strengthen or reaffirm in-group status, while punishing the out-group for overstepping their racial boundaries (see Perry, 2001).

The respondent also identifies hate crimes as message crimes intended to intimidate the victim and the members of his or her shared community. They are symbolic crimes purposefully directed toward a victim because of his or her membership in a group, an affiliation that exists in the perception of the perpetrator (see Perry, 2003). Hwang (2001) argues that what makes hate crimes punishable above and beyond the physical act of criminality is the psychological and emotional impact of hate violence, which goes beyond the crime itself. He argues that the penalties are more severe because we recognize that, based on a history of racial intolerance, the victims are particularly vulnerable and suffer levels of injury far beyond the physical damages. For example, he states that burning a cross on the lawn of an African American is more than a traditional act of arson or vandalism because it bears a clear threat of further escalation of violence when considered in the context of historical precedent (Hwang, 2001). He also argues that this is true whether or not the direct victim understands the intended message of intimidation and racial hatred because hate crimes are symbolic crimes, and responding to them with a focus on the individual level makes little sense. This means that when a shop owner whose store is vandalized with painted swastikas is unaware of the significance behind the symbol, given the swastika's symbolism of racial hatred and violence, its use defines the incident as one of hate violence, regardless of the understanding of the property owner (Hwang, 2001):

> Even though you are not directly targeted, somebody I know like my family, friends, or coworkers, if it affected them, it has affected me. I know them, and I can tell that I can be targeted sometime too. . . . So even though I'm not directly targeted, I can feel it. At my acquaintance's church there was racist graffiti on it, they would paint over it, and then there would be racist graffiti on it again, and they would paint over it again. They are doing that because they don't want a Korean church in their neighborhood. So even though it's not directly at me it's at my friend's church. . . . She ended up leaving the church since she said they never would win and wished that her church would move to a different location. (interview with Mary, second-generation Korean American, Yorba Linda, California)

The respondent, recognizing her own vulnerability as a member of the targeted community, talks about this incident as an indirect victim of hate crime. The determination of the offenders to "drive out" the church members from the surrounding community is strongly communicated through the repetitious act of vandalism. Her friend's church was not only vandalized once, but repeatedly. One intended impact was clearly intimidation. According to the respondent, since the leaders were not considering relocating in response to the repeated acts of vandalism, the respondent's friend, feeling intimidated and concerned for her safety, stopped attending this church. Although there are laws that prohibit vandalism and defacement of certain locations and institutions, including houses of worship, cemeteries, schools, public monuments, and community centers, the most common types of hate crime statute at the state level deal with institutional vandalism (Levin & McDevitt, 2002):

> I remember when we first moved to California we were living in Long Beach and my dad got his car windshield bashed in two or three times within two months. And you know there isn't really anything that anybody could do about it. We never found out who it was. It was probably a racial hate crime thing. This happened in front of our home, and it was the car on the street. We were only living there for only a couple of months. And I don't see any other reason . . . it [the neighborhood] was almost all Caucasian. . . . That definitely made my family leave right away. It was a matter of months that we moved. What we did was move up to San Francisco; it was more of an Asian community. (interview with Ray, second-generation Vietnamese American, Hackensack, New Jersey)

What is perhaps particularly alarming for victims is when hate crimes occur right at their front door. According to the U.S. Commission on Civil Rights (1992), harassment and vandalism were the most common forms of "move-in violence." These assaults occurred in a number of neighborhoods, including suburban communities, where middle-class and professional Asian Americans lived in low-income homes that recent Southeast Asian refugees found affordable (Fong, 2002). The incidents included egg throwing, shattering windows with rocks or BB guns, and more serious acts of vandalism, including firebombing. Levin and McDevitt (2002) call these incidents *defensive hate crimes*. According to Levin and McDevitt, defensive hate crimes occur when the perpetrator targets an individual or a group of individuals who are perceived to be a personal threat: "the Black family that just moved into an all-white neighborhood, the white college student who has begun to date her Asian classmate, or the Latino who was recently promoted at work" (p. 78). Defensive hate crimes are intended to send a message to those who try to "take over," for example, the message that blacks are not welcome in this neighborhood and Latinos should not apply for that promotion. It is in this manner that these crimes are like terrorist acts, intended to instill fear and horror. This hate crime, in the form of a property offense, sends a clear unwelcome message to the victim and to the victim group (Levin & McDevitt, 2002).

> When me and my friend decided to drive to California from the East Coast, we decided against taking a southern route because we knew there were chapters of the KKK [Ku Klux Klan] there. I've heard stories where it is

Klan country, where people would come up to you at the gas station and say this is Klan country. So, to avoid the south area, we went to another route. My friend is Vietnamese, so we thought two Asian guys in a red Celica may draw too much attention driving down south. I heard these stories from my one friend who was traveling with other whites, and he was the only Filipino. The sign for the county, I guess it was an add-on, it said, "This is KKK Country." So, the white friends put him in the back of the van and covered him with a sheet. They did this to protect him. Just in case, to keep him out of trouble. . . . He was pretty scared from just the sign with the Dixie flag of the Southern army with the handmade sign that said, "This is KKK Country." So, it was a wake-up call. You don't think it happens, but in the South, there is still a good amount of KKK members around. (interview with Matt, second-generation Filipino American, New Brunswick, New Jersey)

Given the history of racism in the Deep South, along with the identifying white supremacy symbols of power, it is no wonder that these men feared for their safety. The KKK long terrorized communities and spread hatred against minorities. With the end of the Civil War came a brief period of reconstruction, during which the newly freed slaves sought some measure of economic and political equality. The KKK, an organization founded after the Civil war for the purpose of protecting and furthering Southern tradition, such as the separation of the races (Streissguth, 2003), responded with a campaign of terror and violence, in which many African Americans were targeted and lynched when economic times were hard, whenever progress was threatened in the area of civil rights and equality before the law, and when African Americans committed "unacceptable" behavior such as whistling at white women (Levin & Rabrenovic, 2004; Streissguth, 2003). Klan activity has spread beyond the South (Southern Poverty Law Center [SPLC], 2008), and the KKK is one of the extremist groups monitored by civil rights organizations such as the Southern Poverty Law Center (SPLC). According to the SPLC, KKK activity has been directed not only toward African Americans, but at also at other groups, including Jews, gays and lesbians, immigrants, and, more recently, Roman Catholics (see SPLC, 2008). In one of the earliest cases won by Morris Dees and the SPLC against a hate group, the Klan was forbidden to continue its violent attacks against Vietnamese (Wu, 2002). In 1981, Vietnamese fishermen along the Texas Gulf Coast took the KKK to court (Wu, 2002). The entire shrimp industry was suffering, and the Klan blamed the Asian refugees for the decline. Dees and the SPLC continue to be an active voice in the fight against hate, and the SPLC is one of the leading advocates in the preservation of civil rights.

Approximately 5 percent of all hate crimes are committed by members of organized hate groups like the KKK, Aryan Nations, or the White Aryan Resistance (Levin, 2002). Although organized hate groups are blamed for a small fraction of all hate crimes, they are associated with some of the most brutal assaults and heinous crimes. Two of the three white men who were convicted of the vicious 1998 murder of African American James Byrd Jr. in Jasper, Texas, were identified as white supremacists. After picking up handicapped Byrd, who was hitchhiking, they beat him unconscious, chained him by the ankles to their pickup truck, and dragged him along the road for more than two miles to his death. Investigators found in the possession of one of the assailants a KKK manual, and the other two had white supremacist body tattoos depicting the Confederate Knights of America (Levin & Rabrenovic, 2004). The two men identified as white supremacists were sentenced to death by lethal injection.

These groups are known for their extremist beliefs, for their history of violence, and for terrorizing their targeted populations. Facing the possibility of a serious confrontation, the respondent's friend's reaction was telling of the panic and terror extremist groups like the KKK invoke in victimized populations. Although the idea to "duck and cover" from danger may be construed as a "cowardly" act from a male normative standard, the risk of being sought out by the KKK would be too great a cost to pay. Recalling this story and the graphic picture of what could happen, the respondent, when deciding which route to take to his destination, also avoided driving the southern route, a territory known for increased KKK activity, out of concern for his safety and that of his driving companion. It is also worth noting that since hate crimes against Asian Americans are underreported in the media (NAPLC, 1999), Asian Americans continue to rely on shared stories for protection and to warn others of the imminent threat and danger they face from hate violence:

> Won-Joon Yoon wasn't in this country long and it was shocking that it happened at the church I attended. It seemed like a senseless random shooting by a guy that I would consider to be of the white extremist type that targeted other Asians and other minorities. I don't know if it was totally random, but the picking of him was random, not the targeting of the group. . . . You wouldn't think this or believe this, but sometimes the extremist beliefs come from the most normal people. . . . It was brushed aside as a random senseless act and that was it. . . . Having a personal tie to that church made it feel like it hit home . . . the victim could have been her [my wife], it could have been anyone in that situation, a Korean international student there or any Asian in general. (interview with Jeff, second-generation Korean-European American, Brea, California)

The preceding respondent expresses shock over the murder of his fellow church member and the reality of his own endangerment as a racial minority. Although Won-Joon Yoon was randomly selected, that is, indiscriminately as an individual, he was intentionally targeted as a racial minority, or a nonwhite person. Since the killing of any nonwhite person in this shooting would have fulfilled the offender's mission, the respondent himself and his wife were also in grave risk of murder. Since victims are interchangeable so long as they are members of the targeted community, the specific person is immaterial to the perpetrator in a hate crime offense. Most hate crimes are committed by offenders who are strangers to their victims (Levin & McDevitt, 2002).

Since the victim cannot rationally diminish the risk of future endangerment or change the characteristic that makes him or her a victim, those who survive the attack express feelings of anger and vulnerability (see Lawrence, 1999). Although a person may avoid risky places that lead to risky or criminal behavior, it's another thing to avoid a particular geographical area because of one's race. Because the victim did nothing personally to cause the attack and was attacked by a stranger, there was nothing Won-Joon Yoon could have done to prevent the murder; for all members who are under threat of an attack, leaving home puts them at risk of being victimized. Wherever they are, members of the targeted community carry with them the reason for their potential victimization.

Victor Hwang (2001), attorney for the Asian Law Caucus, argues that "isolated hate crimes are particularly venomous because of their seemingly random nature and the inability of the victim to rationalize its occurrence" (p. 49). Rationalization, he states, is an important defense in a logical world. And, as thinking beings, it is important for victims to be able to assign reasons to why bad things happen so that they can learn from their experiences and avoid a repeat occurrence. When a person is, however, unable to explain the incident or prevent it from happening again, the victim is subjected to further trauma. Feelings of helplessness over the incident can also be exasperated by the fact that the perpetrators are rarely caught.

Hwang (2001) also emphasizes that victims of hate crime are attacked not as individuals, but as symbols. They are attacked to send a message to the rest of their community: "They are stripped of their individuality, their personhood, and diminished to their race" (p. 50). The repeated message of violence aimed at Asian Pacific Americans is, "You are the foreigner, you do not belong here, you are not an American" (p. 50).

> About 10 years ago, there were these race issues in East Brunswick . . .
> letters were being sent to families and phone calls were being made saying that all the Asians should get out of the neighborhood. . . . Some of the neighbors got together and filed a complaint . . . but the police took it as a prank. . . . This went on for about four to six months . . . even though you would think at that time people's sensitivity would have been heightened, a lot of teenagers and younger kids at the time thought they had the right to jump on the band wagon. . . . I could go to the supermarket and be subject to racial slurs from people half my age . . . initially, I was very shocked. . . . Once I got in a huge argument with the parent of a child who

was yelling racial slurs at me . . . and the mom's reaction was that he's too young to understand and he doesn't mean anything by that. I told her by that fact that you are not addressing it you are ignoring it and telling him that it is OK. . . . As far as protection, you can't help but feel a little foolish about telling the police that a kid yelled a racial slur at me especially knowing that nothing will happen . . . but things like that . . . the victims can't really do anything until the victim is actually physically hurt . . . like someone who is getting stalked until he or she is hurt or raped. . . . Obviously, it's hurtful. I was in my 30s and to be subject to ridicule by 10 or 12 year olds . . . you get angry. (interview with Mark, second-generation Chinese American, East Brunswick, New Jersey)

As hate incidents were spreading throughout East Brunswick, during the 1990s, this community was experiencing a rapid expansion of Asian ethnics. Hate messages communicated through letters and phone calls were intended to do more than express hostile views. According to the preceding respondent, these messages were clearly intended to intimidate and "drive-out the Asians from the community." In spite of the fact that some of the neighbors reported the incident to the police, these hate incidents were diminished as mere pranks. It is one thing to classify these racially motivated incidents, no matter how loathsome, as nonprosecutable offenses, but it is another to tell the community under attack that they are harmless acts committed for fun.

According to Weiss (1992), although addressing hate crime is a multifaceted problem that requires a multifaceted approach, including the participation of a variety of groups, such as coalition groups, the successful involvement of other groups depends largely on the commitment of law enforcement officials. More specifically, dealing with this problem from a law enforcement perspective requires monitoring trends so that it is possible to intervene before incidents explode into more serious acts. Police departments in England and Wales collect data on racial incidents, which include "any incident which is perceived to be racist by the victim or any other person" (Iganski, 2002, p. 7). Although these incidents aren't necessarily identified as offenses, even these data understate the true extent of the hate crime problem. Levin and McDevitt (2002) also argue that collecting statistics on bias incidents is important since they serve as an early warning for the community and local officials of potential hot spots of racial tension. Less than a year before Benjamin Smith killed Won-Joon Yoon, Ricky Birdsong and injured nine others in a shooting rampage over the Fourth of July weekend in 1999, Smith had become notorious in Bloomington for spreading hate letters in the campus community.

Community involvement and interagency cooperation play a key role in the prevention of hate crimes (Ferry, 1993). Although the respondent in the preceding extract expected East Brunswick to be a more responsive community, what he found instead was an environment that fostered and condoned more hate. He was subjected to racism on more than one occasion within a short time period, but what particularly upset the respondent was his encounter with a young child and the parent's unwillingness to discipline her child for the racist remark. Although one may argue that a young child in his or her innocence is unable to understand the weight of his or her actions, the child's remarks suggest that there is a true climate of hate.

According to Levin and Rabrenovic (2004), when hatred is widely shared among members of society, it becomes part of the culture—the way of life for that society. They argue that although humans have a predisposition to view outsiders with some skepticism, "hating outsiders, or those from specific groups, is taught" (p. 68). For example, they state that white supremacists were not born to loathe blacks and Latinos. They learn such ideas either early in life, from their parents, or later, from their friends, classmates, teachers, religious leaders, and the mass media. Children are therefore indoctrinated from an early age to hate, and the first few years of life have a disproportionate influence on the way that individuals will think about other people. By age three, most children are already aware of racial and ethnic differences. By the time they are five, they have learned negative stereotypes about various groups. Thus Levin and Rabrenovic (2004) argue that children are socialized to hate in exactly the same way they are socialized to accept other beliefs about what should be valued.

Hate crimes not only shower fear on the entire targeted community, but fracture interethnic or interracial relations within the larger society. Some Interviewees, including some who were not direct victims of hate crime, expressed fear for their safety and livelihood. These kinds of responses are not surprising since an attack against an individual often leaves the targeted community feeling intimidated, isolated, and unprotected (Kelly, Maghan, & Tennant, 1993).

For respondent Ray's family, this meant moving out of their Caucasian-dominated neighborhood in order to ward off further attacks. The family relocated to San Francisco, a city with a thriving Asian ethnic population.

Bias-motivated crimes can have negative impacts on communities because they fracture a community's sense of harmony and commonality by creating group-based divisions that not only hinder social interaction, but also incite intergroup violence (Wang, 1997). Failing to recognize and adequately address hate crime can also inflame isolated incidents into widespread community tension and intergroup conflict, potentially polarizing cities (Anti-Defamation League, 1994). Bias crimes not only violate a community's general concern for the security of its members and their property, but also the shared value of equality among citizens in a heterogeneous society—the egalitarian ideal and antidiscrimination principles that are fundamental to the American legal system and culture (Lawrence, 1999).

CONCLUSIONS: UNDERSTANDING THE COLLECTIVE IMPACTS OF HATE CRIME

Hate crimes impact society on three interrelated levels: the direct victim, the targeted community group (the victim's shared community), and intergroup relations. Those who suffer from hate crimes experience difficulty in coping with their victimization (see Garofalo & Martin, 1993). They experience a strong sense of violation similar to rape victims (Weiss, 1992). Victims of hate crime also suffer from high levels of distress, including post-traumatic stress disorder, depression, sleep disorders, withdrawal, feelings of helplessness, and serious interpersonal problems (Herek & Berrill, 1992; Weiss, 1992). Some victims who survive attacks also endure suffering long after the initial incident and turn their frustration and anger inward by expressing self-hatred and group denial.[3] Hate crimes also have harmful effects on communities by fracturing communities' sense of harmony and commonality and by creating group-based divisions that hamper social interaction and provoke intergroup violence (Wang, 1997).

The narratives in this chapter demonstrate that hate crimes harm, and that hate crimes, as message crimes, terrorize targeted populations. What, then, makes hate crimes message crimes? First, victims of hate crimes are not attacked as individuals, but as symbols; for racial minorities, they are attacked for their perceived stigmatized differences as the Other, nonwhite. Second, victims are, therefore, interchangeable. Although Won-Joon Yoon in the shooting spree was randomly selected, that is, indiscriminately as an individual, he was intentionally targeted as a racial minority, or as a non-white person. It's the idea that any victim will do as long as he or she bears the mark of "difference" or is nonwhite. Wherever they are, members of the targeted community carry with them the reason for their potential victimization. And since potential victims cannot change the characteristic that makes them a potential target, there is nothing they can do to prevent a future attack (Levin & McDevitt, 1993). Third, as symbolic crimes, victims are attacked to send a message to the rest of the targeted community. For Asian Americans, it's the message of the "perpetual foreigner": "beware; you are inferior, you do not belong here, and you are not American."

Although the Asian Americans in this chapter vary in their responses, these narratives demonstrate that hate violence permeates their minds, is anticipated, and is carefully managed. The narratives compellingly demonstrate that the mere threat of hate crime can penetrate every part of the targeted member's daily life, that Asian Americans exert a considerable amount of time and energy adjusting their lives in fear of a potential hate crime attack. Unlike the FBI's UCR data, which count hate crimes as incident based, this chapter explicitly reveals how the harm of hate crime extends beyond the immediate victim to the victim's shared community.

Moreover, the narratives are telling of the cumulative and collective impacts of hate crime and its continuous nature—how hate crimes, as message crimes, continue to terrorize targeted populations long after the initial attack.

NOTES

1. Despite their high levels of education, Asian American men receive lower salaries when compared to their white male counterparts. In 1990, highly educated Asian American males received 10 percent less than white males even when they were more likely to hold advanced degrees. Asian American men were also less likely to hold a job as executives, administrators, or managers when compared to white men (23% versus 31%; Espiritu, 1996). The use of "family income" by politicians has also obscured this disparity, given that Asian American families have more workers per family than white families (Takaki, 1998).

2. See *United States v. Ebens*, 800 F.2d 1422,1427 (6th Cir. 1986).

3. Having an entire racial population blamed for the action of one individual is also a common phenomenon for African Americans (Mann, 1993).

REFERENCES

Abelmann, N., & Lie, J. (1995). *Blue dreams: Korean Americans and the Los Angeles riots.* Cambridge, MA: Harvard University Press.

Anti-Defamation League. (1994). *Hate Crimes Law: A Comprehensive Guide.* New York: Author.

Baird, R. J., & Rosenbaum, S. E. (Eds.). (1992). *Bigotry, prejudice and hatred: Definitions, causes and solutions.* New York: Prometheus Books.

Falk, G. (2001). *Stigma: How we treat outsiders.* New York: Prometheus Books.

Federal Bureau of Investigation. (2006). Hate crime statistics: 2006. Retrieved October 10, 2008 from http://www.fbi.gov/ucr/hc2006/abouthcs.htm

Ferry, T. (1993). Community involvement and interagency cooperation in the prevention of hate crimes. In R. Kelly (Ed.), *Bias crime: American law enforcement and legal responses* (pp. 132–142). Chicago: Office of International Criminal Justice, University of Illinois at Chicago.

Fong, T. P. (2000). The history of Asians in America. In T. Fong & L. Shinagawa (Eds.), *Asian Americans: Experiences and perspectives* (pp. 13–30). Upper Saddle Back, NJ: Prentice Hall.

Fong, T. P. (2002). *The contemporary Asian American experience: Beyond the model minority* (2nd ed.). Upper Saddle Back NJ: Prentice Hall.

Garofalo, J., & Martin, S. E. (1993). The law enforcement response to bias-motivated crime. In R. J. Kelly (Ed.), *Bias crime: American law enforcement and legal responses* (pp. 64–80). Chicago: Office of International Criminal Justice, University of Illinois at Chicago.

Green, D. P., Strolovitch, D. A., & Wong, J. S. (1998, September). Defended neighborhoods, integration, and racially motivated crime. *American Journal of Sociology, 104*, 372–403.

Herek, G. M., & Berrill, K. T. (1992). *Hate crimes: Confronting violence against lesbians and gay men.* Newbury Park, CA: Sage.

Hwang, V. (2001). The interrelationship between anti-Asian violence and Asian America. In P. W. Hall & V. M. Hwang (Eds.), *Anti-Asian violence in North America: Asian American and Asian Canadian reflections on hate, healing, and resistance* (pp. 43–66). Lanham, MD: AltaMira Press.

Iganski, P. (2002). Introduction: The problem of hate crimes and hate crime laws. In P. Iganski (Ed.), *The hate debate: Should hate be punished as a crime?* (pp. 1–14). London: Profile Books.

Kang, J. (1993). Racial violence against Asian Americans [Note]. *Harvard Law Review, 106*(8), 1926–1943.

Kelly, R. J., Maghan, J., & Tennant, W. (1993). Hate crimes: Victimizing the stigmatized. In R. J. Kelly (Ed.), Bias crime: American law enforcement and legal responses (pp. 24–44). Chicago: Office of International Criminal Justice, University of Illinois at Chicago.

Kim, C. J. (2000). *Bitter fruit: The politics of black-Korean conflict in New York City.* New Haven, CT: Yale University Press.

Kleg, M. (1993). *Hate prejudice and racism.* New York: State University of New York Press.

Lawrence, F. (1999). *Punishing hate: Bias crimes under American law.* Cambridge, MA: Harvard University Press.

Levin, J. (2002). *The violence of hate: Confronting racism, anti-Semitism, and other forms of bigotry.* Boston: Allyn and Bacon.

Levin, J. L., & McDevitt, J. (1993). *Hate crimes: The rising tide of bigotry and bloodshed.* New York: Plenum Press.

Levin, J. L., & McDevitt, J. (2002). *Hate crimes revisited: America's war on those who are different.* New York: Plenum Press.

Levin, J., & Rabrenovic, G. (2004). *Why we hate.* New York: Prometheus Books.

Lopez, H. (1997). Racial restrictions in the law of citizenship. In N. Gates (Ed.), *Critical race theory: Racial classification and history* (pp. 109–125). New York: Garland.

Mann, Coramae Richey (1993). Unequal Justice: A Question of Color. Bloomington: Indiana University Press.

Min, P. G. (1999). Major issues relating to Asian American experiences. In F. L. Pincus & H. Ehrlich (Eds.), *Race and ethnic conflict: Contending views on prejudice, discrimination, and ethnoviolence* (2nd ed., pp. 195–204). Boulder, CO: Westview Press.

National Asian Pacific Legal Consortium. (1997). *1997 audit of violence against Asian Pacific Americans.* Washington, DC: Author.

Omi, M., & Winant, H. (1994). *Racial formation in the United States: From the 1960s to the 1990s* (2nd ed.). New York: Routledge.

Perry, B. (2001). *In the name of hate: Understanding hate crimes.* New York: Routledge.

Perry, B. (2003). Where do we go from here? Researching hate crime. *Internet Journal of Criminology.* Retrieved September 11, 2008, from http://www.internet journalofcriminology.com/Where%20Do%20We%20Go%20From%20Here.%20 Researching%20Hate%20Crime.pdf

Pulera, D. (2002). *Visible difference: Why race will matter to Americans in the twenty-first century.* New York: Continuum.

Southern Poverty Law Center. (2008). *Active U.S. hate groups.* Retrieved December 20, 2008 from http://splcenter.org/intel/map/hate.jsp

Streissguth, T. (2003). *Library in a book: Hate crimes.* New York: Facts on File.

Takaki, R. (1998). *A history of Asian Americans: Strangers from a different shore* (Rev. ed.). New York: Back Bay Books.

Tuan, M. (1998). *Forever foreigners or honorary whites?* New Brunswick, NJ: Rutgers University Press.

United States v. Ebens, 800 F.2d 1422,1427 (6th Cir. 1986).

U.S. Census Bureau. (2000). *State and county quick facts: Somerset County, New Jersey.* Retrieved December 20, 2008 from http://quickfacts.census.gov/qfd/states/34/34035.html

U.S. Census Bureau. (2002). *United States Census 2000.* Washington, DC: U.S. Department of Commerce Economics and Statistics Administration.

U.S. Commission on Civil Rights. (1992). *Civil rights issues facing Asian Americans in the 1990s.* Washington, DC: Commission on Civil Rights.

Wang, L. (1997, November). The transforming power of hate: Social cognition theory and the harms of hate-related crime. 71 *Southern California Law Review* 47–136.

Weiss, J. (1992). Ethnoviolence: Impact upon and response of victims and the community. In R. J. Kelly (Ed.), *Bias crime: American law enforcement and legal responses* (pp. 174–185). Chicago: Office of International Criminal Justice, University of Illinois at Chicago.

Wu, F. (2002). *Yellow: Race in America beyond black and white.* New York: Basic Books.

CHAPTER 7

CRIME AND PREJUDICE: NEEDS AND SUPPORT OF HATE CRIME VICTIMS

Peter Dunn

My house was burned down and I ended up sleeping rough in hostels and one night on a bench. It is a constant whispering and bullying campaign. They call me names, saying I'm a paedophile and saying that I'm gay. Eggs, stones and footballs are thrown at the windows. None of the allegations is true and there has never been any evidence against me.

Victim Support, 2006, p. 51

This quote is from a man who suffered years of hate victimization by his neighbors, which culminated in his house being burned down. He was interviewed as part of Victim Support's research into the support needs of victims of hate crime. One hundred and seven people, most of whom were black, Asian, gay, lesbian, transgender, or refugees and asylum seekers, were interviewed in four parts of Britain: Lambeth, Cardiff, Stoke on Trent, and Oldham in Greater Manchester. Victim Support (2006) wanted primary research to provide the evidence base for the development of their services to victims of hate crime, and the project, which produced the report *Crime and Prejudice: The Support Needs of Victims of Hate Crime*, was funded by Cooperative Insurance Services.

RESEARCHING THE SUPPORT NEEDS OF VICTIMS OF HATE CRIME

This chapter describes the findings of the *Crime and Prejudice* report, and it discusses some of the implications of the findings for criminal justice policy and service delivery in the context of what else is known about the effects of hate crime and the harm it can cause. To provide a context for the discussion, it may first be helpful to consider some of the problems inherent in researching victimization, and hate victimization in particular.

The limitations of official crime data are widely documented. Most hate incidents do not get reported to the police, so crime statistics greatly underestimate the extent of hate crime (Bowling, 1998; A. Mason & Palmer, 1996). Differences in the definitions of hate crime undermine the usefulness of statistical information, particularly in making comparisons between different jurisdictions (Hall, 2005; Perry, 2003). Ratcliffe shows that even concepts such as race are social constructs that cannot be subject to clear, agreed definitions (Ratcliffe, 2004). This is perhaps even more of a problematic issue with sexual orientation. The way that construct has been assembled in itself both reflects and perpetuates discriminatory norms (G. Mason, 2002).

Victimization surveys like the British Crime Survey also may not elicit accurate information about hate crime. Referring to racist crime, Bowling (1998) points out that the cumulative effect of hate crime ensures that it "becomes part of people's everyday experience and they don't remember to mention it in interviews" (p. 161). Chahal and Julienne (1999) suggest that some people deny being victims of racist crime, perhaps because it means facing up to their continuing vulnerability. Spalek (2006) points out that victimization surveys "tend to exclude many potential victims, those who are at most risk from crime" (p. 53)—including children and young people.

To try to take all these factors into account, Victim Support decided not to give in to pressure from its funders, the media, and even some of its own people for answers to statistical questions like, How many hate crimes? Are there more hate crimes committed now than were committed last year? and What proportion of hate crimes are reported? Instead, we decided to take a qualitative approach to the research, focusing on people's accounts of what happened to them; how they were affected; how the criminal justice system responded; and what, if anything, would help them recover—from their victimization and from its aftermath, which sometimes included secondary victimization by the criminal justice system. Victim Support's own collective experience of helping victims of crime confirmed Iganski's (2001) view that "understanding the harm involved will arguably inform effective interventions with victims" (p. 636).

KEY THEMES ARISING FROM THE RESEARCH

The quote with which this chapter starts says a lot about the nature of hate crime: who can be targeted, why, and what the emotional and practical effects are; how it is both physically and verbally enacted; how bigotry and ignorance lead perpetrators to conflate and confuse terms (gay equals pedophile), and so on.[1] It also illustrates the long-term nature of hate crime, that is, how it tends not to stop unless it is stopped by effective interventions from the police, sometimes working with a support organization, and how the effects of hate crime can be cumulative. Hate crime often ends in the loss of a home and an income; and the destruction of the well-being and security that, in Western democracies, we are led to believe we should all be able to take for granted. Often, the loss of good health and, sometimes, the loss of life are also features of hate victimization. These are themes that are explored in the *Crime and Prejudice* report and that are central to an understanding of the harm of hate crime. A further, very significant theme is fear, engendered by being previously victimized and fearing repeat attacks, or by hearing about what has happened to other people. This is illustrated by someone who had repeatedly experienced racist attacks:

> I kept my children in the house, to protect my children so that they are safe. Because I hear that in other areas . . . people are having their houses burned or people are being killed. (Victim Support, 2006, p. 50)

Anger is a powerful emotion that was described by several of the people interviewed by Victim Support's researchers:

> I get angry and keep it inside until I get home. Then I bang doors and windows and let it all out, because I don't want them to see how it affects me. (Victim Support, 2006, p. 50)

This person seems to have been determined to retain some control of the situation by not appearing to her attackers to be affected by their behavior. For some victims, anger is inwardly directed, and it can become guilt, a disabling, rather than motivating, emotion:

> I get quite guilty that I didn't make a stand, you know, because normally I just try to ignore the situation. I feel guilty for not telling them that their behaviour is out of order and also for having let them get away with it, thinking they weren't doing anything wrong, because I know in most cases they will never get caught simply for the lack of evidence. (Victim Support, 2006, p. 52)

This person, a gay man, seems to be at the point where his guilt at not doing anything about the incidents he was subjected to could become a motivator to report what was happening. But as the research illustrates, for many victims, this will only happen if they have an expectation of a supportive and effective response from the criminal justice system and the voluntary organizations associated with it. Such a response is often lacking, and it is not surprising, therefore, that many people's expectations are so low that they have no confidence to report incidents, particularly if they have previously sought help and been let down:

Nothing was ever done, nobody went any further, nobody wanted to find out what actually happened. (Victim Support, 2006, p. 53)

Some participants described a desire to do something about it and confront the attackers. A man who had experienced regular homophobic abuse accomplished this very effectively:

I would also like to see these leaflets [on homophobic crime] made available . . . the family around the corner, two boys and a girl, I couldn't walk past the house, because I would have verbal abuse every time. The moment I took that leaflet round to the mother and went "right, read, I suggest you read it to your children, you better explain to them, that you can lose your home, you can be evicted!" Then bingo, it stopped! (Victim Support, 2006, p. 52)

Loss

Significant loss was described by most of the 107 participants in the Victim Support research. Loss of home, livelihood, income, health, and security were common:

I had a small shop in Manchester and similar incidents happened, but they were much worse. I had to close down that shop and I lost out on a lot of money because I can't sell it on. (Victim Support, 2006, p. 52)

I thought if I was going to get harassed when I go out, then I'd rather stay inside. It got to the point where I stopped working and I started claiming benefits. (Victim Support, 2006, p. 51)

Loss of security was a recurring theme. Participants described feeling that they could not sleep soundly at night and that their children were emotionally affected. Several participants described loss of normal health, with depression, high blood pressure, and anxiety being common consequences of their victimization. Some cited medical opinion in support of such attributions. Loss of any sense of normality was also something experienced by many participants. Indeed, victimization had become a feature of normal life. This is a function of both the number and regularity of incidents:

I have somewhat become desensitised to the sheer number of times this happens. It used to happen literally on a daily basis, you know I would just walk out of the house, go into town, and in a space of three or four hours, there would be three or four incidents. (Victim Support, 2006, p. 52)

Other research has also suggested that the harm of hate crime lies partly in its regularity and frequency—the fact that it is often a continual process, not a one-off incident. Unfortunately, the criminal justice system is more used to dealing with individual offences than ongoing processes of victimization. This may help explain why victims' lack of satisfaction with the criminal justice system is a theme that arises in almost all hate crime research.[2] The harm caused by the incessant nature of repeat hate-motivated victimization was noted by Bowling (1998), who observed that "the repeated incidence of harassment is bound to have a cumulative effect" (p. 189).

Shaw's (2001) research illustrates the way that the repeated nature of victimization aggravates the seriousness of each incident. She suggests that chronic victims experience a sense of loss of their normal life so powerful that it is similar to bereavement. Using the Kubler-Ross model of the four stages of bereavement, she argues that because victimization for them is constant, they never get the chance to work their way successfully through the four phases to recovery. The loss they experience is the loss of their life as it was and of their life as it should be. Discussing Tom, a victim of racist vandalism and burglary who was victimized almost daily, Shaw writes, "This incident affected his fear for his personal safety. The loss is in both material and emotional terms. This is the nature of the bereavement suffered through chronic victimisation. . . . There appears to be no boundary to his perception of what he could potentially be a victim of and by whom he could be victimized. This creates despair as the whole perception of life is changed" (p. 177).

Barnes and Ephross (1994) suggest that a particular effect of hate crime, as opposed to non-hate-motivated victimization, is loss or lowering of self-esteem. This is not surprising, as hate victimization is bound to be experienced as yet another manifestation of discriminatory, unjust, and oppressive social norms that are in themselves damaging to self-esteem.

Fear

Participants feared repeat attacks, and hearing about the victimization of other people profoundly affected their assessment of their own safety:

I kept my children in the house, to protect my children so that they are safe. Because I hear that in other areas . . . people are having their houses burned or people are being killed. (Victim Support, 2006, p. 50)

It made me scared to be in the house. I felt unsafe. (Victim Support, 2006, p. 50)

For some victims who have experienced victimization on the street, at work or school, and in their home, nowhere is safe. Fear is therefore a constant and unavoidable feature of life. Fear of going out, which can be exacerbated by fear of being attacked while away from home or fear that your home will be attacked if you are absent from it, can cause illness, loss of employment, and isolation.

Fear can also be instrumental in preventing people from reporting incidents and receiving support. Fear of reprisals, or of not being believed, are known to exert a strong influence on willingness to report (Bowling, 1998, Chahal & Julienne, 1999; Hall, 2005; A. Mason & Palmer, 1996). In the Victim Support study, people described being fearful of getting caught up in the criminal justice system:

> Because of the fear of retaliation. And let's be perfectly blunt about it, there would be retaliation and I would get no support. (Victim Support, 2006, p. 53)

The issue of fear of reprisals was also noted by support organizations and community groups:

> If you sit for hours in Brixton police station and people can see you—it's frightening, and they fear repercussions. (Victim Support, 2006, p. 45)

Only 10 percent of the participants in the Victim Support research saw their case go to court. This low figure is disturbing because a large number of participants had been recruited via their local Victim Support service. These participants would in most cases have reported the incident and been referred to Victim Support by the police. However, many other participants had not reported incidents. Where participants had reported incidents to the police, the offender was rarely caught or prosecuted. Over three-quarters of participants said they would be willing to give evidence if the offender were caught. Many expressed frustration that no action was taken against the offender, even when the offender was previously known to the police. Fear can prevent people from obtaining support even if they are willing to report incidents.

Anger and Frustration

For some participants, their anger about their victimization was exacerbated by their experience with criminal justice agencies, some of which seemed to compound the sense of powerlessness that hate crime engenders. The participant who described getting angry and struggling to "keep it inside until I get home" did not want the offenders to see how affected she was by their behavior. She seems to be describing a need to regain some control of the situation, control having been taken away from her by the victimization. While this is identified by other research as well, little seems to have been written about the nexus between hate victimization and the potential for victims to harness their anger as a means of regaining some control of their situation.

Rather than help people regain control, in some instances, criminal justice agencies did the opposite:

> What affected me more was the attitude of the police officer, who took it so lightly. (Victim Support, 2006, p. 66)

> Please don't give me any verbal abuse after 5 [pm], because I won't be able to get hold of [the relevant person to speak to]. (Victim Support, 2006, p. 65)

Some people wanted to engage with the criminal justice system, perhaps as a way of working out their anger toward the offender, and certainly out of a sense of obligation to society:

> It is one of the main ways of tackling these sorts of crime—catching people and making them go through the court process. Although I actually cringe at the prospect of going through the court process, I feel a moral duty. (Victim Support, 2006, p. 52)

One of the most pernicious aspects of hate crime is its power to distort and damage people's usual emotional responses to those close to them. Writing about how children learn and unlearn prejudice, Stern-LaRosa and Bettman (2000) quote a father who was disturbed by his own unhelpful reaction to his son, who had been racially victimized: "I blamed him for something that wasn't his fault . . . it was racism that caused that situation, not my son. I directed my anger at my son, but it was the racist situation I was really mad about—and my own sense of powerlessness to protect my son from this kind of hate" (p. 119).

Guilt

We might ask, Why would people feel guilty for being victimized? Research demonstrates that guilt is a common reaction to victimization, and to hate-motivated victimization in particular. Factors that feature in guilt reactions to victimization include the feeling that one must somehow be responsible for what happened or must have deserved it; the internalization of repressive norms leading to shame about being different; and blaming oneself for not being able to avoid the incident. A participant in the Victim Support research was verbally abused on a bus shortly after the London terrorist bombings in 2005:

> I felt guilty . . . and became scared and very upset. They shouted "Muslims, what do you want to do today?" (Victim Support, 2006, p. 52)

DiPlacido (1998) reviewed U.S. research on the effects of homophobic crime and noted the significance of internalized homophobia, which can result in lesbians and gay men accepting derogatory heterosexist norms. Herek and Berrill (1992) noted the damage that people's emotional well-being can sustain as a result of internalized homophobia. It is not difficult to see why the interaction of internalized homophobia and homophobic crime is so effective in undermining people's belief in themselves and their right not to be victimized. Add racism or disablism to the mix, and the damaging effects are likely to be even more acutely felt. Perry (2003) observed that research has really only scratched the surface of these issues, with "little understanding of the specificity of violence experienced by people who occupy multiple positions of culturally defined inferiority" (p. 33).

Some victims experience guilt for not being able to prevent further victimization. In this way, people can end up taking on the unrealistic and intolerable burden not only of responsibility for preventing their own repeat victimization, but of perhaps preventing the victimization of other people as well:

> I get quite guilty that I didn't make a stand. . . . I feel guilty for not telling them that their behaviour is out of order and also for having let them get away with it. (Victim Support, 2006, p. 52)

Victims' guilt can be compounded by the well-intentioned but nevertheless sometimes unhelpful interventions of families. In the Victim Support research, families were usually cited by participants as sources of support, but in a few notable examples, family reactions made things worse. This was particularly true of victims of homophobic crime:

> [The least helpful] was my father: "what was I doing on Clapham Common at that time of night?" etc. (Victim Support, 2006, p. 54)

Similarly, the sister of a victim of racist crime suggested she should stop wearing her *hijab* because it would otherwise continue to draw attention to herself as a Muslim.

Damage to Health and Well-being

Some participants reported that the hate victimization they experienced had directly damaged their health:

> My blood pressure rose up to 225. Basically I went into shock. (Victim Support, 2006, p. 50)

The quote offered in the first paragraph of this chapter, from the person who had been victimized so regularly that he or she stopped going out and had to give up work, illustrates the way in which people who are repeatedly hate victimized can drift into isolation and withdrawal from normal life. This is particularly likely when the victimization is as frequent as that described in the same paragraph—every time the person goes out of his or her home.

The issue of shock immediately following an incident has profound implications for the provision of help and support, which many victims might not have yet identified a need for in the immediate aftermath:

> But a lot of people don't want help [at first]. It's only later on that people become emotionally withdrawn. (Victim Support, 2006, p. 63)

Very few victims who had been offered support reported that the offer was repeated at a later stage, yet a few days or a week after an incident might be the time when someone becomes able to accept help.

Parents who were attacked at home expressed concern for the emotional welfare of their children:

> We have developed a terrible sense of insecurity, but the worst of all is my little one. Since this last attack he wakes up almost every night with nightmares, crying, and any small noise distracts his attention. (Victim Support, 2006, p. 51)

Lack of help for children affected by hate crime was mentioned by several participants, some of whom voiced uncertainty about the extent to which they were able to understand their children's needs:

> I feel that even though I am thick-skinned my children should have been offered some kind of counselling because I still don't know how the incident has affected them. (Victim Support, 2006, p. 61)

IMPLICATIONS OF THE RESEARCH FINDINGS FOR THE SUPPORT NEEDS OF VICTIMS OF HATE CRIME

This section of the chapter uses the Victim Support research and its recommendations, with reference, as well, to other U.S., Australian, and U.K. studies, to explore in more detail some of the implications of the harm caused by hate crime for criminal justice and voluntary organization responses to hate-motivated victimization. These implications can be grouped into four areas: reporting, crime prevention and reduction, the provision of support for victims, and policing.

Reporting

Most victims who do not report hate crime do not receive support or protection from further victimization (Victim Support, 2006). The underreporting of hate crime and the reasons for it are well documented (Bowling, 1998; Hall, 2005; A. Mason & Palmer, 1996; McGhee, 2005; Perry, 2003). They include fear of reprisals, fear of not being believed, an expectation that nothing will happen as a result, not knowing how to report, and language difficulties. Most of these reasons are common to any stigmatized group subject to hate crime, but there are some additional factors specific to certain groups. Some lesbians and gay men may fear being "outed" if they report. For some, this could have very serious consequences, such as for young gay people living with parents who have fundamentalist religious views. People seeking asylum may have previously only experienced the police as violent agents of state repression, or they may fear that their status in this country might be unfairly investigated if they report. The Victim Support research shows that such fears are often based on very real experiences, as illustrated by some of the service providers interviewed:

> Cross examination is bad . . . the [criminal justice system] is stacked against getting victims or witnesses into court. So if on top of the difficulties which are faced by anyone you get someone insecure about their sexuality, it is even more difficult. (Victim Support, 2006, p. 46)

The report noted that "in several instances the police who arrived at the scene reportedly treated the victim as a suspect with respect to the perpetrator, or questioning the victim about their personal legal status, or that of their car when it was involved in the reported crime. In one case, the victim himself was arrested" (Victim Support, 2006, p. 66). In this way, it may be that minority communities are still very much "overpoliced and underprotected." This was acknowledged by the 1999 report of the Macpherson inquiry into the bungled police investigation of the racist murder of Stephen Lawrence in London in 1993. Since that time, a range of initiatives by police, voluntary organizations, and local authorities have been developed to encourage victims to report hate crime and to increase the levels of protection available.

Third-party reporting enables hate crime victims to report an incident without having to contact the police. People can fill in a form available from housing offices, libraries, surgeries, and so on, or can complete a form online. They are asked for details of the incident, and if they wish to give their contact details, they can be offered support. Anonymous information is made available to the police and is used to build up a picture of hate incidents locally to identify patterns and hot spots. The great value of third-party reporting is that it gives people the option of obtaining help without having to deal with the police, and they can be helped to report the incident to the police if they feel able and willing to do that.

The fragmented and sometimes parochial nature of third-party reporting schemes was noted by the researchers. For example, in only one of the four fieldwork areas was there a third-party reporting scheme that set out to meet the needs generated by all categories of hate crime; the other local schemes focused mainly on racist crime.

Unfortunately, none of the 107 hate crime victims who participated in the Victim Support research had used third-party reporting. Few of the local specialist community groups contacted by the researchers were familiar with third-party reporting or knew how to help victims use it. Voluntary organizations, such as the local Victim Support service, "were perplexed by the widespread failure of these centers. They suggested that the key problems are a lack of capacity-building of the reporting sites, and a lack of outreach" (Victim Support, 2006, p. 46). As well as being a function of lack of publicity and promotion, the underuse of third-party reporting might also be illustrative of some of the harmful effects of hate crime. It may be that people become too depressed, undermined, or isolated as a result of their experiences to be able to make use of such systems. The use of third-party reporting requires as a prerequisite some knowledge of and confidence in the criminal justice system, voluntary organizations, or local authorities, and it requires sufficient self-esteem to regard oneself as having the right to receive help. The report recommended "greater publicity for third party reporting schemes . . . particularly through outreach, training, and support to community organisations" (Victim Support, 2006, p. 72).

Crime Prevention and Reduction

Many of the participants in the Victim Support research talked of the need for more attention to be given to the prevention of hate crime. Significantly, when they were asked what more could have been done to help them, many referred to the need to tackle the root causes of hate crime before talking about better support for themselves. They talked about the need for better awareness-raising, particularly with young people, and about the harm that hate crime causes; and their desire for better measures to tackle offenders:

> Work more hard to take crime off the streets. Work hard to stop racism and improve community relations because all of us must get on together. (Victim Support, 2006, p. 68)

Nothing in the Victim Support research raises questions about the suitability of everyone accepting some reasonable responsibility for avoiding being victimized. Yet some initiatives to reduce crime or prevent repeat victimization—to interrupt the *process* of hate victimization—have themselves replicated the harm that hate crime causes by placing an inappropriate onus on victims to prevent their own revictimization. While everyone has a personal responsibility for his or her own well-being and avoidance of crime, some communities are propelled by policing methods and crime prevention initiatives into taking on an inappropriate burden of responsibility for it. This is explored by Stanko and Curry (1997), who argue that the right to walk safely in public spaces has "special meaning within law and order politics in western societies" (p. 514). Hate crime denies people that right—and often the right, as well, to live safely in one's home—on the basis of their presumed membership in a particular group of people that Perry refers to as the subjects of "culturally defined inferiority" (Perry, 2003, p. 33). Policing and crime prevention that, for example, call on lesbians and gay men to be cautious about being out in public and to "police" themselves work against the reduction of homophobic violence. This is because such a strategy shifts responsibility for crime prevention onto the victim-to-be, who may be able to do nothing further to avoid being victimized. For example, two people of the same sex bringing up children together will inevitably be highly visible to homophobic neighbors even if they don't hold hands and kiss outside their home. Homophobic violence then becomes normalized, something to be gotten used to and avoided, rather than something that must be eradicated. It ignores the strategies that people have already adopted for their self-protection, such as the pressure we all experience sometimes to avoid "appearing to be gay" in certain public areas. It also ignores the gendered nature of violence and the greater vulnerability of women to violence that takes place in private, rather than in public, spaces such as rape and domestic violence.

As Stanko and Curry (1997) point out, the promise by the police of "sensitive treatment" if a crime is reported is not enough because the response is often just the giving of advice. This means that lesbians, gay men, and transgender people have to learn to live with the ontological insecurity of being "at risk at all times" (p. 520).

We need to think about what this approach can help us learn about improving protection for other "at-risk" groups as well, for example, learning-disabled people. Their vulnerability to abuse in institutions is replaced, or perhaps added to, by their vulnerability to hate crime if they move from institutional care into independent housing "in the community" and thereby become more visible.

Engel (2001) described a Miami newspaper report from 1954 about the murder of a gay man, which demanded that homosexuals be punished for prompting "normal" people to commit such deeds. It is hoped that nowadays, everyone, with the exception of the most extremist bigot, would be appalled by such a suggestion, but crime reduction initiatives that exhort minority communities to be responsible for their own protection from violence and

harassment may be only a few small steps away from that approach. Mc
Devitt, Balboni, Garcia, and Gu (2004) found, from their research comparing
the effects of hate-motivated versus non-hate-motivated crime, that victims
"did not believe they could do anything to prevent future victimisation . . .
bias crime victims [may] feel largely powerless to protect themselves in the
future" (p. 53).

Support Services

The differential impact of hate crime is important because it may have
implications for the way in which victims of hate crime are helped and supported. The Victim Support research set out to provide data about support
needs and what works, and what does not work, for hate crime victims. Added
value was given to the data by testing out some potential recommendations
in cooperative enquiry workshops run in each of the four fieldwork areas. In
the workshops, we discussed the implications of the findings with local community groups, criminal justice agencies, and service providers.

Participants had made numerous suggestions about how services could be
improved, and these were discussed at the workshops. Following are three
quotes that may be helpful examples:

> Victim Support should employ a few Asian people to go to these places, to
> taxi bases [Asian taxi drivers had talked of being harassed daily and physi-
> cally attacked frequently]. They should put leaflets any place where you
> are vulnerable to this kind of attack. (Victim Support, 2006, p. 63)

> You are not going to get the gay community to go to Victim Support for
> help, unless they know that there is a gay support worker there. There is
> no point whatsoever talking about homophobic abuse to someone who has
> never experienced it, because, quite frankly, they don't know what you are
> talking about. (Victim Support, 2006, p. 59)

> I just thought that if the police are doing nothing about it, then they
> [Victim Support] are bound to act the same because they are linked. (Vic-
> tim Support, 2006, p. 59)

The first quotation illustrates the need for effective outreach in responding to hate crime victims. For example, there is no point sending a letter
offering support to someone who has reported a hate incident, who has recently fled to England from Iraq and who cannot read English. Sending a
letter that includes terms like *homophobic crime* or *hate crime worker* could
put a victim in danger if the letter is seen by the victim's bigoted parent
or sibling. Given the small proportion of hate crimes that are reported to
the police, support organisations will only meet the needs of a tiny (and
probably already privileged) minority of hate crime victims, unless they
practice effective outreach with the communities who are most at risk in

their area. Yet racist assumptions are often made that prevent outreach from being prioritized, for example, the assumption that Asian communities are self-supporting. Sometimes such assumptions appear to be supported by a superficial reading of research data. A participant in the Victim Support research said,

> I had my family, who were there for me, to console me. . . . Being of Asian background, we tend to think who is going to go to Victim Support? We've got close-knit families—who are Victim Support for us. (Victim Support, 2006, p. 59)

Yet the research also gave examples of Asian people who were not supported by their families, such as the woman whose sister urged her not to wear her *hijab* anymore. So, effective services are those that recognize the diversity that exists within diversity, and which do not assume homogeneity of needs within a particular community. If the idea of talking to Asian taxi drivers about hate crime at taxi ranks seems simple and obvious, service providers should ask themselves, So why haven't we done it yet?

The second quotation, about the gay community not using mainstream support services, could at first seem depressing because the participant seems to be suggesting that heterosexual people cannot effectively support gay people. But it might instead be pointing to the need for a more effective approach, which would involve three main areas of action:

- The importance of support organisations doing outreach to demonstrate an interest in supporting minority communities and a knowledge of those communities
- The need to ensure that support is provided by people who have the competence to support hate crime victims (competence being the interaction of knowledge, skills, and understanding, which are not necessarily gained by personal experience)
- The importance of being seen to be relevant to minority communities, in this instance, demonstrating "gay-friendly" credentials

Competence would involve being able to understand the harms that hate crime causes, which victims may not necessarily wish to speak about or be able to articulate. Self-esteem, isolation, depression, and guilt are emotions that participants in the Victim Support research mentioned, and these can result when one's identity is called into question. The way in which hate crime can undermine identity has been noted elsewhere (cf. Iganski, 2001; G. Mason, 2002). A participant in Stanko and Curry's (1997) research said, "You think you're very solid . . . but [an attack] makes you question your own sexuality: is what I do or who I am really bad or sick?" (p. 526). The issue for support services personnel is how to ensure they can convey the basic degree of empathy required to provide effective support. Without good training and insightful, skilled supervision, this will be difficult for them if they have had no personal experience of being made, through victimization, to accept that they are unchangeably marked out as "legitimate" targets for violence, abuse, and harassment.

Janoff-Bulman and Frieze (1983) suggest that psychological distress in victims results from the shattering of three basic assumptions that most people hold about themselves and the world around them: personal invulnerability (the sense that we have autonomy), a perception that the world is meaningful and ordered, and a view of the self that is positive. They argued that "coping with victimisation is . . . a process that involves rebuilding one's assumptive world," and they noted that "even relatively 'minor' victimisations can result in a great deal of suffering and disruption" (pp. 1–2).

According to Janoff-Bulman and Frieze (1983), assumptions are shattered, and victims no longer see the world as being a safe place. Victims are confronted with the reality of human malevolence and their own vulnerability, and this can be paralyzing. The trauma of victimization activates a negative self-image. Recovery from victimization involves coming to terms with the fact that bad things happen, but that does not mean the world is all bad. They suggested that one component of helping victims recover is finding some purpose in the victimization or attributing the victimization, in part, to personal behaviour, which can be changed in the future as a means of regaining autonomy and control. The significance of this for hate crime services and hate crime prevention is that if victims can attribute their victimization to an aspect of their behavior, they will recover more quickly because they can change their behavior. But if their victimization is attributed to a central aspect of their identity that they cannot change, such as ethnicity or sexual orientation, recovery becomes more difficult.

While many of Janoff-Bulman and Frieze's (1983) findings have been supported by later research, particularly concerning victims' immediate responses to victimization, Spalek (2006) points out that there are a number of problems with their conceptualization of the shattering of basic assumptions and the measures that victims can take to regain a sense of autonomy. The analysis appears based on middle-class, European approaches to how society is ordered and how it functions. There is no recognition that the very many women whose lives are completely controlled by men will have never had the opportunity to feel a sense of autonomy, or the fact that people who have lived in places where violent conflict is a fact of daily life are unlikely to have ever perceived the world as a meaningful and ordered place. Spalek comments that "services supporting the victims of crime, developed largely from these mainstream analyses, will insufficiently help victims who belong to minority ethnic communities" (p. 86). She argues that the secular nature of victim services, which do not address spiritual needs, makes services less attractive to some minority ethnic communities for whom religious affiliation is a fundamental aspect of their self-identity.

The third quotation, suggesting that support organizations will work in the same way as the police because they are linked, illustrates the way in which support services need to be able to work with the police in partnership, but be sufficiently independent to be able to challenge unsatisfactory police practice when needed—and be seen to be independent. Where support services challenge police inertia, victims appreciate it:

> [Most helpful?]—Victim Support, because progress has only been made since they have gotten involved. (Victim Support, 2006, p. 57)

The Police

Of the participants in the Victim Support research who reported a recent incident to the police, most said they did so to obtain justice and to help prevent further attacks. Some described a positive experience with the police, but most were highly critical of the response they received:

> Police helped—they were supportive—helping me to keep calm. (Victim Support, 2006, p. 65)
>
> They took my statement and promised to contact Neighbourhood Watch but nothing happened. (Victim Support, 2006, p. 66)
>
> Make sure a female officer interviews transgender people because I felt uncomfortable having a male officer interviewing me who had a narrow minded male attitude. (Victim Support, 2006, p. 61)

While most participants described an unsatisfactory experience with the police, those who were visited by a specialist hate crime police officer tended to be very satisfied with the response:

> If you have a gay police officer, they know the problem, because nine times out of ten they've already experienced it, and they know what help is required. (Victim Support, 2006, p. 65)

This type of feedback from victims should be good news for the police. It shows that progress can be made, and it builds on existing evidence that effective investigation of crime does not follow from a bureaucratic or authoritarian response to victims.

Criticism of police policy was voiced at the cooperative enquiry workshops. For example, some police forces have a policy of not investigating possible minor offences that victims might have committed if the victim has reported a hate crime—the hate crime takes priority. Yet other forces were not able to make any clear statement on this issue, which perhaps explains why a participant whose car windshield had been smashed by someone shouting racist abuse found himself being questioned by the police about the car's legality. The report noted that in other areas of policing, there is written national guidance on officers' use of discretion, such as not dealing with the immigration status of women who are being trafficked as sex workers.

The majority of those who reported a hate incident were disappointed by the lack of progress in prosecuting offenders. In all instances, participants attributed responsibility for this to the police. They were not aware that the Crown Prosecution Service (CPS), not the police, makes the final decision as to whether an offender is prosecuted. The report recommended that local hate crime partnerships should work harder on involving the CPS to facilitate better communication with victims.

CONCLUSIONS

The Victim Support research report *Crime and Prejudice* set out to gather the views of victims of mainly racist, homophobic, and transphobic crime on how hate victimization had affected them, how the criminal justice system and voluntary organizations responded, what was helpful and what was not helpful in those responses, and what could be improved. Service providers, community groups, and criminal justice agencies were also interviewed. The initial findings were discussed with local organizations at four cooperative enquiry workshops in the fieldwork areas, and this provided additional data that enriched the report's recommendations.

Some issues were raised by the research that were beyond the scope of the project. For example, we were very much aware that categories such as race, sexual orientation, disability, and so on, are by no means mutually exclusive. The fact that several of the participants in the research were people who, as Perry (2003) puts it, "occupy multiple positions of culturally defined inferiority" (p. 33) reminded us of this, but their numbers were small. So we cannot draw conclusions from the *Crime and Prejudice* report about the intersectionality of racist, homophobic, gender-based, and disablist violence. As Perry (2001) points out, "gay men of colour are the 'outsiders' on both the axes of gender and racial identity" (p. 129).

Key themes from the *Crime and Prejudice* research report echo the findings of other research into the effects of hate crime. Victims spoke about the sometimes crippling fear of repeat victimization, the damage to health, loss of income and well-being, and feelings of hopelessness and powerlessness. The data did not establish if these effects are particularly acutely felt by victims of hate-motivated crime, and that would have been beyond the scope of the project. However, the insights of participants about their experiences of reporting hate incidents, and receiving—or not receiving—support, all indicate that specialist competencies and working methods are required to support victims of hate crime effectively. The research underlined the need for proactive outreach work; a close partnership between criminal justice agencies, support services, and community groups; specialist personnel who have an enhanced level of knowledge of the complex effects on victims that may be particular to hate victimization; and publicity for the services available so that victims can obtain support without first having to report to the police. None of the participants had used third-party reporting, and few community organizations knew about it. This suggests that otherwise promising initiatives are unlikely to work effectively unless resources are made available to publicize their existence.

Similarly, participants showed how the policing of hate crime requires different approaches. Participants who were satisfied with the police response were those who had been seen by a specialist hate crime officer. Support services and community groups need to work closely with the police so that they can influence police policy and practice. But they should not be so close that it becomes difficult for them to challenge police inaction or unsatisfactory practice, or so that they appear to victims to be part and parcel of the criminal justice system. The research suggests that where the police have made resources available for improving their response to hate crime, significant progress has been made.

The research supports the view that crime prevention initiatives that seek to place responsibility on victims for avoiding victimization by monitoring their visibility are inappropriate and unlikely to be effective. This is because they ignore the limited opportunities that most hate crime victims have for avoiding revictimization. Such initiatives collude with violence by accepting its inevitability, instead of working to eradicate it; and they ignore the gendered nature of violence.

The research showed how inappropriate a one-size-fits-all response to hate victimization can be. All who are concerned with responding to and combating hate crime need to be aware of the diversity within diverse groups, and to think through the implications of this for their work.

NOTES

1.   However, Hall (2005) cites both Stonewall's and Lemos's research in arguing that educating bigots about the groups they despise can sometimes lead to them being even more committed to their views.

2.   Victim Support's research recorded, significantly, high levels of satisfaction among victims with specialist hate crime police officers, who were probably better trained than their nonspecialist colleagues to understand and respond to the process of repeat victimization that hate crime very often involves.

REFERENCES

Barnes, A., & Ephross, P. (1994). The impact of hate violence on victims: Emotional and behavioural responses to attacks. *Social Work, 39*, 247–251.

Bowling, B. (1998). *Violent racism: Victimisation, policing, and social context.* Oxford: Oxford University Press.

Chahal, J., & Julienne, L. (1999). *We can't all be white! Racist victimisation in the UK.* York, England: Joseph Rowntree Foundation.

DiPlacido, J. (1998). Minority stress among lesbians, gay men and bisexuals. In G. M. Herek (Ed.), *Stigma and sexual orientation* (pp. 138–59). Thousand Oaks, CA: Sage.

Engel, S. (2001). *The unfinished revolution: Social movement theory and the gay and lesbian movement.* Cambridge: Cambridge University Press.

Hall, N. (2005). *Hate crime.* Cullompton, England: Willan.

Herek, G., & Berrill, K. (1992). *Hate crimes: Confronting violence against lesbians and gay men.* Newbury Park, CA: Sage.

Iganski, P. (2001). Hate crimes hurt more. *American Behavioral Scientist, 45*, 626–638.

Janoff-Bulman, R., & Frieze, I. (1983). A theoretical perspective for understanding reactions to victimisation. *Journal of Social Issues, 39*, 1–17.

Macpherson, W. (1999). *The Stephen Lawrence Inquiry: Report of an Inquiry by Sir William Macpherson.* Cm 4262-1, London: Home Office.

Mason, A., & Palmer, A. (1996). *Queer bashing: A national survey of hate crimes against lesbians and gay men.* London: Stonewall.

Mason, G. (2002). *The spectacle of violence: Homophobia, gender and knowledge.* London: Routledge.

McDevitt, J., Balboni, J., Garcia, L., & Gu, J. (2004). Consequences for victims: A comparison of bias- and non-bias-motivated assaults. In B. Gerstenfeld & D. Grant (Eds.), *Crimes of hate: Selected readings* (pp. 45–57). Thousand Oaks, CA: Sage.

McGhee, D. (2005). *Intolerant Britain? Hate, citizenship and difference.* Maidenhead, England: Open University Press.

Perry, B. (2001). *In the name of hate.* New York: Routledge.

Perry, B. (2003). Where do we go from here? Researching hate crime. *Internet Journal of Criminology.* Retrieved September 11, 2008, from http://www.internetjournalof criminology.com/Where%20Do%20We%20Go%20From%20Here.%20Researchi ng%20Hate%20Crime.pdf

Ratcliffe, P. (2004). *Race, ethnicity and difference: Imagining the inclusive society.* Maidenhead, England: Open University Press.

Shaw, M. (2001). Time heals all wounds? In G. Farrell & K. Pease (Eds.), *Crime prevention studies: Vol. 12. Repeat victimisation* (pp. 165–198). Monsey, NY: Criminal Justice Press.

Spalek, B. (2006). *Crime victims: Theory, policy and practice.* Houndmills, England: Palgrave Macmillan.

Stanko, E., & Curry, P. (1997). Homophobic violence and the self "at risk": Interrogating the boundaries. *Social and Legal Studies, 6*, 513–532.

Stern-LaRosa, C., & Bettman, E. (2000). *Hate hurts: How children learn and unlearn prejudice.* New York: Scholastic.

Victim Support. (2006). *Crime and prejudice: The support needs of victims of hate crime: A research report.* London: Victim Support.

CHAPTER 8

IDENTITY, OTHERNESS, AND THE IMPACT OF RACIST VICTIMIZATION IN THE ENGLISH COUNTRYSIDE

Neil Chakraborti and Jon Garland

Within the United Kingdom, a substantial body of literature has developed in recent decades that has helped to increase levels of understanding of the complexities of racist victimization and to highlight issues such as the underreporting of racist incidents and victims' dissatisfaction with criminal justice agency responses (see Bowling, 1998; Clancy, Hugh, Aust, & Kershaw, 2001; Fitzgerald & Hale, 1996). However, the vast majority of previous research has tended to focus on more urbanized environments, which typically contain substantial minority ethnic communities. Such a focus has overshadowed the difficulties facing minority ethnic households living in rural and isolated areas, where communities are generally more intransient and feelings of isolation and alienation may be at a premium.

The neglect of the countryside as a legitimate source of criminological enquiry has been a feature of contemporary academic discourse (Moody, 1999) and may be largely attributable to the enduring influence of certain dominant images of the rural. While such images are likely to vary between countries, a number of writers have observed a tendency within England to romanticize rurality by drawing parallels with problem-free, "idyllic" environments (Cloke, 1997, 2004; Cloke & Milbourne, 1992; J. Little & Austin, 1996). Positive associations are seen to surround different aspects of rural lifestyle and landscape, thereby reinforcing nostalgic representations that refer to the distinctive, timeless, and ultimately desirable qualities of the rural that provide a welcome escape from the hassles of modern-day living. Typically, this conception is encapsulated in the oft-used term the *rural idyll*, which, in the words of Cloke and Milbourne (1992), "presents happy, healthy and problem-free images of rural life safely nestling with both a close social community and a contiguous natural environment" (p. 359). Within such an idyllic context, studies of crime, deviance, and, more specifically, "race" are perceived to be superfluous and better suited to urban environments.

A related factor behind the absence of detailed enquiry into racialized exclusion and victimization within rural England lies in the extent to which the countryside is seen to capture the very essence of Englishness. Despite the widespread industrialization and urbanization that has affected the majority of the English population during the past 100 years or so, the countryside has maintained an enduring strong association with English national identity. When conceived in such a way, the rhetoric of rural living has the capacity to evoke powerful feelings of patriotism and nationalism, characterized, for example, by images of "England's green and pleasant land," which serve to further reinforce dominant stereotypes (Milbourne, 1997, p. 95). Consequently, such imagery conjures notions of a homogenous, "quintessentially English" haven to which the more superficial, problem-ridden urban world should aspire.

However, growing awareness of the social and spatial complexities of rural life, developed primarily through the work of rural geographers, has helped to cast doubt on the relevance of traditional representations of the English countryside. Instead, attention has increasingly been focused on the extent to which such representations have been used as exclusionary devices to decide who does and does not belong in the countryside. This is perhaps best articulated in Philo's (1992) description of the rural *othering process*, where he sees the unwarranted focus on the interests of powerful rural groups as resulting in the active exclusion of different social strata from what he refers to as the zone of "sameness," a zone where mainstream values or ideals, such as Englishness, whiteness, heterosexuality, and middle-class occupancy, are to be upheld. For Philo and other writers who have explored the possibility of a more diverse rurality (see, e.g., Murdoch & Pratt, 1997; Sibley, 1997), certain groups are ostracized from mainstream society on account of a variety of "undesirable" social characteristics alien to the norms of conventional rural society. Consequently, the interests of rural "others" run the risk of being marginalized within the apparent hegemonic condition—or what Scutt and Bonnett (1996) neatly refer to as the *cultural reservoir*—that is central to romanticized constructions of the countryside.

In a challenge to these popular (mis)conceptions, and with specific reference to minority ethnic Others, a series of small-scale studies have begun to explore issues of "race," exclusion, and victimization in rural and isolated parts of the United Kingdom (de Lima, 2001; Derbyshire, 1994; Jay, 1992; Robinson & Gardner, 2004). This localized research has been instructive not only in highlighting the problem of racist prejudice, but also in encouraging the development of context-specific responses; indeed, as Dhalech (1999) acknowledges, although racism is inherently a similar phenomenon in both urban and rural areas, the way that it is both experienced and expressed will vary, and therefore different solutions will be required. It has also helped to illustrate that for ethnic minorities living in the less urbanized parts of the country, problems of racism can in fact be more distressing and prolonged as they find themselves living in a "double-bind" situation: on one hand, minority ethnic groups are "invisible," in that their needs are not accounted for within existing rural policy and service provision; on the other hand, they are all too visible to local residents as a result of being one of few individuals or households from a minority ethnic background. Accordingly, it is not just the experience of racism per se that these groups find harmful, but also the lack of interaction with mainstream and voluntary services, which can intensify feelings of isolation and exclusion.

This chapter draws on the authors' own studies of "race" in the English countryside to assess the nature of rural village life and the experiences of minority ethnic households within this context. It will suggest that ideas relating to "Englishness" are still strongly associated with notions of the rural idyll, which is itself conflated with "whiteness." Though racism itself is not simply an inevitable or homogeneous experience that affects all rural minority ethnic households to the same extent or in the same way (see, e.g., Chakraborti & Garland, 2004a; Robinson & Gardner, 2004), we will see that episodes of racist victimization are by no means uncommon, and it is argued that developing an understanding of the nature of the risk of victimization may actually assist in the reconstruction of the perception of rural minority ethnic communities as "communities of shared risk," which takes note of the scattered and vulnerable nature of such populations. Such a conceptualization may help to develop a fuller appreciation of the realities of rural life for those communities.

The authors' research was conducted over a four-year period across rural towns and villages based within three English counties—Suffolk, Northamptonshire, and Warwickshire[1]—and similar methodologies were employed in the respective locations (for a more detailed account of the research methods utilized in each study, see Garland & Chakraborti, 2004, 2007). Postal questionnaire surveys were distributed to rural minority ethnic households, designed to assess respondents' views on a range of quality of life issues, including perceived problems in their locality; levels of concern about, and experiences of, racist victimization; reasons for reporting, or not reporting, racist incidents; and satisfaction with local agencies. Just over 250 responses were received in total from the respective research sites, and although questionnaires in themselves provide only partial and decontextualized insights into the *process* of victimization, it was felt that distributing questionnaires would at least facilitate the process of making contact with hard-to-reach households and help to indicate the types of key issues to be further explored during the qualitative phase of the research. This qualitative phase included a total of 60 in-depth, semistructured interviews conducted with rural minority ethnic households based within the three counties, undertaken as a way of gaining a deeper appreciation of the process of racialized othering from those with direct experience of these issues.[2] A further 10 interviews and 12 focus groups were arranged with long-term white rural residents to investigate the processes of exclusion that can work to marginalize minority ethnic households from their wider rural communities, while 60 in-depth, semistructured interviews were also undertaken with individuals from a selection of organizations that have some degree of responsibility for policy making and service provision for local communities in the three counties.[3]

REASSESSING THE ENGLISH COUNTRYSIDE

As alluded to previously, idyllicized portrayals of the English countryside are used to perpetuate a popular cultural myth of the cozy English village community, replete with strong ties of kinship, shared values, and a sense of belonging (Chakraborti & Garland, 2004b; Neal & Agyeman, 2006). Complementing this myth is a depiction of villages as crime-free locales, where there is a certain shared sense of identity complemented by strong feelings of belonging (Francis & Henderson, 1992), ideas that are often reflected in traditional notions of community more generally (Bauman, 2001). However, and as an emerging body of research has highlighted, these notions fail to reflect the fragmented and complex nature of contemporary village life. As Cloke and Little (1997) suggest, rural communities are often more cautious, conservative, and essentially "circumspect" in nature than many residents like to admit, and incomers from the city, and indeed even those from neighboring towns and villages, are viewed with distrust and suspicion. This point is vividly illustrated by the following two observations from a white senior police officer from south Warwickshire and a white male in north Warwickshire, expressed to the authors during the course of their research:

> These old, established communities—if you've come from the outside, like the next village, you're never regarded as an insider. That is the nub of the problem.
>   Most of England, historically, has been suspicious of foreigners, and it also applies to people who are, you know, short-sighted, blonde, long-legged, all that sort of thing.

This form of "localism," involving an inherent distrust of the Other, was, according to the two interviewees, reserved for all of those who are perceived to be different in some form. They argued that minority ethnic incomers to the village are treated no differently from others whose faces are not familiar. Therefore, while acknowledging the common marginalization of the

Other in the rural, they suggested that any discrimination directed against those from different ethnic backgrounds was merely a symptom of this intense "localism," and not racism per se: it was caused simply by the fact that outsiders simply did not fit in with the standard norms of the community. A. Little (2002), in his detailed study of the politics of community, indicates that the problem may be deeper than one of mere difference by suggesting that communities "still command certain behaviour from members and indeed this may take the form of expectations of obligation, reciprocity and so on" (p. 4). Therefore anyone new to a tightly knit and small social network may take time to understand the patterns of local behavior and particularistic rural customs, and will experience coercion to learn and abide by them. As Giddens (1994) notes, rather than being open and tolerant, such traditional communities can be limiting and oppressive toward individualism, while exerting a "compelling pressure towards conformism" (p. 126) on anyone perceived to be somehow different.

In the course of the authors' studies of rural racism in various regions, this intolerance has been vocalized by a number of those interviewed and has certainly been evident in the testimony of both white and minority ethnic participants. However, the fact that someone may look visibly different appears to act as a catalyst for forms of racism peculiar to environments where white communities are simply not familiar with, or used to, people with markedly different physical features, as the following research quotations demonstrate:

> In certain communities people will actually stand and openly stare at people just because they've got a different skin color. And I don't think that's in a particularly antagonistic way, I think it's just because people don't have an understanding because they're not exposed. (senior police officer, south Warwickshire)

> I always think back to the very first, umm, ethnic girl that I had in a class, and no one knew how to refer to her. They were sort of saying, "Well, it's, er, you know the one I mean: the little girl in the red cardigan." (white female schoolteacher, north Warwickshire)

The discomfort when talking about minority ethnic people illustrated in the last quotation was evident in a number of the testimonies from white rural dwellers, whether agency representatives or "ordinary" members of the public, when interviewed by the authors for their studies. Whether intentional or not, such behavior reflects attitudes that have, in a broader context in England during the early part of the twenty-first century, manifested themselves most visibly in village campaigns against the Labour government's policy of dispersing asylum seekers into rural areas. As Bright (2004) describes, these campaigns are often conducted amid a "climate of mistrust, fear and ignorance" (p. 13), in which rural residents believe that their "cultural identity" will be eroded by the arrival of asylum seekers, the misunderstood "alien Other."

This othering of those who are visibly different takes place in a rural environment in which, as Saunders, Newby, Bell, and Rose (1978) suggested 30 years ago, long-standing hierarchical social structures persist, and consequently, "traditional forms of authority seem to ensue" (p. 62). Such stratified social systems, with their in-built hierarchies, may have been in place for decades, if not centuries, and are almost impenetrable to newcomers. If minority ethnic families try to get involved in aspects of village life, then they may find themselves victims of this rigid system and unable to become part of traditional village activities. As Magne (2003) found when investigating rural racism in Devon in southwest England, only around one-third of her minority ethnic research participants were involved in community-related activities, and fewer than half participated in community life in any way at all. Reasons given for this lack of participation included fear of cultural and linguistic problems, cultural connotations that caused concern about participation in organizations, and exclusion by virtue of the fact that village life is intertwined with church life.

The inherently exclusive nature of basing so much rural community activity around the church (and most usually the Church of England) creates barriers that those from different religions find very difficult to penetrate. However, the authors' own studies found that rural minority ethnic households were generally reluctant to form their own religious or cultural organizations within their towns or villages. This may be attributable, as one interviewee suggested, to the fear of adverse reaction from the white population:

> If we did all get together the white population might think, "We have got a problem here, brown people getting together," and it probably wouldn't work in our favor. It might be a negative thing, they might try and beat us up. (female interviewee of mixed heritage, north Warwickshire)

Other "traditional" social activities have exclusionary implications for rural minority ethnic households. The "customary" visit to the village pub, for instance, especially on a Sunday, causes problems for those whose faith dictates that they should not drink alcohol. For other households interviewed by the authors, the process of gaining acceptance into village life revolved around social status and issues relating to class. They felt that having a "respectable" occupation, such as being a medical or legal practitioner, helped to ease the process of integration into the community, as it reassured local residents of the person's professional and social credentials. As a district councilor in south Warwickshire stated to the authors,

> The ethnic minorities we have got are well-educated professionals, therefore they're not perceived as spongers off the state or anything like that. They're really part of the community.

Thus, if a minority ethnic villager conforms to the more established, and more "customary," norms, values, and expectations of rural society, then they may find acceptance into village life more easily achievable. By having a professional employment status, minority ethnic people in wealthier rural settlements "reassure" white residents that they are not "scroungers" of state benefits, but instead are net economic contributors to the community. Their well-educated backgrounds also conform to middle-class notions of respectability and thus offer another route for acceptance, something that minority ethnic residents in lower-status occupations, or with few qualifications, have additional difficulty with.

However, the "process of acceptance" into rural communities for minority ethnic people is one of *assimilation*, rather than integration. Often, it appears that white rural communities expect minority ethnic households to adopt the preexisting (and essentially white English) cultural, social, and religious norms that characterize village life, whatever the implications of this may be. If they do so, minority ethnic individuals can attain the status of an "honorary white person," as the following quotation demonstrates:

> There's a chap who lives just down the road from me, he was saying. "It's all right love, we don't see you as one of them. You're one of us." I don't want to be one of you, thank you very much. I'm me, thank you. (female interviewee of mixed heritage, Mid-Suffolk)

This "honorary" status, whether accepted or not, is temporary and ephemeral in nature and can be just as easily withdrawn in the same way that it is conferred on the recipient (Karner, 2007). It is more often than not based on an exclusionary construction of rural identity centered within an imagined, rather than actual, formulation of rural community life (Anderson, 1991). As we shall see in the next section, conceiving of the English countryside in this manner neglects to acknowledge, whether by accident or design, the realities of rural racism, which undermine the traditional notions of rural village communities that appear so symbolically significant to many of their residents.

CULTURES OF RACISM AND EXCLUSION IN THE COUNTRYSIDE

An important, though commonly overlooked feature of rural racism is the way in which expressions of prejudice can be conveyed in different ways to different groups. For instance, while often relatively guarded, at least initially, with regards to their use of language when referring to more established minority ethnic groups, many of the white respondents interviewed during the authors' studies felt that it was perfectly acceptable to use inflammatory language toward Gypsy Travellers; indeed, it appeared that these groups were regarded as "fair game" for vitriolic abuse, in much the same way that asylum seekers have also been scapegoated by sections of the English public and the tabloid press in the last decade. While only a handful of white research subjects had actually come across asylum seekers in the flesh, they nevertheless had formed strong, and mostly negative, opinions about this group, perhaps reflecting the influence of the xenophobic and somewhat histrionic coverage of asylum in certain sections of the tabloid press that have contributed to the perception of asylum seekers as modern-day 'folk devils' (Garland, 2004).

These sentiments are illustrative of the lack of familiarity with difference that characterizes many rural and isolated areas (see, e.g., Chahal & Julienne, 1999; Cloke, 2004). This does not just apply to the presence in the countryside of those from a minority ethnic background, but it also affects those who, for whatever reason, do not conform to the rural "norm," including those who lead an alternative lifestyle, or who are of minority sexuality (Kirkey & Forsyth, 2001), or who experience poverty or homelessness (Cloke, 1997). Indeed, a number of minority ethnic interviewees from the three counties studied mentioned the tacit pressure that exists in such close-knit communities to fit in. For minority ethnic rural households, this pressure heightened their own sense of being "othered" and excluded, and many noted that their discomfort was compounded by being stared at constantly or by being the subject of suspicion. For instance, one minority ethnic interviewee recalled instances when he had been asked to leave local shops or stores as his mere presence had appeared to unnerve or unsettle staff, who were afraid that he was about to steal something. Others reported that when they went near the counter, shop assistants would respond by closing the register, or that white customers would refuse to stand behind them in the queue.

Such "low-level" forms of racist harassment were reported to be commonplace by many minority ethnic participants in the three research projects undertaken by the authors and formed part of a continuum of incidents that are a constant feature of living in the rural. The types of "low-level" incidents described include verbal abuse, unnecessary or persistent staring, the throwing of eggs or stones, "the knocking on doors and then running away, ," the blocking of driveways with cars, being sprayed with air freshener, and being the subject of racist "humor," reflecting patterns of racist harassment noted in other contexts (see, e.g., Bowling, 1998; Jay, 1992; Rowe, 2007). Other less frequent, but equally disturbing, incidents of "high-level" racism were also reported by minority ethnic participants, including criminal damage, physical assault, and even attempted petrol bombing. One Indian male living in Northamptonshire reported to the authors that his attacker yelled,

"You black bastard, you fucking Paki!" and he started pounding me. Then he gave me a couple of blows and by this time I was already fazed by what's happened and he was a big guy. He literally put me in a head lock, and he was shaking me about and I was trying to get free. I nearly passed out.

This incident left the victim badly shaken as well as in need of hospital treatment. Others reported being spat at, kicked, and having their hair or clothes set alight, while some had suffered regular damage to their property, including having windows smashed; cars damaged, or even defecated on; doors kicked in; and property daubed with racist graffiti. The recipients of this harassment were not just those from visible minority ethnic backgrounds but also included those of white Irish or American descent, or asylum seekers and Gypsies.

The experience of mixed-heritage rural residents and their families is also worth noting here. Some of those from a mixed-heritage background who were interviewed by the authors spoke of receiving racist abuse and intimidation from white villagers while also being the subject of some hostility from African Caribbean or Asian populations. This often left the recipient feeling confused and hurt, compounding his or her sense of social isolation. Moreover, the white parents or even grandparents of mixed-heritage children related that they too had been the victims of verbal and physical harassment, reflecting the way in which "mixed-race" relationships are still unacceptable and unpalatable to some. Equally, a substantial number of Muslim research participants felt that they had been subjected to a higher number of incidents of harassment following the 9/11 terrorist attacks in the United States and those of July 7, 2005, in England, and also that, more generally, there was a level of "racial tension" that had not existed in the countryside previously. A concern expressed by non-Muslim south Asians was that they, too, had been the subject of Islamophobic hate since 9/11 from those who were not minded to distinguish between those from different Asian backgrounds (see also Chakraborti, 2007). It is therefore important to acknowledge the impact that global events such as 9/11 can have even in the "localist," isolated, and "inward-looking" environment of the rural. Indeed, there have been incidents in the countryside in which those from the majority white population have also been the target of anti-Muslim prejudice, such as the case of the white, non-Muslim male who had to leave the county of Norfolk in 2004 because of the Islamophobic harassment he had suffered for supposedly "looking like a terrorist" simply by virtue of the fact that he sported a beard (Ashworth, 2005).

It has been suggested by some commentators (see, e.g., Derounian, 1993) that the more hostile forms of rural racism may be located not in the sections of white communities who can trace their rural family lineage back centuries, but instead in the attitudes of new village residents—the so-called white-flighters—who have "escaped" from the urban (with its perceived "negatives" of crime and large minority ethnic populations) to what they view as the peaceful and ethnically homogenous countryside. These "refugees from multiculturalism" (Jay, 1992, p. 22) are therefore both surprised by, and resentful of, the presence of minority ethnic residents in their villages, and it is these feelings that have been manipulated by the far-right British National Party (BNP) in its specifically rural "Land and People" campaign, with its emphasis on the preservation of the essentially white nature of English rural communities.

However, the BNP's correlation of the countryside with English national identity is in itself resonant of wider ideas of Englishness, whose formulation can be traced back to the nineteenth century and the development of a new nationalism based on "the characteristics of landscape, and in the forms of a (rapidly vanishing) rural life" (Kumar, 2003, p. 209). In a society experiencing urbanization and industrialization at a bewildering pace, the rural was seen as the true heart of England, where the essence of national character had not been corrupted. The countryside's gently rolling hills, divided by meandering brooks and dotted with the spires of village churches, were often evoked, particularly at times of war, as the "soul" of the English nation, which must be preserved at all costs (Colls, 2002). As Billig (1995, p. 71) suggests, if the history and self-image of a nation are constructed from a certain narrow view of both people and places, then it becomes very difficult for a number of minority groups to offer a different, and less monocultural, version of that nation:

> National histories tell of a people passing through time—"our" people, with "our" ways of life, and "our" culture. Stereotypes of character and temperament can be mobilized to tell the tale of "our" uniqueness and "our" common fate. . . . Different factions, whether classes, religions, regions, genders or ethnicities, always struggle for the power to speak for the nation, and to present their particular voice as the voice of the national whole.

This feeling of "not fitting in" can lead to a sense of isolation, something that Magne (2003) found was exacerbated by difficulties in forming cross-cultural friendships and a lack of contact with other co-ethnic people. This sense of isolation caused some of those interviewed by the authors for their own research to feel as if they existed "apart" and were excluded from the village life around them. As Johnston (2000) suggests, this may be part of the way that some communities define themselves, by finding "suitable enemies" against whom they can rally. In the case of rural villages, often the most easily identifiable scapegoat is the outsider, and especially the person who looks so obviously different from everyone else. The villager who is seen to threaten the essentially white character of the community will be the one who is excluded by those who feel challenged by his or her presence.

CONCLUSIONS: UNDERSTANDING THE SIGNIFICANCE OF "RACE" IN THE COUNTRYSIDE

This chapter has examined the nature of English rural communities and, in particular, the relationship between such communities and their minority ethnic inhabitants. It has been suggested that these communities—so often portrayed as warm, convivial, and friendly—can in fact be insular and conservative in nature, and suspicious toward those deemed outsiders. For community "insiders," rural villages can be places where kinship and shared identities can be played out and enjoyed; for those subject to the othering process, such places can be cold and unwelcoming. The process of othering can often be coupled by feelings of hostility, which can manifest themselves through both high- and low-level forms of harassment that cause distress and anxiety for victims. Such incidents are rarely one-off events, however, and instead occur as part of a pattern of victimization that can continue over a sustained period of time, leaving the victim feeling isolated and vulnerable, as he or she cannot access the kinds of in-built support networks that characterize more numerically substantial minority ethnic communities in urban locations.

Moreover, we have also seen that othering can take a variety of forms and can affect minority ethnic households in different ways. Far from being a homogeneous experience, the othering process can differ widely in terms of its nature, extent, and impact, depending on a range of factors, such as the victim's ethnicity or professional status, or the type of rural space involved. While not a focal point of this chapter (and for a more detailed examination of the *heterogeneity*, as opposed to the *homogeneity*, of the othering process, see Chakraborti & Garland, 2004a), the sheer diversity of this process in terms of how it can operate differently at times, depending on the particular minority group, region, and village, should not be understated. Similarly, and fairly self-evidently, it is clear that not every minority ethnic individual living in a rural town and village will be a victim of racial harassment. Indeed, the authors' research revealed that some households, albeit a small minority, felt that they had not encountered any forms of racial prejudice, and as discussed previously, this was particularly applicable to those perceived to be from a relatively higher social class or from a more affluent background, whose position in rural society was seen as more secure by virtue of the fact that they were seen to be actively contributing to (as opposed to "sponging from") their community.

Whether the othering process experienced by minority ethnic individuals and families in rural areas is in any way similar to the othering process reserved for any outsider, irrespective of ethnicity, is debatable. While there may be some similarities between the two (in that the "fear of the unknown" may underpin them both), there are key differences, too. An especially troubling feature of rural communities is the tendency of some white residents to expect minority ethnic groups to assimilate into village life, complete with its traditional, specifically rural, and therefore quintessentially white, English customs and practices. However, these customs and practices are embedded in a notion of the countryside that is seen as the true embodiment of English values, and it is therefore easier for white English newcomers to be accepted into village communities, though it may take some years. However, there are certain barriers—cultural, religious, linguistic, social—that are ever present for some minority ethnic people and are thus extremely difficult to overcome. This can result in a sense of isolation and exclusion from local (white) communities, which is exacerbated by the lack of presence of other minority ethnic people nearby and by the pernicious effects of racism.

Nevertheless, there still appears to be a widespread reluctance to admit that racism is a problem of any significance in the English countryside. Indeed, acknowledging its very existence is something that some white rural residents can find unpalatable, due to the fact that their self-identities are formulated around notions that their communities are warm and welcoming to outsiders. To suggest that perpetrators of racist harassment are "ordinary" members of village populations is an assertion that is commonly met with expressions of incredulity and resentment from rural communities and stakeholders, as the authors found firsthand during their own research studies (see, e.g., Garland & Chakraborti, 2004). However, as Ray, Smith, and Wastell (2004) found, the racist sentiments held by the offenders they studied "are widely shared in their local communities" (p. 364) and are not solely the province of small sections of the population who can be conveniently dismissed as "extremist." These findings are similar to those from Mason's (2005) examination of the relationship between perpetrators of racist hate crime and their victims, which found that

> it is the low-level, persistent and virtually unremarkable nature of harassment that enables it to shape the daily lives of its recipients, and their communities in so many undesirable ways. (p. 838)

It is this "everyday" nature of much racist harassment that can cause difficulties for the police and other service providers, who may fail to appreciate the gravity of such harassment. At the same time, it is not just the victimization that can go unrecognized, but also the needs of the rural minority households themselves. Commonly, the provision of appropriate services to victims of racism can suffer because many agencies simply do not feel that allocating scarce human and financial resources toward small rural minority ethnic populations should be a policy priority (de Lima, 2001; Garland & Chakraborti, 2004). It appears as though they simplistically assume that if there are no substantial minority ethnic communities in rural localities, then there can be no substantial problem of racism. For those agencies responsible for issues of rural community safety, it seems that if rural minority ethnic communities are not evident in the way that they define and view "communities" (i.e., simply as large numbers of easily identifiable, homogenous people living in close geographical proximity), then their concerns need not be prioritized, thereby missing, or inadvertently disregarding, minority ethnic groups that need assistance, but whose presence in the countryside is sparse (see Hughes, 2004, for a succinct and perceptive analysis of the dangers of basing policy on "simple," or "primitive," notions of community).

Indeed, the term *minority ethnic community* may be something of a misnomer in a rural context, as the research has pointed to the existence of essentially scattered, isolated households who lack peer group support and the types of network that tend to be associated with the formation and sustenance of such a community. Instead, what we have are relatively small (though growing) rural minority ethnic populations characterized by diversity and heterogeneity in terms of their ethnic, cultural, and religious identities; their professional and economic status; and their capacity to engage with the norms and customs of their wider rural community. What links them together, though, is their susceptibility to racist victimization. While racism is by no means an "inevitability" for the rural minority ethnic household, each of the authors' research studies has shown that both the fear and the experience of racism are persistent problems for the vast majority of such households and can have serious physical, emotional, and financial implications.

Clearly, then, to fully understand issues of "race," exclusion, and victimization in a rural context, it is important to move away from geographically based notions of community and toward those that examine the issue from other angles (Hughes, 2007). A useful suggestion in this regard is provided by Kelly (2003), who suggests that for all types of community, "the prime defining feature is that the members *believe* themselves to be linked to the other members" (p. 41, emphasis added). While different minority ethnic groups do share these bonds (at least within each group), an added factor that may help in the formulation of this conceptualization of community is that of risk. For instance, a factor that underscores the lives of all of the diverse minority ethnic populations in rural areas is that they are at risk on a daily basis of experiencing racist harassment (Taylor, 2003). Johnston (2000) argues that populations should be thought of in terms of the risk that they face of becoming victims of crime, meaning that one could have high- or low-risk communities, or those of *shared risk*, who face a common problem collectively. In the case of rural minority ethnic groups at risk of racist exclusion and victimization, they could be conceived of as communities of shared risk, a concept that bypasses the need for such populations to live in the same shared space and that can be used as a tool to encourage rural support agencies to identify minority ethnic groups and their problems. Without this focus on numbers and geography, but with the added emphasis on risk, this alternative definition of rural minority ethnic communities may help to raise their profile in the countryside, where previously, they were often all but invisible. These communities may then ultimately, and belatedly, be afforded the recognition that their situation deserves.

NOTES

1.   All three counties are predominantly rural in nature, with two of them, Warwickshire and Northamptonshire, situated in the middle of England, while the other, Suffolk, sits on the east coast. According to the 2001 Census, the areas studied in Warwickshire had a minority ethnic population of 4 percent or less, while in Northamptonshire, the minority ethnic population of the study area was less than 2 percent, and in Suffolk, it was approximately 3 percent (Office for National Statistics, 2005).

2.   The research was designed to generate a sample containing a suitably wide cross section of different perspectives, as opposed to a representative reflection of each county's minority ethnic population. The profile of interviewees in each county was relatively evenly distributed in terms of ethnicity and included people from the following ethnicities: black Caribbean, Indian, Pakistani, Bangladeshi, Chinese, black African, Irish, Iranian, mixed heritage, white American, Peruvian, Kosovan, and Gypsy Traveller.

3.   Interviewees included the following individuals and organizational representatives based in the three counties: race equality support officers, the police (including senior representatives and probationers), youth workers, social services, Victim Support, district and parish councils, social services, citizens advice bureaus, local education authorities, Gypsy Traveller education services, councils for voluntary service, primary care trusts, asylum and refugee groups, housing associations, and local councilors.

REFERENCES

Anderson, B. (1991). *Imagined communities: Reflections on the origin and spread of nationalism.* London: Verso.

Ashworth, H. (2005, April 22). Racism drives man out of county. *Eastern Daily Press,* p. 11.

Bauman, Z. (2001). *Community.* Cambridge: Polity Press.

Billig, M. (1995). *Banal nationalism,* London: Sage.

Bowling, B. (1998). *Violent racism: Victimisation, policing and social context.* Oxford: Oxford University Press.

Bright, M. (2004, January 15). Plea to stem rural fears over asylum. *Observer,* p. 13.

Chahal, K., & Julienne, L. (1999). *"We can't all be white!" Racist victimisation in the UK.* York: Joseph Rowntree Foundation.

Chakraborti, N. (2007). Policing Muslim communities. In M. Rowe (Ed.), *Policing beyond Macpherson: Issues in policing, race and society* (pp. 107–127). Cullompton, England: Willan.

Chakraborti, N., & Garland, J. (2004a). England's green and pleasant land? Examining racist prejudice in a rural context. *Patterns of Prejudice, 38 (4),* 383–398.

Chakraborti, N., & Garland, J. (2004b). Introduction: Justifying the study of racism in the rural. In N. Chakraborti & J. Garland (Eds.), *Rural racism* (pp. 1–13). Cullompton, England: Willan.

Clancy, A., Hough, M., Aust, R., & Kershaw, C. (2001). *Crime, policing and justice: The experience of ethnic minorities—findings from the 2000 British Crime Survey* (Research Study No. 223). London: Home Office.

Cloke, P. (1997). Poor country: Marginalisation, poverty and rurality. In P. Cloke & J. Little (Eds.), *Contested countryside cultures: Otherness, marginalisation and rurality* (pp. 252–271). London: Routledge.

Cloke, P. (2004). Rurality and racialised others: Out of place in the countryside? In N. Chakraborti & J. Garland (Eds.), *Rural racism* (pp. 17–35). Cullompton, England: Willan.

Cloke, P., & Little, J. (Eds.). (1997). *Contested countryside cultures: Otherness, marginalisation and rurality*. London: Routledge.

Cloke, P., & Milbourne, P. (1992). Deprivation and lifestyles in rural Wales. *Journal of Rural Studies, 8 (4)*, 359–371.

Colls, R. (2002). *Identity of England*. Oxford: Oxford University Press.

de Lima, P. (2001). *Needs not numbers: An exploration of minority ethnic communities in Scotland*. London: Commission for Racial Equality and Community Development Foundation.

Derbyshire, H. (1994). *Not in Norfolk*. Norwich, England: Norwich and Norfolk Racial Equality Council.

Derounian, J. (1993). *Another country: Real life beyond rose cottage*. London: National Council for Voluntary Organisations.

Dhalech, M. (1999). Race equality initiatives in south west England. In P. Henderson & R. Kaur (Eds.), *Rural racism in the UK: Examples of community based responses* (pp. 11–21). London: Community Development Foundation.

Fitzgerald, M., & Hale, C. (1996). *Ethnic minorities, victimisation and racial harassment* (Research Study No. 39). London: Home Office.

Francis, D., & Henderson, P. (1992). *Working with rural communities*. Basingstoke, England: Macmillan.

Garland, J. (2004). The same old story? Englishness, the tabloid press and the 2002 football world cup. *Leisure Studies, 23*(1), 79–92.

Garland, J., & Chakraborti, N. (2004). Racist victimisation, community safety and the rural: Issues and challenges. *British Journal of Community Justice, 3 (2)*, 21–32.

Garland, J., & Chakraborti, N. (2007). "Protean times"? Exploring the relationships between policing, community and "race" in rural England. *Criminology and Criminal Justice, 7 (4)*, 347–366.

Giddens, A. (1994). *Beyond left and right: The future of radical politics*. Cambridge: Polity Press.

Hughes, G. (2004). The community governance of crime, justice and safety: Challenges and lesson-drawing. *British Journal of Community Justice, 2*(3), 7–20.

Hughes, G. (2007). *The politics of crime and community*. Basingstoke, England: Palgrave.

Jay, E. (1992). *"Keep them in Birmingham": Challenging racism in south west England*. London: Commission for Racial Equality.

Johnston, L. (2000). *Policing Britain: Risk, security and governance.* Harlow, England: Longman.

Karner, C. (2007). *Ethnicity and everyday life.* London: Routledge.

Kelly, L. (2003). Bosnian refugees in Britain: Questioning community. *Sociology, 37 (1),* 35–49.

Kirkey, K., & Forsyth, A. (2001). Men in the valley: Gay male life on the suburban-rural fringe. *Journal of Rural Studies, 17 (4),* 421–441.

Kumar, K. (2003). *The making of English national identity.* Cambridge: Cambridge University Press.

Little, A. (2002). *The politics of community: Theory and practice.* Edinburgh: Edinburgh University Press.

Little, J., & Austin, P. (1996). Women and the rural idyll. *Journal of Rural Studies, 12 (2),* 101–111.

Magne, S. (2003). *Multi-ethnic Devon: A rural handbook—the report of the Devon and Exeter Racial Equality Council's Rural Outreach Project.* Devon, England: Devon and Exeter Racial Equality Council.

Mason, G. (2005). Hate crime and the image of the stranger. *British Journal of Criminology, 45 (6),* 837–859.

Milbourne, P. (1997). Hidden from view: Poverty and marginalisation in rural Britain. In P. Milbourne (Ed.), *Revealing rural "others": Representation, power and identity in the British countryside* (pp. 89–116). London: Pinter.

Moody, S. (1999). Rural neglect: The case against criminology. In G. Dingwall & S. Moody (Eds.), *Crime and conflict in the countryside* (pp. 8–28). Cardiff: University of Wales Press.

Murdoch, J., & Pratt, A. C. (1997). From the power of topography to the topography of power: A discourse on strange ruralities. In P. Cloke & J. Little (Eds.), *Contested countryside cultures: Otherness, marginalisation and rurality* (pp. 51–69). London: Routledge.

Neal, S., & Agyeman, J. (2006). Remaking English ruralities: Processes of belonging and becoming, continuity and change in racialised spaces. In S. Neal & J. Agyeman (Eds.), *The new countryside: Ethnicity, nation and exclusion in contemporary rural Britain* (pp. 99–126). Bristol, England: Policy Press.

Office for National Statistics. (2005). *Census 2001: The most comprehensive survey of the UK population.* Retrieved April 1, 2008, from http://www.statistics.gov.uk/census2001/census2001.asp

Philo, C. (1992). Neglected rural geographies: A review. *Journal of Rural Studies, 8,* 193–207.

Ray, L., Smith, D., & Wastell, L. (2004). Shame, rage and racist violence. *British Journal of Criminology, 44 (3),* 350–368.

Robinson, V., & Gardner, H. (2004). Unravelling a stereotype: The lived experience of black and minority ethnic people in rural Wales. In N. Chakraborti & J. Garland (Eds.), *Rural racism* (pp. 85–107). Cullompton, England: Willan.

Rowe, M. (Ed.). (2007). *Policing beyond Macpherson: Issues in policing, race and society.* Cullompton, England: Willan.

Saunders, P., Newby, H., Bell, C., & Rose, D. (1978). Rural community and rural community power. In H. Newby (Ed.), *International perspectives in rural sociology* (pp. 55–85). London: John Wiley.

Scutt, R., & Bonnett, A. (1996). *In search of England: Popular representations of English-ness and the English countryside* (Working Paper No. 22). Newcastle upon Tyne, England: Centre for Rural Economy, University of Newcastle upon Tyne.

Sibley, D. (1997). Endangering the sacred: Nomads, youth cultures and the English countryside. In P. Cloke & J. Little (Eds.), *Contested countryside cultures: Otherness, marginalisation and rurality* (pp. 218–231). London: Routledge.

Taylor, K. (2003). Hatred repackaged: The rise of the British National Party and antisemitism. In P. Iganski & B. Kosmin (Eds.), *A new antisemitism? Debating Judeophobia in 21st-century Britain* (pp. 231–248). London: Profile Books.

CHAPTER 9

THE HARMS OF VERBAL AND TEXTUAL HATRED

Nicole Asquith

It is in the comparative analysis of free speech doctrine and the regulation of vilification that the vast differences in governmentality and jurisprudence of Western nations are most stark. While the First Amendment of the U.S. Constitution plays a part in the free speech doctrine of all Western nations, it is the United States, alone, that has a constitutional proscription against abridging *all* speech. Unlike the United States, Canada, South Africa, the United Kingdom, and Australia all weigh the damage of "words that wound" (Matsuda, 1993) against the possible damage to democracy and individual freedom arising out the marginalization of its citizens, or, equally, the damage of speech regulation. However, even in the United States, some speech is protected. Speech that facilitates economic and status relationships continues to be abridged (such as insider trading, defamation, libel, union elections, and product advertising). The Supreme Court has also consistently ruled against the free speech of gay men and lesbians.[1] And, more recently, so, too, the speech of perceived terrorists has been curtailed. These special classes of speech are regulated with the understanding that the protection *of* capitalism and the protection *against* homosexuality and terrorism warrant special intervention from the state. In this chapter, I ask why it is that these speech acts are perceived to be—and are constructed as—more damaging to democracy than that of vilification against marginalized citizens of Western nations. Of all the nations mentioned previously, Australia, as with the United States, also stands alone, however, in a very different way to the United States. Unlike other Western nations, Australian citizens do not have a legislative or constitutional commitment to free speech. Quite the opposite. With the exception of a very limited implied right to freedom of political communication—which has been constructed in constitutional law as primarily relating to the organization and operation of elections (*Australian Capital Television Pty Ltd v. the Commonwealth*, 1992)—speech and text in Australia are regulated not only to manage the economy and terrorism, but more important for this chapter, the harms caused to democratic participation by racial, ethnoreligious, and sexuality vilification.

Traditional Millian theory posits that free speech is the most important mechanism to achieve a greater tolerance of difference and thus create a dynamic marketplace for truth to flourish.[2] In responding to maledictive hate,[3] theorists such as Gelber (2002) and Butler (1997) have recommended that marginalized speech actors engage with a process of speaking back, of returning the gaze to make perpetrators' contributions to the marketplace of ideas marginal and aberrant. However, as will be demonstrated by an analysis of maledictive force and effects, the ideal speech situations of communicative action theory, and the recasting of terms of abuse by "speaking back," require both rational speech actors—something clearly absent in many acts of maledictive hate—and an institutional validation of the authenticity of marginalized subjects and their speech. Constructing new truths in the marketplace of ideas is both socially and politically contingent. As such, the capacity for marginalized subjects to contribute to the marketplace rests on their ability to be able to speak with authority and to be authorized to speak. Yet, validation as authorized speech actors can be withheld from marginalized groups such that, even when individuals feel empowered to speak back to their victimizers, their speech and writing may be forestalled, gagged, frustrated, and disabled by the social and historical context of their outsiderhood. Furthermore, speaking back is offered by those who oppose the regulation of speech as inherently noninstitutional: as an act of individual agency. This failure to read institutional responses as a process of speaking back—which recontextualizes social relationships, as they exist at the time of enactment—fundamentally devalues the contributions that the state, and law, can make in managing maledictive hate when it is embodied in dynamic constitutional law, government policy, and equitable social interactions.

Malediction is critical to the effectiveness of most hate violence. In previous research, maledictive hate was found to occur in 80 percent of all reported cases of antisemitic and heterosexist violence.[4] Explicit, personalized abuse constitutes one of the identifying characteristics of hate violence and establishes it as a practice unique to this form of interpersonal violence. Maledictive hate acts as a warning and as a justification: a prelude of things to come, and—if addressees respond—a justification for the transformation of malediction into physical and sexual violence. Too often in accounts of hate violence, escalation from malediction to physical or sexual assault occurs when those named in hate violence respond to their victimizer's heed and take on the label spat out in hate. Embracing outsiderhood is proof enough that disorder is contained *in* the marginal body and that order must be reinstated by physical containment *of* the body.

Rather than employing a simplistic Millian or equally unresponsive post-structuralist theoretical framework to account for this transformation from speech to action, Bourdieu's critical engagement with Austinian speech act theory (Bourdieu & Thompson, 1991) and Langton's (1993) twist on speech act theory have been foregrounded in this chapter. Employing such frameworks does not mean that I privilege state intervention over a radical reworking of social institutions and social interactions—for that would fall prey to the misrecognition of state power as arbitrary. However, it will also be shown that "speaking back" from unauthorized or deauthorized social positions is as ineffective as state intervention that is purely symbolic or overly zealous; both are incapable of bringing about real change to the lived experiences of survivors of heterosexist, anti-Muslim, and antisemitic hate violence.

PERFORMATIVE "SPEECH" ACTS

In 1955, Austin (1980) presented a series of lectures titled *How to Do Things with Words*. This work reconstructed the field of linguistic philosophy at that time and, later, reconstructed the debate over the regulation of pornography and "hate speech" in the United States. In an attempt to short-circuit the limitations imposed by the First Amendment on the regulation of "content," MacKinnon (1997) and critical race theorists (Matsuda, 1993) have recontextualized the maledictive hate of pornography and "hate speech" as conduct, rather than mere words. Central to this conversion from malediction to conduct was the redeployment of Austin's (1980) analysis of perlocutionary and illocutionary performative speech acts. In *How to Do Things with Words*, he argues that

> we first distinguished a group of things we do in saying something, which together we summed up by saying we perform a *locutionary act*, which is roughly equivalent to uttering a certain sentence with a certain sense and reference. . . . Second, we said that we also perform *illocutionary acts* such as informing, ordering, warning, undertaking, &c., i.e., utterances which have a certain (conventional) force. Thirdly, we may also perform *perlocutionary acts:* what we bring about or achieve *by* saying something, such as convincing, persuading, deterring, and even, say, surprising or misleading. (p. 109)

From this seemingly simple classification of speech and the ways in which speech can be action, theorists such as Bourdieu, Butler, and Langton have developed a sophisticated system for assessing the force and effects of subordinating and silencing malediction. However, particularly for Bourdieu and

Langton, it is Austin's deeper analysis of the forms of *illocutionary* speech that provides the basis for their claims about the authority to speak and the power of authorized speech. Austin, in his analysis of performative acts, details five classes of illocutionary utterances (Austin, 1980), two of which Langton has reclassified as *authoritative illocutions:* verdictives (exercise of judgment) and exercitives (exercising of power; Langton, 1993).

The first of these classes of illocutions relates to the "delivering of a finding, official or *unofficial*, upon evidence or reasons as to value or fact" (Austin, 1980, p. 153, emphasis added). Verdictive illocutions aim to rank and value the addressee and thus establish a verdict on the "truth and falsity, soundness and unsoundness and fairness and unfairness" (Austin, 1980, p. 153) of their subjectivity or contributions to the marketplace of ideas. In maledictive hate, verdictive illocutions include naming and pathologizing individuals within a hierarchy of social positions according to their proximity to dominant representations of the body and identity. The second class of illocutions are exercitive performatives, and unlike verdictive illocutions, they are a judgment that it "is to be so, as distinct from a judgment that it is so: it is advocacy that it should be so, as opposed to an estimate that it is so; . . . it is an award as opposed to an assessment; it is a sentence as opposed to a verdict" (Austin, 1980, p. 155). More than verdictives, exercitives require an authorized or conventional force to bring about the objective of the "speech" act. Furthermore, where verdictives are temporally present or an assessment of the past, exercitives are statements about how the future should look: an advocacy of things to come. As such, if exercitives are spoken with authority or by an authorized delegate, they are capable of influencing addressees in more ways than verdictives.

HARMS OF HATE: SUBORDINATION AND SILENCE

Langton argues that authoritative illocutions are capable of achieving two types of action: subordination and silencing. There is an important relationship between subordination and silencing. Many free speech theorists suggest that the best way to dismantle explicitly subordinating malediction—which ranks individuals and groups, legitimizes inequitable treatment toward them, and withdraws rights and privileges from them—is with more speech (see, e.g., Allen & Jensen, 1995; Butler, 1997; Gates et al., 1994; Gelber, 2002; Heyman, 1996). However, as Langton (1993) highlights, fighting maledictive hate with more speech is an impossible task when marginalized individuals or groups are also silenced. She argues that "free speech is a good thing because it *enables people to act*. . . . Speech that silences is bad, not just because it restricts the ideas available on the shelves, but because it constrains people's action" (p. 328). However, when gay men, lesbians, Muslims, and Jews are unable to make recognizable contributions to the marketplace—as authorized participants in discussions and as experts on the subject of hate—they are not only silenced, they are also subordinated.

Addressees are subordinated when maledictive hate "rank[s] certain people as inferior . . . legitimate[s] discriminatory behavior towards them . . . [and] deprive[s] them of powers and rights" (Langton, 1993, p. 307). Being ranked as inferior, and having that assessment legitimated (e.g., through the devaluation of violence against gay men or lesbians, or the conflation of Muslim with terrorist), also creates the conditions for withholding rights and privileges, such as the banning of same-sex marriage and adoption or guardianship by same-sex couples (as is the case in Australia), or for regulatory controls that make religious faith the new racial profile for governmental policy, institutional practices, and localized interactions.[5]

The second set of actions achieved in performative malediction is silencing. Langton (1993) suggests that if speech (or text) is action, "then silence is the failure to act" (p. 314) or the failure of speech to count as an action. This failure to act can be seen in the locutionary gag, perlocutionary frustration, and illocutionary disablement. While Langton privileges the latter form of silencing (illocutionary disablement)—perhaps due to her need to operate within the confines of First Amendment jurisprudence—all three forms of silencing have sufficient force to harm marginalized subjects.

The primary form of silencing is the locutionary gag. This is where speech or text is unavailable because the conditions for articulating are made "unspeakable" (or unwritable). The principal way silence is secured is through the loss of mechanical means (such as limited access to a public forum or a physical incapacity) to create speech or text. Silence as the result of mechanical loss is a significant factor in any traumatic incident. Traumatic memory, unlike automatic memory or narrative memory, resides largely in corporeal sensation and dysfunction. Recollecting traumatic memory calls on different parts of the brain than those required to speak and construct narratives of experiences (Brison, 1999). Brison suggests that this is one reason why many survivors of trauma (such as hate violence) lose the ability to articulate a coherent narrative of the encounter, and why memories of these events can appear as "full of fleeting images, the percussion of blows, sounds, and movements of the body" (Culbertson, as cited in Brison, 1999, p. 42).

The second way that Langton (1993) suggests that silence can be secured is through perlocutionary frustration. While locutionary silence is the failure to make a sound, perlocutionary frustration is achieved by letting a person speak but not letting those speech or textual acts have the intended effect. Austin (1980) argues that *by* saying something—in contrast to the illocutionary force created *in* saying something—"often, or even normally . . . certain consequential effects upon the feelings, thoughts, or actions of the audience, or of the speaker, or of other persons" are produced (p. 101). These perlo-cutionary effects may be that the audience is persuaded, or intimidated, or convinced by the speaker's arguments. Perlocutionary silence or frustration is a regular part of everyday life such that "one invites, but nobody attends the party; one votes, hoping to oust the government, but one is outnumbered" (Langton, 1993, p. 315); one refuses consent in sex, and it is ignored. How-ever, for marginalized subjects, perlocutionary frustration is more likely to be integral to their life experiences because their marginality results in the con-struction of their identity as flawed, suspect, and inadmissible (e.g., the "don't ask, don't tell" policy of the U.S. military). For a perlocutionary statement to be successful, it must be articulated by a social actor recognized as a "speaker" with authority. If marginalized subjects are proscribed from positions of au-thority (even on the subject of marginality), then the effects of their speech and writing are bound to be frustrated.

The final form of silence is presented by Langton as the most serious way that the objectives of marginalized subjects are disabled. An illocutionary malediction is one that does something *in* the saying or writing. Illocution-ary disablement occurs when "when one speaks, one utters words, and fails not simply to achieve the effect one aims at, but fails to perform the very action one intends": one refuses to accept hate speech, and it is transformed into "fighting words"; one refuses consent in sex, and it is transformed into an eroticized "yes" (Langton, 1993, p. 321). In illocutionary performatives, not only are addressors required to speak with authority (or, at least, with a veneer of expertise), but they are also required to be authorized to speak. Consequently, those with no recognized authority or expertise, or those who are not delegated to speak on a given topic, can have their speech, text, and actions disabled.

SPEAKING WITH AUTHORITY AND THE AUTHORITY TO SPEAK

When Judith Butler (1997) turned to Austin's work four years after Lang-ton's analysis of sexual violence, it was to interrogate the use of perlocution-ary effect and illocutionary force as a theoretical and legal tool in regulating subordinating and silencing maledictive hate. Butler rejects a straightforward reading of illocutionary force and the idea of a state-sponsored response to maledictive hate. She advocates an appropriation of maledictive hate, which creates new contexts of meaning and thus deauthorizes, then reauthorizes, the words or text. In the space between meaning and intent—between speaking and acting—Butler (1997) argues that there is a slippery reiterative moment where there is an opportunity for a reversal, an appropriation, or an expro-priation that undermines the hatred and intentions of the speaker or writer and offers new meanings, new intentions, and the chance of linguistic agency.

Butler (1997) further argues that illocutionary force is reserved for few occasions in contemporary societies as it relies on prior convention to convey what is said (the meaning and intent) *and* the physical, corporeal power to bring about the uttered intent or meaning. She suggests that there are moments of illocutionary force but that any analysis of malediction that claims this rare moment as the primary social process closes or fixes the possibilities of changing or uncoupling the hurtful connections between meaning and intent and the ability to act on that meaning and intent. Butler (1997) contends that every utterance is unstable and open to reinterpretation. In fixing the meanings of maledictive hate within a state framework such as law, she argues, we undermine the possibility of inscribing new meanings and therefore hinder the addressee's linguistic agency.

Regulating some hateful speech, for Butler (1997), is a partial task of interrogating "words that wound" because contexts and meaning change over time and place and because some performatives actually gain their force from the break with prior contexts (e.g., "queer" in the mouths of gay men and lesbians, or "nigger" in the mouths of African Americans). Bourdieu rejects Butler's (1997) position, claiming instead that social power is invested in all speech acts prior to this utterance of "words that wound" (Bourdieu & Thompson, 1991). They highlight that the conventional means that bring about linguistic success are not embodied in language use—nor is convention authorized internally to language; rather, convention is effective because of the social conditions external to language, that is, the social conditions of those who get to speak, those who are allowed to speak (but within limitations), and those who are silenced completely. Bourdieu argues that the illocutionary forces of performative utterances do not gain their efficacy from "the fact that they seem to possess in themselves the source of a power"; rather, this efficacy "resides in the institutional conditions of their production and reception" (Bourdieu & Thompson, 1991, p. 111). This theoretical approach has the advantage of foregrounding the social construction of authority and thus the social conventions required for individuals to wield hate as an act of power.

In this sense, language is a social structure instituted *prior* to any utterance by the speaker (or writer), and maledictive hate is a habit that requires generational reinscription for it to do its social magic. Intergenerational reinscription (whether of hate or respect) requires structural processes—not just social interactions—for hate or respect to pass to the next generation. In this sense, as Langton (1993) argues, speaking (or writing) with authority requires social recognition of one's position as a specialist on the subject under discussion, while being authorized to speak requires a social delegation of power to define the subject of discussion, and whether the subject is in fact a valid, legitimate matter to be discussed at all.

SPEECH ACT THEORY AND ANTI-VILIFICATION LEGISLATION IN AUSTRALIA

Given that institutional validation or recognition has been the most potent form of social recognition available in Western democratic states, it appears counterproductive to suggest that a privatized response is the principal and most successful way to eliminate maledictive hate. Although a small number of individuals and communities may at times feel empowered to engage with perpetrators of hate violence without the intervention of the state,[6] prioritizing this form of response not only constructs others unable to act in this manner as socially deficient, but it also constructs social change as a localized process. Unlike privatized individual or community responses to maledictive hate, state intervention can establish the ground rules of social engagement for all citizens. This is not to say that marginalized groups have no role in the elimination of maledictive hate or that individuals and communities cannot make significant changes to the experience of hate; rather, it is to argue that these groups require state support and intervention for their voices to be perceived as being authorized and as having the requisite expertise or authority to be contributors to the issues raised by hatred.

Without a First Amendment to hamper their intervention, since 1995, Australian state and federal governments have adopted a variety of mechanisms to seek remedies for the damages caused by maledictive hate. While these laws have been constructed as great symbols of the intent of Australian government, unfortunately, this intervention has been largely obviated. In part, the lack of success of Australian vilification law is due to the conditions under which intervention is tolerable to the electorate, but also because Australian governments (unlike their counterparts in the United Kingdom, South Africa, and Canada) have abrogated their responsibility as active participants in this adjudication of maledictive hate in favor of an individualized, privatized system of civil law. In particular, anti-vilification measures, such as the *New South Wales Anti-Discrimination Act 1977*[7] and the Commonwealth of Australia's *Racial Hatred Act 1995*,[8] seek to regulate only complaints of vilification submitted by individuals who are recognized members of the victim groups named in the legislation. In practice, this means that only a Jew can make a complaint of antisemitic vilification, or only gay men and lesbians could make complaints of sexuality vilification. Furthermore, under these Acts, a case of vilification can only be met if the speech or text incites—or could possibly incite—another person to hate. Vilification in Australia is judged not on the basis of the intent of perpetrators; rather, harm is assessed through the eyes of the reasonable third person of law. While an objective assessment is preferable to the subjective assessment of intent, the reasonable third person is also problematic. Finally, Australian models for regulating maledictive hate, while requiring a public act of hatred, are adjudicated in camera. This effectively hinders the capacity for these institutional responses to maledictive hate to create a social commitment to—that is, perlocutionary effects for—the elimination of vilification.

The right to demand a life free from targeted violence requires state interventions that establish a set of standards for good citizenship. Law should never be solely an exercise in symbolism; it must also be able to change the circumstances of hatred. Too often, institutional measures, such as the *Anti-Discrimination Act 1977* (NSW) and the *Racial Hatred Act 1995* (Cth), are presented as symbols of the intent of state and federal governments, rather than as mechanisms for real social change. The containment of these legislative responses to acts of symbolism stems primarily from the adjudicating framework employed to seek redress for marginalized subjects. In particular, these institutional measures only partially capture the acts of hatred experienced by marginalized subjects because these civil procedures only relate to public speech and textual acts that incite *others* to hate. These regulatory measures only trap those acts that create effects on others, rather than those that create force against the primary addressee. This is the reverse of the regulatory system in the United States, which can only ever regulate maledictive hate that is constructed as action (such as illocutionary speech acts of "fighting words"). In Australian regulatory systems, it is not enough that one person hates, that hatred must be able to infect another's mind. Governments in Australia have deemed that the damage of vilification is not contained in the initial authoritative *illocution;* rather, the damage is contained in the maledictive, *perlocutionary* infection of another. This preference for secondary effects over primary force significantly devalues the damage done in the one-on-one engagement between addressee and addressor.

The second major concern in relation to the regulatory frameworks adopted by Australian governments is their use of the objective, reasonable third person to assess the harm caused by maledictive hate. To adjudicate the secondary effect of malediction, governments have established the *ordinary reasonable person* as the third person in every encounter of vilification—whether or not there is an actual third person present in the encounter. In *Harou-Sourdon v. TCN Channel Nine* (1994; as cited in McNamara, 2002) the Tribunal of the Equal Opportunity Commission set the reasonable person as one who is neither "immune from susceptibility to incitement" nor compelled to act with "racially prejudiced views." Given that the objective approach requires an analysis of the social and historical contexts that play a part in each incident of vilification, it appears counterintuitive to start from a position of the ordinary reasonable person not being inclined to racist or heterosexist views. Australia was founded on the racist proclamation of *terra nullius* (empty land); it did not give indigenous Australians full citizenship until 1967; it maintained a white Australia immigration policy until 1967; it criminalized sodomy (in Tasmania) until 1998. How, then, can we expect that the ordinary reasonable person is somehow immune from this socialization? Takach (1994) suggests that vilification legislation was introduced to remedy a perceived social problem. However, in the conversion from social policy to a legal framework, the objective approach "may not take into account the viewpoint of the very group[s] that the . . . legislation is designed to support" (p. 41).

Finally, as both Gelber (2002) and McNamara (2002) argue, civil complaint systems that require *public* acts of discrimination, harassment, and vilification to be adjudicated primarily through a *private*, in camera conciliation process fail to achieve either the objective of establishing a symbol of the intent of governments or the production of real social change. While vilification must be a public act, remedies to vilification are confined largely to private conciliation, where neither parties (nor the tribunals hearing the matter) are permitted to speak publicly about the proceedings. Gelber (2002) argues that confining these acts of vilification to the public sphere, and the conciliation of these acts to the private sphere, fundamentally undermines the stated goals and objectives of the legislation, as decisions reached are not made public and do not serve as symbols of unacceptable behavior.

Each of these imperfections in the regulatory frameworks in Australia limit the ability for marginalized subjects to seek justice. However, they offer some limited remedies to maledictive hate, albeit partial and available in a few privileged cases. Adopting Austin's performative speech act theory may, however, assist in ameliorating some of the more debilitating impediments of Australian vilification law. This is not to make a case for textual analysis as the *only* tool in adjudicating malediction; rather, speech act theory could serve as an additional framework to clarify the purpose, intent, and consequences of malediction and, as a result, lead to a more effective system that is based on the force *and* effect of malediction, instead of the assessment of the reasonable third person.

CONCLUDING REMARKS

The primary defense to free speech—that which Gates (1994) argues constitutes "armchair absolutists' Old Reliable" (p. 23)—is a slippery slope. Over the last six years, since the attacks on the World Trade Center and the Pentagon, many Western nations have lost traction on the free speech slippery slope, perhaps with the belief that regulating the speech and text of terrorists will forestall similar attacks. Whether this curtailment of speech and writing has been successful or not, for some, this regulation is a clear demonstration of the slippery problems associated with abridging speech. However, if we are to accept that the slope is slippery, then we must also accept, as Gates (1994) point out, that

> a more accurate account of where we currently stand is somewhere halfway up the side of the mountain; we already are, and always were, on that slippery slope. (p. 23)

This view of free speech theory—from the side of the mountain, rather the pinnacle—highlights the negotiated nature of speech regulation and the social effort required to manage speech and text and their force and effects. We must also contextualize the slippery slope: where does the slope lead; what is its gradient; who and how many are making the trek up its slope; and is there a commitment to trekking the slope for time immemorial, even when the costs are high and borne disproportionately?

The state (in all Western nations) has defined the illocutionary acts of terrorists as unspeakable and unwritable because they *may* cause harm or may represent the beginnings of harm; that is, that the perlocutionary effects of *speech*, rather than the illocutionary force of speech *acts*, are sufficient to warrant curtailment. In effect, they are what Iganski (2002) considers *in terrorem*. Maledictive hate—especially threats of death—are speech and textual acts that *do* things in the saying and create a set of consequences for the addressees. Equally, these acts of malediction are, in effect and force, *in terrorem*. Yet, while the former set of speech and textual acts is regulated, its complementary partner in malediction is constructed as ethereal, as somehow less harmful than threats of terrorism.

It has been suggested throughout this chapter that the simple remedy proposed by traditional Millian theory—that maledictive hate can be countered by additional speech acts in the marketplace of ideas—fails to account for the legitimated power of illocutionary force. When viewed through Austinian speech act theory, Australian anti-vilification laws appear either to ignore or devalue the force of authoritative illocutions, preferring instead to privilege the perlocutionary effects of malediction. This not only reduces anti-vilification legislation to ineffectual, symbolic law, it also indicates to those citizens most at risk of social death that their governments are largely unconcerned by the violence of their everyday lives, except when it incites others to action. It has been suggested that the limited success achieved to date through civil anti-vilification complaint procedures can be remedied by the employment of a more nuanced interpretation of the textual properties of maledictive hate and the illocutionary force of authorized speech. The reformation of institutional measures will ensure that the symbolism is converted into an authorized redistribution of justice.

ACKNOWLEDGMENTS

The findings reported in this chapter were developed from data provided by the NSW Anti-Discrimination Board, the Executive Council of Australian Jewry, and the Lesbian and Gay Anti-Violence Project. Without the support and assistance from staff members and elected representatives of these organizations, this research would never have been possible. Furthermore, I am grateful to Ms. Sonya Stanford for her insights and comments on earlier drafts of this chapter.

NOTES

1. For example, *Toward a Gayer Bicentennial Committee v. Rhode Island Bicentennial Foundation* (417 F. Supp. 632 U.S. Dist. RI, 1976), *Council on Religion and the Homosexual v. PT&T* (70 Cal. PUC 471, 1969), *Solmitz v. Maine School Administrative District* (495 A. 2d 812 Sup. Ct. Maine, 1985), and *San Francisco Arts and Athletics, Inc. v. United States Olympic Committee* (483 U.S. 522, 1987), as cited in Siegel (1995).

2. For a full discussion of Millian free speech theory, see Gates (1994), Heyman (1996), Allen and Jensen (1995), and Ten (1980).

3. In this chapter, I have made a break with traditional analyses of violence against gay men, lesbians, Muslims, and Jews, particularly in relation to the terms used to define "mere words." In the construction of "hate speech" (and, of course, in the deployment of speech act theory), most analyses gloss over the fact that these practices include spoken and written forms of hatred. To remedy the shortcomings of the term *hate speech*, I have resurrected the term *malediction*—and *maledictive hate*—for its verbal and textual properties and for its stronger meaning: "the utterance of a curse, the condition of being reviled, and an evil intention or deed" (as defined in the *Shorter Oxford English Dictionary*, Oxford University Press, 2002).

4. See Asquith (2008). The claims and recommendations made in this chapter are based on a quantitative and textual analysis of 1,227 complaints of antisemitic and heterosexist hate violence, discrimination, and vilification lodged with the Lesbian and Gay Anti-Violence Project, the Executive Council of Australian Jewry, and the New South Wales Anti-Discrimination Board between January 1995 and December 1999. This initial research has been enhanced by the textual analysis of 173 articles relating to the Cronulla riots published in Australian newspapers between December 10, 2005, and January 19, 2006.

5. As per the *Marriage Act of 1961* (Cth), as amended in 2004 by the Parliament of Australia.

6. In the analysis of complaints lodged by gay men and lesbians to the Lesbian and Gay Anti-Violence Project, only 17 percent of complainants indicated that they felt capable of responding to their perpetrators or of fighting back (Asquith, 2008).

7. *Anti-Discrimination Act of 1977* (NSW), Parliament of New South Wales, Australia (No. 48 of 1977).

8. *Racial Hatred Act of 1995* (Cth), Parliament of Australia (No. 101 of 1995).

REFERENCES

Allen, D. S., & Jensen, R. (Eds.). (1995). *Freeing the First Amendment: Critical perspectives on freedom of expression.* New York: New York University Press.

Anti-Discrimination Act 1977 (NSW), Parliament of New South Wales, Australia (No. 48 of 1977).

Asquith, N. L. (2008). *Text and context of malediction: A study of antisemitic and heterosexist hate violence.* Saarbrucken: VDM Verlag.

Austin, J. L. (1980). *How to do things with words* (2nd ed.). London: Oxford University Press.

Australian Capital Television Pty Ltd v. The Commonwealth, 108 ALR 577 at 618 (1992).

Bourdieu, P., & Thompson, J. B. (1991). *Language and symbolic power.* Cambridge: Polity Press.

Brison, S., J. (1998). The autonomy defense of free speech. *Ethics, 108*(2), pp. 312–341.

Butler, J. (1997). *Excitable speech: A politics of the performative.* New York: Routledge.

Gates Jr, H. L. (1994). War of words: critical race theory and the First Amendment. In Gates, H. L., A. P. Griffin, D. E. Lively, R. C. Post, W. B. Rubenstein & N. Strossen (Eds.), *Speaking of Race, Speaking of Sex.* New York and London: New York University Press.

Gelber, K. (2002). *Speaking back: The free speech versus hate speech debate.* Philadelphia: John Benjamins.

Gilman, S. (1991). *The Jew's Body.* New York and London: Routledge.

Harou-Sourdon v. TCN Channel Nine, EOC 92-604 (1994).

Heyman, S. J. (Ed.). (1996). *Hate speech and the Constitution.* New York: Garland.

Iganski, P. (2002). How hate hurts. In G. Csepeli & A. Orkeny (Eds.), *Gyulolet es politika (Hate and Politics)* (pp. 25–35). Budapest: Friedrich Ebert Stiftung—Minoritas Alapitvany Kisebbsegkutato, Intezet.

Langton, R. (1993). Speech acts and unspeakable acts. *Philosophy and Public Affairs, 22,* 293–330.

MacKinnon, C. (1997). Not a moral issue. In K. J. Maschke (Ed.), *Pornography, sex work, and hate speech* (pp. 2–31). New York: Garland.

Matsuda, M. (1993). Public response to racist speech: Considering the victim's story. In M. Matsuda, C. R. Lawrence, R. Delgado, & K. Williams Crenshaw (Eds.), *Words that wound: Critical race theory, assaultive speech and the First Amendment* (pp. 17–52). Boulder, CO: Westview Press.

McNamara, L. (2002). *Regulating racism: Racial vilification laws in Australia.* Sydney, NSW: Sydney Institute of Criminology.

Nemes, I. (1997). Antisemitic hostility. In C. Cunneen, D. Fraser & S. Tomsen (Eds.), *Faces of hate: Hate crime in Australia* (pp. 44-74). Sydney: Hawkins Press.

Racial Hatred Act 1995 (Cth), Parliament of Australia (No. 101 of 1995).

Siegel, P. (1995). Why lesbians and gay men need traditional First Amendment theory. In D. S. Allen & R. Jensen (Eds.), *Freeing the First Amendment: Critical perspectives on freedom of expression* (pp. 224–252). New York: New York University Press.

Takach, R. (1994). Gay and lesbian inequality: the anti-vilification measures. *Australasian Gay and Lesbian Law Journal, 4,* 30–49.

Ten, C. L. (1980). *Mill on liberty.* New York: Oxford University Press.

CHAPTER 10

HATE CRIME AS A HUMAN RIGHTS VIOLATION

Barbara Perry and Patrik Olsson

For what are generally obvious reasons, the last several decades have seen extensive global interest in the issue of human rights. We say "obvious" in light of such egregious violations as the Nazi Holocaust, the genocide in Rwanda, and even the threats posed by contemporary antiterrorist legislation in Western nations like the United States. Each successive wave of such assaults on the integrity and well-being of human beings has been met variously with calls for human rights legislation, declarations, and other statements of the sanctity of rights.

Beginning more recently, say, in the last two to three decades, there has also been a growing recognition of the harms of what has come to be known as hate crime. In part, this acknowledges the potential for the escalation from racial or other animus-based violence into the sorts of atrocities associated with genocide. It is also, perhaps, a tacit acknowledgment of hate crime as itself a human rights violation. This chapter aims to make that connection much more explicitly than has been the case to date. In short, we answer the standard question, What is the harm of hate crime? not with the similarly standard answers appealing to psychological or physical or even civic harm; rather, the response is that hate crime *is* the harm, insomuch as it is more often than not motivated or intended to violate the basic rights of minority groups and individuals.

Human rights scholarship tends to concern itself with gross violations of human rights, and largely those perpetrated or tacitly condoned by the state, thereby without immediate interventions to prevent the violations. On the other side of the equation, hate crime scholars have concerned themselves with the physical or psychological—rather than rights-based—harms associated with bias-motivated violence. Rarely do the two fields of inquiry talk to one another. As an illustrative example, consider the fact that no articles in *Human Rights Quarterly* have referred to hate crime, while none in the three years of publication of the new *Journal of Hate Studies* refer to human rights—a simple but quite telling pair of observations. Perhaps the one exception to this has been Evelyn Kallen's (2003, 2004) recent work focusing on rights and social justice in Canada. In *Social Inequality and Social Injustice*, for example, Kallen (2004) includes a chapter titled "The Experience of Degradation, Abuse and the Harmful Impacts of Hate." This is as close as any scholar comes to conceptualizing the mundane, everyday violence associated with hate crime in terms of the limitations it poses for the free exercise of rights. Yet even here, the analysis is brief and conducted predominantly through illustration and example, rather than grounded argumentation.

This chapter aims to initiate a dialogue that broadens our understanding of hate crime, seeing it as running along the same continuum as, for example, the "ethnic cleansing" in Kosovo or the "social cleansing" of vulnerable children in the urban settings of Colombia. While not of their magnitude in some respects, hate crime nonetheless shares the underlying dynamics and, more important, violation of the human dignity to which we are all entitled through United Nations (UN) conventions, treaties, and declarations.

In what follows, we open with a brief introduction to what is meant here by a human rights framework. This includes a discussion of the historical evolution of the doctrine of human rights that has dominated legal and academic work since the inception of the UN Declaration of Human Rights in 1948. It also includes a summary of what might be said to be the cardinal principles of human rights and the related bundles of constitutive rights. This introductory section is followed by a précis of the ways in which the harm associated with hate crime has generally been addressed. To date, this scholarship has tended to see the harm as a consequence, rather than as a constituent element, of hate crime, something outside the act, rather than inherent in the act. Then we turn to the heart of the chapter, which is the argument that hate crime is, by nature, a sustained and systematic violation of human rights and is thus to be condemned on its own merits, and not only on account of its consequent harms.

A HUMAN RIGHTS FRAMEWORK

If there is any single point of consensus in the debates around human rights, it is that the twentieth century witnessed a revolution in rights (Ignatieff, 2001; Kallen, 2003, 2004). Clearly the concept of human rights did not suddenly appear on the global scene at that time; rather, the modern notion traces its lineage to ancient Greek notions of citizenship. Nonetheless, we take as the artificial and arbitrary starting point the effort to create and win support for the UN human rights documents of the early twentieth century. This remains the most widely known and subscribed to rights document and thus has informed rights discourse and practice universally.

The abuses of the first part of the twentieth century—the Armenian genocide and the Holocaust, in particular—sounded an alarm internationally. Here were two extreme cases that illustrated the human propensity to inflict unspeakable harm on other human beings. Global shock at the atrocities—torture, "medical" experimentation, mass murders—associated with these genocides culminated in the adoption by the UN General Assembly of the Convention on the Prevention and Punishment of the Crime of Genocide (December 9, 1948). Quickly on its heels followed the adoption of the Universal Declaration of Human Rights (UDHR; December 10, 1948), a document that would provide the blueprint and moral guide for the protection of human rights globally. Moreover, it is Article 1 of the UDHR that encapsulates the cardinal principles from which all subsequent articles derive:

> All human beings are born free and equal in dignity and rights. They are endowed with reason and conscience and should act towards one another in a spirit of brotherhood.

As stated, the UDHR formalizes three tenets of global human rights: freedom, equality, and dignity. Kallen (2004) offers a succinct definition of each of these:

> the right of every human being to participate in the shaping of decisions affecting their own way of life and that of their society (freedom to decide); reasonable access to the economic resources that make that participation possible (equality/equity of opportunity); and affirmation of the essential human worth and dignity of every person, regardless of individual qualities and/or group membership (dignity of person). (p. 15)

Simply put, human rights are those rights that accrue to all people by virtue of them being human beings. They speak to the inherent and inalienable right to claim human dignity, equally, regardless of group identity or membership or any other characteristic. The contemporary human rights regime regards human rights as universal claims to safeguard human dignity from illegal and unjustified coercion or the threat thereof.

While the UN has perhaps suffered from a somewhat tarnished image in recent years, the underlying notion of human rights continues to enjoy universal acknowledgment. Indeed, Bunch (1990) makes the observation that

> the concept of human rights is one of the few moral visions ascribed to internationally. Although its scope is not universally agreed upon, it strikes

deep chords of response among many. Promotion of rights is a widely accepted goal. (pp. 486–487)

The veracity of her claim is apparent, first, in the diversity of the 191 nations that are signatories to the various conventions inspired by the UDHR:
Canada, Uganda, Venezuela, Turkey, and Papua New Guinea, to name but
a few very distinct members. Of course, the extent to which these nations
practice what they've agreed to is an empirical question—witness the fact
that such countries as Afghanistan and Rwanda are member states. But involvement with the UN is nonetheless an indicator of at least rhetorical recognition of the value of human rights. Second, it is also the case that many
of these member states have consciously modeled their own human rights
documents on the UDHR.

The UDHR is not a legally binding document, but rather a morally binding document since it is meant to provide guidance and moral leadership to
member states who oblige themselves to respect and promote the contents
of the document. It was intended to promote collaboration in the global af-
firmation and protection of fundamental human rights. However, a cursory
review of recent and ongoing ethnic conflicts and genocides suggests that
the UDHR has failed to fulfill its promise (M. Perry, 1998):

> As important and hopeful as the story is, however, there is little reason to
> believe that many basic human rights are really any more secure now than
> they were before 1945. In this final decade of the twentieth century, the
> furious slaughter of innocents continued—most famously in Rwanda and
> in the former Yugoslavia. Even slavery, thought by many to have died with
> the nineteenth century, remains alive and well at the end of the twentieth—
> especially the enslavement of women and children. Torture, too, remains
> pervasive. (p. 4)

And so, too, of course, does hate crime—often the predecessor to genocide—
remain pervasive and worthy of examination through a human rights lens.

THE HARMS OF HATE CRIME

As noted at the outset, there is an identifiable body of scholarship that
takes seriously the individual and collective impacts of animus-based violence.
However, this literature has tended to emphasize the individual emotional or
physical injury associated with such acts. For the sake of simplicity, we identify two interrelated dimensions of the impact of hate crime for individuals
and collectives: impact on immediate victims and impact on other members
of the victim's group. Only one of these has received serious attention, and
that very narrowly. Moreover, neither set of accounts considers the immediate harm of hate crime, which is the abrogation of victims' human rights.

It is the first of these that has garnered scholarly attention. Research suggests that first and foremost among the impacts on the individual is the physical harm: bias-motivated crimes are often characterized by extreme brutality (Levin & McDevitt, 1993). Additionally, the empirical findings in studies of the emotional, psychological, and behavioral impact of hate crime are beginning to establish a solid pattern of more severe impact on bias crime victims, as compared to nonbias victims (see, e.g., Herek, Cogan, & Gillis, 2002; McDevitt et al., 2000). Such comparative analyses of bias- and non-bias-motivated victims must be replicated to enhance the credibility of such findings.

A largely unknown aspect of the victim's experience is the impact of victimization on his or her perceptions of the offender and his or her group. If we are to understand the collective and cumulative effects of ethnoviolence on broader intergroup relationships, it is important to first understand how victimization—even the act of offending—affects the perceptions of the individuals directly involved in the offense. This is something about which we have little, if any, information. When we move beyond the experiences of the immediate victim, we enter the realm of speculation. Many scholars point to the "fact" that hate crimes are "message crimes" that emit a distinct warning to all members of the victim's community: step out of line, cross invisible boundaries, and you, too, could be lying on the ground, beaten and bloodied (see, e.g., Iganski, 2001). Consequently, the individual fear noted previously is thought to be accompanied by the collective fear of the victim's cultural group, possibly even of other minority groups likely to be victims. Weinstein (as cited by Iganski, 2001) refers to this as an *in terrorem* effect: intimidation of the group by the victimization of one or a few members of that group. However, we know of no empirical study that explicitly surveys large numbers of victims' reference communities to determine the veracity of this assumption.

One related area that has received scant attention has been the observation that anxiety triggered by the victimization of one's cultural group can easily erupt into periods of retaliatory violence. In the United States, Chief Justice Rehnquist acknowledged this, writing for the majority in *Wisconsin v. Mitchell* (1993). He argued for the recognition of hate crime as a special class of offense because of the likelihood that it would, in fact, initiate yet more violence. This effect was evident in New York following the murder of a young African American man by a crowd of Italian youth in Bensonhurst in 1989, where the murder was followed by days of racial skirmishes. A more recent example occurred in Carson City, Nevada, in 2002, where a group of 12 American Indian males attacked two Latino males, apparently in response to an earlier assault on a Native American in which they were thought to have taken part. McDevitt et al. (2000) include a retaliatory motive in their typology of hate crime offenders, based on their observation that a notable proportion of offenders reported that their offence was a response to a prior (perceived or real) offence perpetrated against them.

Even if the victim's cultural group does not directly retaliate against the hate crime perpetrators or their reference community, it is argued, hate crime may yet have deleterious effects on the relationships between communities. Cultural groups that are already distant by virtue of language differences or differences in values or beliefs are rendered even more distant by virtue of the fear and distrust engendered by bias-motivated violence. Intergroup violence and harassment further inhibit positive intergroup interaction.

Clearly both the individual and broader social effects of hate crime are themselves important indications of the significance of hate crime. They suggest that bias-motivated violence causes disproportionate harm to its immediate and vicarious victims. However, this conceptualization does not go far enough. It does not acknowledge the distinct way in which the harm is even more immediate, in fact, inherent in the act. Hate crime is itself the distinct harm, to the extent that it constitutes a violation of human rights, a threat to human dignity. It is to the development of this line of argument that we now turn.

HATE CRIME *IS* THE HARM: HUMAN RIGHTS VIOLATION

There is a tendency in the literature on human rights to focus on gross violations, or what Sandholtz (2002) refers to as "massive and sustained" campaigns of human rights violations. In so doing, scholars attend primarily to violations perpetrated by the state or by those aspiring to displace/replace the current regime (Bunch, 1995; Peterson & Parisi, 1998). In this formula, only systematic, organized violence and oppression appear on the stage. Rightly, writers point to the widespread and brutal genocides of German Jews, or Rwandan Tutsis. And, it is something that happens "over there," in conflict-ridden African or Middle Eastern nations, or "down there," in revolutionary Central and South American countries. Yet such emphases deny the human rights implications of the mundane but perhaps more common incidents of what we now refer to as hate crime. In many respects, this phenomenon, too, is "massive and sustained." For members of marginalized communities—like gays or aboriginal peoples, for example—it is massive, to the extent that it is a constant threat; it can be a daily risk.

For these same communities, it also represents a sustained assault. It is normative; it is endemic in a broader culture that maligns and stigmatizes the Other. Unlike most typical "street crime," violence motivated by racial or gender or religious animus, for example, is not a "one-off" event; rather, for many victims, it represents an ongoing pattern of harassment and brutality. Consider the case of "move-in" violence, wherein people of color, in particular, are often subject to ongoing vandalism, verbal harassment, arson, and even death threats until they see no option other than to leave otherwise "white" communities. In addition, one of the authors of this chapter has found in her own work with Native American victims of hate crime that such experiences are common across their life span, not only during their youth, in the classroom, in the school yard, or on the local streets (B. Perry, in press).

The sustained nature of hate crime alone suggests very strong parallels to human rights violations. Even more dramatic, however, is the argument that it is likewise a *systematic* violation of human rights. What we suggest here is that hate crime undeniably lies along the same continuum of violence and oppression as do genocidal patterns. Moreover, we say that it is systematic quite consciously, in contrast to random and episodic. There is nothing "random" about hate crime. Its victims are chosen purposefully on account of who they are perceived to be (Young, 1995):

> Any woman, for example, has a reason to fear rape. Regardless of what a black man has done to escape the oppressions of marginality or powerlessness, he lives knowing he is subject to attack or harassment. The oppression of violence consists not only in direct victimization, but in the daily knowledge shared by all members of oppressed groups that they are *liable* to violence, solely on account of their group identity. (p. 83)

Thus, while not organized (necessarily) or operating (directly) under the aegis of the state, hate crime is nonetheless systematic and targeted and might thus properly be understood as a human rights violation.

Hate crime is what Stanko (1990, 2001) refers to as *targeted violence*. Specifically, Stanko (2001) uses this term to capture the vulnerability of members of particular groups because of their "relational disadvantage" to their attacker(s). The notion makes explicit the fact that racial or gendered or anti-immigrant violence, as examples, are nested in a structural complex of relations of power grounded simultaneously in often intersecting identities. The interactions between subordinate and dominant groups provide contexts in which both compete for the privilege to define difference in ways that either perpetuate or reconfigure hierarchies of social power. Such confrontations—including violent ones—are inevitably informed by the broader cultural and political arrangements that "allocate rights, privileges and prestige" (Sheffield, 1995, p. 438).

This "embeddedness" of violence is also reflected in Iris Marion Young's (1995) use of the term *systematic violence*, referred to previously. By this she means the "unprovoked attacks on . . . persons or property that have no motive but to damage, humiliate or destroy the person" (p. 83). The parallels with Stanko's understanding of targeted violence are especially evident in Young's observation that systematic violence is, in fact, permissible, if not encouraged, by the social context in which it occurs—a context that marginalizes and stigmatizes raced and gendered minority groups through multiple and overlapping mechanisms of oppression (Young, 1995). The notion also makes the connection between hate crime and human rights violation explicit—both are perpetrated with a mind to terrorize and disempower victims such that their worth is thrown into question.

For Young—and for us—the oppression of which racial violence is a part is more than the outcome of the conscious acts of bigoted individuals. It represents a network of norms, assumptions, behaviors, and policies that are structurally connected in such a way as to reproduce the racialized and gendered hierarchies that characterize the society in question. Such "oppressive violence" is empowering for its user. It facilitates the ability to set the terms of discourse and action and to impose a particular type of order. Oppressive violence is itself a mechanism of social power by which white males, in particular, assert a narrow vision of hegemonic whiteness. As such, it is a mechanism for reinforcing the privilege of whiteness and the oppression of color, or masculinity, or sexuality, as the case may be. It represents a will to power by which the very threat of otherwise unprovoked violence "deprives the oppressed of freedom and dignity" (Young, 1995, p. 83). In other words, it deprives them of their human rights or, in extreme cases, their lives.

Hate crimes and discriminatory practices against minority groups, indigenous populations, and religious groups are taking place in most societies. The rights violations are often severe and frequently carried out by the transgressor with political or economic power. Vulnerable groups of people are targeted with violent assaults, harassment, and threats because of their religious beliefs, ethnicity, or national origin, or because of features that distinguish them from the mass.

During the ethnic cleansing in Bosnia, hate crimes were frequently practiced, and the objective was to humiliate the victims. The hate-motivated acts perpetrated during wartime often take proportions that are most extreme and seemingly without limits to their brutality. Social psychologist Neil Kressel (2002) points out, in *Mass Hate: The Global Rise of Genocide and Terror*, how Muslim and Bosnian Croat women were brutally raped and consciously humiliated by Serbian soldiers in the most degrading and dehumanizing ways, to show the disgust for the enemy. Such hate crimes are often related to ongoing conflicts—fueled by ideological or religious beliefs to justify the violations—and provide a means by which the perpetrators endeavor to humiliate and degrade the enemy.

Another vulnerable group exposed to state-tolerated hate crime are the so-called street children in the major cities of Latin America. They are called street children because they live, work, and sleep on the streets and are in general ostracized and not accepted by the more privileged citizens of the society. Street children, who only make up for a small proportion of the children who are visible on the streets, have adopted the street as their habitat and consequently escaped from families that are often fraught with domestic violence, neglect, and mental/physical/sexual abuse. The majority of children living on the street are boys, and they commonly pose a perceived if not real threat to, for example, shop and restaurant owners by intimidating the customers by just their appearance and acts.

The extrajudicial killings of street children in South American cities like Bogotá, Rio de Janeiro, and Sao Paulo are examples of hate crimes also known as *limpieza social*, or "social cleansing." Just as with other forms of hate crime, the social cleansings are mainly directed toward the most vulnerable groups of the society, who are already exposed, discriminated against, and unwanted by the society because of their socioeconomic status. The children on the streets live in constant fear of being targeted by armed vigilantes or by the police. The extent of serious human rights violations and hate crimes against children is exceptionally difficult to monitor due to its inherent dynamics. Many cases are not reported because of the lack of witnesses or because victims or their relatives live on the fringes of society and tend to remain anonymous, without resources or knowledge to file complaints or to receive legal assistance.

The perpetrators, or the so-called death squads, are generally made up of off-duty police who have been hired by local businessmen to "take care" of the children who, because of their presence, are disturbing the flow of commerce. Consequently, the social cleansings are primarily intended to eradicate prostitutes, street children, and other stigmatized groups of the society. Instead of establishing supporting structures to help these children to better living conditions, they are apprehended as an embarrassment and problem to society in general. Typically, the perpetrators are organized hate groups, the police, and armed vigilantes. Hate crime and discrimination against less privileged groups of the society increased dramatically during the military dictatorships in such nations as Argentina, Chile, Paraguay, and Uruguay. In each case, the hate crimes specifically targeting dissidents and nonconformist individuals whose identities and beliefs were seen as a threat to the ruling system (Olsson, 2004).

By promoting fear and violence, the agents of the repressive states during the military dictatorships were successful in silencing the citizens' demands for justice and self-determination and also in effectively undermining human rights, peace, and democracy. Yet these repressive regimes share with other "progressive" nations a lengthy history of hate-motivated violence, all of which have the intent of silencing and marginalizing the collective victims. Moreover, consider, now, the core components of human rights as conceived earlier in this chapter: dignity, equality, and freedom. There are very clear ways in which hate crimes challenge victims' abilities to freely pursue these goals. Early in the chapter, we asserted that, according to a human rights framework, all humans have inherent dignity and worth. However, it is also the case that, in practice, dignity and worth come to be socially defined and constructed, arrayed along a continuum in which some members of society are seen to have less worth, such that both the dignity and presumed inequality of subordinate groups are called into question. Hate crime undoubtedly plays a role in reinforcing these limitations.

Western cultures like the United States, the United Kingdom, and even Canada are largely colonizing states grounded in deeply embedded notions of difference and that have been used to justifying and constructing intersecting hierarchies along lines of sexuality, race, gender, and class, to name but a few. These constructions have reinforced similarly changing practices of exclusion and marginalization. They tend to presume essentialist, mutually exclusive categories of belonging, in which one side of the equation—nonwhite, non-Christian, nonheterosexual, for example—is deemed inferior, if not deviant. Associated with these closely guarded divisions are corresponding assumptions about the members within each category; that is, particular traits and abilities are associated with each group. Generally, these traits are posed in oppositional terms, such that the social construction of one group necessarily implies the construction of its opposite. Fine (1997) refers to these opposites as "nested," or as forming a "coherent system." Weis, Proweller, and Centri (1997) similarly refer to the "parasitic construction" of self and other. Neither could exist independently without the other. In creating the self, in carving out an identity, we necessarily create its antithesis. However, as Frankenberg (1993) reminds us, this co-construction is not symmetrical. It implies dominance, normativity, and privilege, on one hand, and subordination, marginality, and disadvantage, on the other. It is those who live on the "wrong" side of the dualism who are, like Orwell's characters, "less equal," less worthy, and thus vulnerable to violence intended to reinforce this.

Also implicit in this construction of difference is the assumption of a good-bad opposition. Not only is the Other different; by definition, he or she is also aberrant, deviant, and inferior. Structures of oppression operate through a set of dualisms—such as good-evil, superior-inferior, strong-weak, dominant-subordinate—wherein the second half of the binary is always marked as deficiency relative to the superior capacities and privileges of the norm. It is important to keep in mind here that difference does not inherently imply inferiority. That evaluation is imposed on the Other by the dominant center. The marking of the Other as deviant is an interpretive act:

> It is assigning a value to a particular difference in a way that discredits an individual or group to the advantage of another that transforms mere difference into deficiency. (Rothenberg, 1995, p. 11)

The marking of difference as deficiency is a social, political process that has the effect of creating hierarchies along divisions such as race, sexuality, and class. Once a group has been defined as inferior or defective or substandard, it is necessarily assigned a subordinate place in society. This construction of the Other facilitates the unequal distribution of resources and power in such a way that it appears natural and justifiable.

Where the popular image of the Other is constructed in negative terms—as it frequently is—group members may be victimized on the basis of those perceptions. Hate crime is thus "bolstered by belief systems which (attempt to) legitimate such violence" so as to "limit the rights and privileges of individuals/groups and to maintain the superiority of one group" (Sheffield, 1995, pp. 438–439). Members of subordinate groups are potential victims *because of* their subordinate status. They are already deemed inferior, deviant, and therefore deserving of whatever hostility and persecution comes their way. In sum, they are damned if they do, and damned if they don't. If they perform their identities on the basis of what is expected of them, they are vulnerable. If they perform in ways that challenge those expectations, they are equally vulnerable.

The violent interactions between subordinate and dominant groups provide a context in which both compete for the privilege to define difference in ways that either perpetuate or reconfigure hierarchies of social power. Simultaneous and oppositional efforts to do difference set up tensions, in which the act of victimization co-constructs the victim and perpetrator. This confrontation is informed by the broader cultural and political arrangements, which "allocate rights, privilege and prestige according to biological or social characteristics" (Sheffield, 1995, p. 438). Perpetrators attempt to reaffirm their dominant identity, their access to resources and privilege, while at the same time limiting the opportunities of the victims to express their own needs. The performance of hate violence, then, confirms the "natural" relation of superiority-inferiority. It is a form of interpersonal and intercultural expression that signifies boundaries. And, significantly, the boundary is "capable of organizing personal interactions in sometimes lethal ways" (Cornell & Hartmann, 1998, p. 185). Ultimately, hate-motivated violence keeps the less worthy in their place and produces personal insecurity and fear.

This leads us to consideration of the next constraint on human rights. Ashworth (as cited in Bunch, 1990) observes that "the greatest restriction of liberty, dignity and movement, and at the same time, direct violation of the person is the threat and realisation of violence" (p. 490). This is the very intent of hate crime: to circumscribe the participation and actions of its victims. The very act of animus-based violence temporarily constrains its victims: they are at the mercy of their brutalizers, often physically unable to retaliate or escape. This is a function of one of the common empirical attributes of hate crime: it frequently involves multiple offenders assaulting one, perhaps two victims (Levin & McDevitt, 1990;

B. Perry, 2001). There is always another pair of hands available to drag the victim down again.

It is also important, however, to consider the other ways in which hate crime threatens the liberty and mobility of victims. As noted in the previous section on the emotional harms of hate crime, many victims—and vicarious victims— are virtually paralyzed by the fear of additional assaults. At the very least, it limits their desire to interact with white people, such that they may choose to limit interactions with others "like" their perpetrators. For others, violence and the threat of violence limits their movements and their perceived options, resulting in withdrawal. It creates "more borders," said one participant in a series of interviews with Native Americans, in that people become fearful of moving out of the relative safety of the reservation. They "stay here for all their lives, because they're afraid to go 'out there' because of what's going on, for all of these reasons." Very similar sentiments were expressed by others:

> That's why people don't leave, why they don't go into the towns to look for a job. They're afraid to go there, so they stay inside. They know—from their experience, or their family's, or their friends'—what can happen. There's too much risk out there. (male, Montana)

In short, hate crime has the intended effect—like most human rights violations—of segregating and marginalizing its victims. The historical creation of ghettoes was, in fact, a product of racial violence pushing blacks, Latinos, and Native Americans into isolated zones of safety. The related violence had its intended effect of moving the nonwhite threat into distinct and isolated communities. Today, racial violence continues to play this role, albeit in slightly different form. Gone are the days of collective violence and race riots intended to chase blacks out of white communities. Far more typical are individual acts of violence directed at those nonwhites who dare to cross the geographical—and often economic—boundaries to "invade" white neighborhoods. In many areas of the country, this has taken the form of the "move-in" violence, noted previously, wherein nonwhite encroachment on "white territory" is met with an array of discouraging behavior, ranging from verbal harassment and vandalism to cross burning, arson, and murder (Green, Strolovitch, & Wong, 1998; Rubinowitz & Perry, 2002). Green and colleagues (1998) observe that

> acts of racial intimidation crime [can be traced] to perpetrators' desire to preserve racially homogeneous residential areas and the ways of life that residents associate with them. The admixture of outright racism, nostalgia, and self-interest that contributes to this desire doubtless varies, but the conjunction of this exclusionary sentiment and the tacit support (or active encouragement) of neighbors leads to a heightened propensity for action when racial homogeneity is threatened. (p. 397)

The danger here is that the effects of residential segregation—like that encapsulated in urban ghettoes or the reservation system—have dramatic implications for other forms of marginalization (Massey & Denton, 1993; Wachtel, 1999). Geographic isolation frequently (re)creates related patterns of social and economic segregation and marginalization. There are what Wachtel (1999) refers to as *reciprocal relationships* between housing segregation and other forums such as health, education, and employment. According to Massey and Denton (1993), residential segregation creates barriers to

> social mobility. Where one lives determines a variety of salient factors that affect individual well-being: the quality of schooling, the value of housing, exposure to crime, (or) the quality of public services. (p. 138)

Thus the tendency to physically marginalize people of color, gay men and lesbians, and others deemed inferior, the attempt to keep them "in their place," finds its parallel in the tendency to also socially marginalize them. Again, in light of the potential for exclusionary violence, this is not a voluntary choice, but the "safe" choice. Rather than risk the threat of being forcibly removed from public places, many victims and potential victims opt to retreat to "their own" stores, bars, restaurants, and even workplaces.

For too many minority group members, the perception, if not the reality, of what awaits them in public places has its intended effect of keeping people in their place. It reinforces the boundaries—social and geographical—across which they are not meant to step. These violent reminders contribute to on-going withdrawal and isolation; in short, racial violence furthers historical patterns of segregation. The hostility, harassment, and violence experienced "out there" produce what Wachtel (1999) characterizes as "voluntary segregation," wherein those subject to the discriminatory and hateful patterns of behavior may choose to return or simply remain in the relative safety of their homes, neighborhoods, or communities in a way that reflects constrained mobility options.

CONCLUSION

Writing specifically about violence against women, Chapman (1990) observes that it is "widespread and global and is tolerated as a social phenomenon in institutions and custom and, to some degree, in law. The results are major human rights violations" (p. 63). As argued throughout, the same can be said about animus-based violence perpetrated against other minority group members. There can be no question that such violence is massive and sustained—an empirical descriptor of human rights violations. However, we have also argued that the two classes of offences are theoretically parallel, running along the same continuum.

If we can agree that, at least as set out in the UDHR, human rights are characterized by the cardinal principles of human integrity, equality, and freedom, then we must also agree that hate crime constitutes an egregious violation of human rights. We have argued here that it violates each of these principles. Hate crime does challenge in very direct ways the security and integrity of its victims. It is explicitly intended to reinforce patterns of structural inequality among and between groups. And it severely limits the mobility of both its direct and vicarious victims.

Thus to shift the discourse of hate crime to the level of human rights is to reinforce the severity of the threat that it represents. Specifically, it names it for what it is: a mechanism of empowerment and disempowerment. The violence of which we speak is not simply about the individual impact of the individual perpetrators; rather, it is an inevitable outgrowth of rigidly structured and hierarchical societies. It is an act of collective empowerment-disempowerment that relies heavily on the history and persistence of relations of advantage and disadvantage.

The legal machinery of even the most democratic states offers little protection to victims of hate crime, to the extent that it represents only a symbol for many victims of hate crime. The law is seldom utilized or operational for vulnerable groups in society because of lack of resources, influence, and knowledge. Yet the law is a complex thing. It is not an immutable behemoth. It is vulnerable to the impact of ongoing struggles between groups. It is itself a site at which raced and gendered relations of power are enacted. Recent reversals on issues such as affirmative action and bilingual education are evidence of its limitations. However, law has been used effectively to extend the rights and protections afforded women, people of color, gays, and ethnic and religious minorities. The Violence against Women Act of 1994 has dramatically expanded the protections and services available to battered women. Successive civil rights acts—nationally and at the state level—have been crucial to the recent political and economic advances of people of color, in particular. It is not unreasonable, then, to consider legislative reform as a means of addressing the negative and exclusionary effects of difference. Consequently, a useful starting point would be the elimination of the types of exclusionary legislation that appear to themselves stigmatize vulnerable communities. For example, as long as the sexuality of gay men and women continues to be criminalized, they will be beyond the protection of the criminal justice system. Thus the primary mechanism for eliminating legal and, indirectly, illegal victimization of gay people will be to decriminalize sodomy, same-sex solicitation, and same-sex sexual activities. However, this will not occur in a vacuum, but within the context of broader initiatives intended to ensure the realization of the civil and legal rights of all people. Coincident with the elimination of discriminatory legislation, then, is the need for inclusive legislation addressing hate crime specifically.

This is the traditional response to the emergence of social problems in most Western nations—to provide a statute to manage the perceived crisis. And there may be some symbolic value to opting for legislation as a means of responding to ethnoviolence. Just as hate crime is an expressive act, so, too, is hate crime legislation an expressive statute. It sends a message to its intended audience(s) about what is to be tolerated. However, hate crime legislation is not without serious limitations. For one, there are significant disparities in hate crime legislation across and even within nations. Foremost among these are inconsistencies in protected classes. Where traditionally oppressed groups are excluded from the legislation—as is often the case with women and gay men and lesbians—the implication is that they are not worthy of the same protections afforded racial minorities. Moreover, the groups that are protected vary dramatically across jurisdictions, so that there is no shared global vision of who should be extended the protections of the law. In a similar vein, the nature of hate crime legislation is itself disparate. Some jurisdictions address bias-motivated violence and intimidation, some account for institutional vandalism, and some allow for penalty enhancement for bias-motivated crime. Moreover, nations are by no means consistent in their inclusion or invocation of such criminal legislation.

The ambiguity of the law is apparent in the latter case. On one hand, the lack of consistency in defining and responding to hate crime by statute prohibits a coherent vision of the problem. On the other hand, the fact that there are multiple jurisdictions and multiple actions available may in fact work to the advantage of victims. Where criminal law fails, civil injunctions, invoking the language of rights, are readily available at the federal level, if not the state level. Rights claims can be powerfully transformative discourses since, according to Hunt (1990),

> they articulate a vision of entitlements, of how things might be, which in turn has the capacity to advance political aspiration and action. . . . Whilst rights-in-isolation may be of limited utility, rights as a significant component of counter-hegemonic strategies provide a potentially fruitful approach to the prosecution of transformatory political practice. (p. 18)

Hunt's final point is the crux: while law can be and has been used effectively to advance the place and protections afforded long disadvantaged groups, its limitations mean that law alone is an insufficient field of discourse. It must be embedded in a broadly based politics of difference that operates at multiple levels, in multiple sites.

Even in light of the limitations discussed previously, then, from a human rights perspective, national and local judiciaries, legislatures, and electoral bodies are all fundamental to the protection and promotion of nondiscrimination and preventing hate crime. They have the ability and function to guarantee the rule and enforcement of the law, helping to establish anti-discriminatory practices and achieve socioeconomic, political, and cultural equality (Olsson, 2003). Both governmental and nongovernmental institutions benefit from comprehensive and coherent legislation or constitutions that guarantee basic rights (social, cultural, economic, civil, and political) and protect the human rights of vulnerable groups in the society.

REFERENCES

Bunch, C. (1990). Women's rights as human rights: Toward a re-vision of human rights. *Human Rights Quarterly, 12,* 486–498.

Bunch, C. (1995). Transforming human rights from a feminist perspective. In C. Bunch (Ed.), *Women's rights, human rights* (pp. 11-17. New York: Routledge.

Chapman, J. (1990). Violence against women as a violation of human rights. *Social Justice, 17,* 54–70.

Cornell, S., & Hartmann, D. (1998). *Ethnicity and race: Making identities in a changing world.* Thousand Oaks, CA: Pine Forge Press.

Fine, M. (1997). Witnessing whiteness. In M. Fine, L. Weis, L. Powell, & L. M. Wong (Eds.), *Off white: Readings on race, power and society* (pp. 57–65). New York: Routledge.

Frankenberg, R. (1993). *White women, race matters: the social construction of whiteness.* Minneapolis: University of Minnesota Press.

Green, D., Strolovitch, D., & Wong, J. (1998). Defended neighborhoods, integration and racially motivated crime. *American Journal of Sociology, 104,* 372–403.

Herek, G., Cogan, J., & Gillis, R. (2002). Victim experiences in hate crimes based on sexual orientation. *Journal of Social Issues, 58,* 319–339.

Hunt, A. (1990). Rights and social movements: Counter-hegemonic strategies. *Journal of Law and Society, 17*(3), 1–20.

Iganski, P. (2001). Hate crimes hurt more. *American Behavioral Scientist, 45,* 626–638.

Ignatieff, M. (2001). *Human rights as politics and idolatry.* Princeton, NJ: Princeton University Press.

Kallen, E. (2003). *Ethnicity and human rights in Canada* (3rd ed.). Don Mills, ON: Oxford University Press.

Kallen, E. (2004). *Social inequality and social injustice: A human rights perspective.* New York: Palgrave Macmillan.

Kressel, N. (2002). *Mass hate: The global rise of genocide and terror* (Updated ed.). Boulder, CO: Westview Press.

Levin, J., & McDevitt, J. (1993). *Hate crimes: The rising tide of bigotry and bloodshed.* New York: Plenum.

Massey, D., & Denton, N. (1993). *American apartheid: Segregation and the making of the underclass.* Cambridge, MA: Harvard University Press.

McDevitt, J., Balboni, J., Bennett, S., Weiss, J., Orschowsky, S., & Walbot, L. (2000). *Improving the quality and accuracy of bias crime statistics nationally.* Washington, DC: Bureau of Justice Statistics.

Olsson, P. (2003). *Legal ideals and normative realities: A case study of children's rights and child labor activity in Paraguay.* Lund, Sweden: Lund University.

Olsson, P. (2004, April). *Children and adolescents in especially difficult circumstances.* Research report presented at the Municipalidad de Educación y Cultura Metropolitana de Lima, Peru.

Perry, B. (2001). *In the name of hate: Accounting for hate crime.* New York: Routledge.

Perry, B. (2008). *The silent victims: Hate crime against Native Americans.* Tucson: University of Arizona Press.

Perry, M. (1998). *The idea of human rights: Four inquiries.* New York: Oxford University Press.

Peterson, V. S., & Parisi, L. (1998). Are women human? It's not an academic question. In T. Evans (Ed.), *Human rights fifty years on* (pp. 133–160). Manchester, England: Manchester University Press.

Rothenberg, P. (1995). Introduction. In P. Rothenberg (Ed.), *Race, class and gender in the United States* (3rd ed., pp. 1-12). New York: St. Martin's Press.

Rubinowitz, L., & Perry, I. (2002). Crimes without punishment: White neighbors' resistance to black entry. *Journal of Criminal Law and Criminology, 92,* 335–427.

Sandholtz, W. (2002). Humanitarian intervention: Global enforcement of human rights? In A. Brysk (Ed.), *Globalization and human rights* (pp. 201–225). Berkeley: University of California Press.

Sheffield, C. (1995). Hate violence. In P. Rothenberg (Ed.), *Race, class and gender in the United States* (3rd ed., pp. 432–441). New York: St. Martin's Press.

Stanko, E. (1990). *Everyday violence.* London: Pandora Press.

Stanko, E. (2001). Re-conceptualizing the policing of hatred: Confessions and worrying dilemmas of a consultant. *Law and Critique, 12,* 309–329.

Wachtel, P. (1999). *Race in the mind of America.* New York: Routledge.

Weis, L., Proweller, A., & Centri, C. (1997). Re-examining "A moment in history": Loss of privilege inside white working class masculinity in the 1990s. In M. Fine, L. Weis, L. Powell, & L. M. Wong (Eds.), *Off white: Readings on race, power and society* (pp. 210–226). New York: Routledge.

Wisconsin v. Mitchell, 508 U.S. 476 (1993).

Young, I. M. (1995). Five faces of oppression. In D. Harris (Ed.), *Multiculturalism from the margins* (pp. 65–86). Westport, CT: Bergin and Garvey.

ABOUT THE EDITOR
AND CONTRIBUTORS

Paul Iganski, PhD, earned his doctorate at the London School of Economics. He is a lecturer in criminology in the Department of Applied Social Science at Lancaster University, England, and formerly Civil Society Fellow at the Institute for Jewish Policy Research, London. He is editor of *The Hate Debate* (2002), coeditor of *A New Antisemitism? Debating Judeophobia in 21st Century Britain* (with Barry Kosmin; 2003), and coauthor of *Hate Crimes against London's Jews* (with Vicky Kielinger and Susan Paterson; 2005). His most recent book is *Hate Crime and the City* (2008).

Nicole Asquith, PhD, is a Senior Lecturer in the Department of Social Sciences and Humanities at the University of Bradford. Her primary research interests relate to the relationship between hate violence and hate speech, and the cross-cultural similarities in the experience of hate violence. This research specialization stems from her work as Client Advocate at the Lesbian & Gay Anti-Violence Project, Co-facilitator of Mary's Place Project, and her collaborative research partnerships with the Executive Council of Australian Jewry and the Metropolitan Police Service. Dr Asquith's work on maledictive speech and violence has been published as *Text and Context of Malediction* (VDM Verlag, 2008) and in the Journal of Sociology 40, 4 (2004), Women Against Violence Journal (July 2002), *New Talents 21C: other contact zones* (Network Books, 2007) and will be included in *Sticks and Stones: Writings and Drawing of Hate* (forthcoming).

Neil Chakraborti, PhD, is a lecturer at the Department of Criminology, University of Leicester. He has published widely on issues of "race," policing, hate crime, and victimization and is coeditor, with Jon Garland, of *Rural Racism* (2004) and coauthor of *Hate Crime: Causes, Impact and Consequences* (2009), again with Jon Garland. His most recent book is an edited collection entitled *Hate Crime: Concepts, Policy, Future Directions* which will be published in Spring 2010.

Kellina M. Craig-Henderson, PhD, is a social psychologist whose research interests and activities have focused on interpersonal and intergroup conflict within dyads, small groups, and organizations as well as the correlates of aggression at each of the preceding levels of analysis. An additional area of inquiry that she has recently initiated involves in-depth analysis of intimate interracial relationships. She is particularly interested in how increases in rates of these types of relationships reflect contemporary race relations and levels of racial prejudice in the United States. Dr. Craig-Henderson has published numerous reports of empirical research, and the National Science Foundation, the Ford Foundation, and the American Psychological Association have provided support for her work. She has presented findings from her research activities at a variety of regional, national, and international research and pedagogical meetings. She is currently serving as a program director at the National Science Foundation in the social psychology program within the Behavioral and Cognitive Sciences Division of the Social, Behavioral, and Economic Sciences Directorate and retains an affiliation with the Department of Psychology at Howard University at the rank of full professor. She earned a PhD in psychology from Tulane University and subsequently served on the faculty in the Department of Psychology and the Afro-American studies and research program at the University of Illinois in Champaign-Urbana as well as in the Department of Psychology at California State University in Long Beach.

Peter Dunn gained an MSc in social work studies from the London School of Economics (LSE) in 1984. He worked as a probation officer until 1999, when he became a policy advisor with the Youth Justice Board. Joining Victim Support in 2001, he was appointed their head of research and development in the following year. Peter left Victim Support in 2007, and he is now once again a student at LSE, researching the effects of hate crime for a PhD in sociology. Peter is a member of the Home Office's Race for Justice Advisory Group; a trustee of London's lesbian, gay, bisexual, and transgender antiviolence charity Galop; and a Fellow of the Royal Society of Arts. He lives in west London with his partner, Henry, and their Siamese cat, Sydney.

Jon Garland, PhD, is a senior lecturer at the Department of Criminology, University of Leicester, England. He has published widely on issues of racism, antiracism, identity, and community safety, and his books include *Racism and Anti-racism in Football* (with Michael Rowe; 2001) and *The Future of Football* (edited with Michael Rowe and Dominic Malcolm; 2000), in addition to books coedited and coauthored with Neil Chakraborti.

Spiridoula Lagou works in social and market research. She was awarded a master's degree in applied social statistics from the London School of Economics in 2005.

Helen Ahn Lim, PhD, is assistant professor in the Department of Criminal Justice at California Lutheran University. She received her PhD from Indiana University, Bloomington. Her research and teaching interests include hate crime, criminology, race, gender, and white-collar crime.

Gail Mason is an associate professor in the Faculty of Law at the University of Sydney, Australia. Prior to this, she was a lecturer in gender studies and criminology. She is the author of *The Spectacle of Violence: Homophobia, Gender and Knowledge* (2002) and has published widely in *Social and Legal Studies*, the *British Journal of Criminology*, and *Hypatia*. Gail's current research centers on the contribution of emotion or affect to the constitution of hate crime as a sociolegal category.

Monique Noelle, PhD, earned her doctorate in clinical psychology at the University of Massachusetts, Amherst, and completed her clinical training at Massachusetts General Hospital (MGH) and Fenway Community Health Center. Past publications have addressed vicarious traumatization in the bisexual, gay, and lesbian community following the 1998 Shepard hate crime murder and issues of clinical supervision. Currently Dr. Noelle maintains a private psychotherapy practice in Cambridge, Massachusetts, and is a clinical assistant in psychology at MGH/Harvard Medical School.

Patrik Olsson, PhD, since the beginning of the 1990s, has been involved in research areas concerning the rights of children and adolescents, information technology and social change, and labor law. His predominant focus has been on the rights of children and adolescents, for example, child labor, human trafficking, children in conflict with the law, children in prison, the right to education, the principles of nondiscrimination, and child participation. Dr. Olsson has conducted extensive research in relation to the sociolegal situation for exposed children in the MERCOSUR countries in South America, but also in Central America and Southeast Asia.

Barbara Perry, PhD, is professor of criminology, justice, and policy studies at the University of Ontario Institute of Technology. She has written extensively in the area of hate crime, including two books on the topic: *In the Name of Hate: Understanding Hate Crime* (2001) and *Hate and Bias Crime: A Reader* (2003). She has just completed a book manuscript for University of Arizona Press titled *The Silent Victims: Native American Victims of Hate Crime* (2008), based on interviews with Native Americans, and one on policing Native American communities for Lexington Press. Dr. Perry continues to work in the area of hate crime and has begun to make contributions to the limited scholarship on hate crime in Canada. Here she is particularly interested in anti-Muslim violence and hate crime against aboriginal people.

Eva Tiby, PhD, is assistant professor of criminology at Stockholm University, Sweden. She has focused on issues concerning victimology in general, and hate crimes in particular, since the early 1990s. Her thesis, "Hate Crime? Lesbian and Gays' Narratives on Victimization" (1999), was based on a triangulated study that contained interviews, narratives, surveys, and media analysis. Since then, she has conducted a replication of some of the issues from the dissertation as well as a study of homophobic hate crimes in the criminal justice system. Tiby has also published studies on the Swedish legislation concerning prostitution, local crime prevention, and young persons' victimization and fear of crime.

Index

African Americans: defensive crimes against, 113; hateful speech against, 167; KKK against, 111–15; legislation concerns, 16; "move-in" violence, 180–81, 186; *vs.* white perpetrators, 19, 115. *See also* Racism/racial violence

African Caribbean populations, 151

American Psychological Association (APA), 19

Anger issues: to anti-BGL crimes, 19, 81–83; by "in-group," 24; second crisis stage, 18; self-hatred, 119; by victims, 7–8, 98–99, 125, 128–29

Animus-based violence, 175, 178, 185, 187

Anonymous reporting, 132, 183

Antibisexual, antigay, and antilesbian (anti-BGL): backdrop, 81–82; "coming out" process, 90–93; families and, 79, 93–95; identity development, 86–89; idiographic nature, 82–83; postvictimization experiences, 19–20; psychological effects, 74, 81–85; rise of, 74–81; SO bias, 74–77; social support, 93–98; sociopolitical context, 100; victim feelings, 19, 81–83, 97, 98–100. *See also* Heterosexism; Homophobia; Homophobic violence; Lesbian/gay/bisexual/transgender

Anti-Muslim prejudice, 15, 129, 130, 151, 163

Anti-Semitism, 98, 168, 180

Anxiety levels: anti-BGL crimes, 19, 81, 83, 97; counseling, 25; with loss, 100; racially motivated, 9, 153; retaliatory violence, 179

Armenian genocide, 177

Asian Americans: harassment, 88; KKK against, 113–15; narrative research, 108–9; as perpetual foreigners, 110; support services, 135–36; as targets, 109–11; *vs.* white supremacy, 115

Asian Indians, 109, 150–51

Asian Law Caucus, 116

Asquith, Nicole, 161–73

Asylum seekers, 123, 132, 147, 150, 151

Attribution errors, 23

Australia: free speech issues, 161–62; personal safety, 57–58; speech act theory, 168–70; victimization survey, 50, 51, 131

Authoritative illocutions, 164, 169

Avoidance behavior, 8, 37–38, 116

Bard, Morton, 18–19
Behavioral consequences, homophobia,
    40–42
Bias victimization: anti-Semitism, 98,
    168, 180; asylum seekers, 123, 132,
    147, 150, 151; as human rights
    violation, 189; negative impacts, 118,
    176, 179; rape crimes, 21, 56, 119,
    134, 181; SO, 74–78; stereotypes,
    109; targets of, 16. See also African
    Americans; Antibisexual, antigay,
    and antilesbian; Asian Americans;
    Discrimination; Homophobia; Racism/
    racial violence
Bisexual issues. See Lesbian/gay/
    bisexual/transgender (LGBT)
Body maps, 54–60, 62–65
Boston Police Department, 7
British Crime Survey (BCS): accurate
    information, 124; emotional harm,
    6–12; offender values, 12; physical
    harm, 1–2; spacial impact, 2–6
British National Party (BNP), 152
Bullying. See Harassment/bullying
Bureau of Justice Statistics, 15

Caucasians. See White offenders
Chakraborti, Neil, 143–59
Children: anti-BGL crime risk for, 85;
    counseling for, 131; as offenders,
    116–17, 118; prejudice in, 129; street
    children, 182–83
Chronic victims, 32, 127
"Closet" privacy, 52–53
"Coming out": behavior changes, 74,
    87–90; process, 52–54, 67, 86, 90–93;
    safety issues, 62, 66, 84, 94
Community Relations Service (CRS),
    26–27
Cooperative Insurance Services, 123
Craig-Henderson, Kellina M., 15–30
Crime and Prejudice: The Support Needs
    of Victims of Hate Crime (Cooperative
    Insurance Services), 123, 139
Crime prevention/reduction, 133–35
Crime Victim Compensation and Support
    Authority (Brottsoffermyndigheten), 35
The Crime Victim's Book (Bard, Sangrey),
    18–19

Crisis theory, 17–18
Cross-cultural friendships, 152
Crown Prosecution Service (CPS),
    139

Danger issues: awareness of, 55–56,
    99–100; behavioral consequences,
    40–42, 95; flouting, 60–62; residential
    segregation, 187; vs. safety, 62–65, 97.
    See also Safety issues
Death squads, 183
Defensive hate crimes, 113
Depression issues: with anti-BGL
    crimes, 19, 81, 82–83; with loss,
    126; PTSD, 19, 25, 119; statistics on,
    8–9
Deviancy feelings, 22–23
Discrimination: emotional distress, 21;
    GLAD against, 50; increases, 183;
    "localism" symptoms, 147; narrative
    research, 38–46, 108–18; occupational
    research of, 33; public acts of,
    170. See also African Americans;
    Antibisexual, antigay, and antilesbian;
    Asian Americans; Bias victimization;
    Homophobic violence; Racism/racial
    violence
"Dotbusters," 109
Dunn, Peter, 123–41

Emotional harm: extended distress, 21;
    to family relationships, 6; mental
    health effects, 16, 25, 86, 101; of
    message crimes, 112; vs. psychological,
    6–12; traumatization effect, 24; trust
    issues, 43–44. See also Anger issues;
    Anxiety levels; Depression issues;
    Psychological harm
Ethnic violence (ethnoviolence):
    cleansing, 182; to minorities, 145–49,
    154–56; "move-in," 180–81, 186;
    repeat victimization, 5. See also African
    Americans; Asian Americans; Racism/
    racial violence
Exercitive illocutions, 164

Family relationships: anti-BGL hate
    crime, 79, 93–95; emotional harm, 6,
    84; support from, 24, 93–95, 100

Fear of crime phenomenon: homophobia, 37–38; repeat attacks, 127–28, 139; from whites, 148

Federal Bureau of Investigation (FBI): hate crime statistics, 15, 77–78; NIBRS, 107; UCR program, 107, 119

Feminism, 50, 56

First Amendment rights: free speech, 161, 164, 171; maledictive hate, 168; of offender, 19; performative speech acts, 163–64

Foreigner issues: message crimes, 108; news media, 110; "perpetual foreigner," 119; suspiciousness, 146–47; targeting, 109–11, 115. *See also* Immigrants/ immigration

Foucaultian discipline, 62, 64–65

Free speech, 161, 164, 171

Garland, John, 143–59

Gay Men and Lesbians against Discrimination (GLAD), 50

Gay rights/issues. *See* Lesbian/gay/ bisexual/transgender (LGBT)

Genocide, 19, 175, 177–78, 180

Ghettoes, 186–87

Gordon, Paul, 2

Group *vs.* individual fear, 179

Guilt feelings: from anger, 125; identity issues, 136; survivors, 95; victims, 18, 82, 129–30

Gypsy Travellers, 150

Harassment/bullying: accountability for, 89; financial influences, 153; identity issues, 12, 21, 85; Muslims, 15, 129, 130, 151, 163; "othering," 153; prior history, 84–85; sexual, 56, 59. *See also* Antibisexual, antigay, and antilesbian; Homophobia; Homophobic violence; Message crimes; Offenders; Verbal hatred; Victims/victimization

Harou-Sourdon v. TCN Channel Nine (1994), 169

Hate crime law, 1–2, 6, 80

Hate Crime Statistics Act, 107

Hate crime study (Sweden), 33–34

Hate speech, 163–64

Health/well-being: damage to, 17, 125, 130–31; of LGBT people, 75, 100; reconstructing, 25; responsibility for, 134

Hesse, B., 2

Heterosexism: anger feelings, 98–99; political, 100–101; psychological effects, 74, 81. *See also* Antibisexual, antigay, and antilesbian; Homophobia

Heterosexual behavior, 52–53, 59, 62, 93

Hierarchical social structures, 148

High school students, 91–92

The Holocaust, 175, 177

Homophobia: internalized, 130; research questions, 32–33; in Sweden, 31–46. *See also* Heterosexism

Homophobia, consequences: behavioral, 40–42; fear of crime phenomenon, 37–38; levels, 45–46; physical, 38–39; psychological, 37, 39–40; public service faith, 44; resignation/ resistance, 45; trust issues, 43–44; work and career, 42–43

Homophobic violence: abuse, 126; body maps, 54–60, 62–65; effects, 50–51; flouting danger, 60–62; managing behavior, 65–66; personal excerpts, 57–58; rise of, 55; safety issues, 62–65; sexual visibility, 52–54. *See also* Antibisexual, antigay, and antilesbian

Homosexuality. *See* Antibisexual, antigay, and antilesbian; Homophobia; Lesbian/gay/bisexual/transgender

Horowitz's Psychological Scale, 7

How to Do Things with Words (Austin), 163

Human multiplicity, 63

Human rights violations: definition of, 181–87; framework, 176–78, 183–84; impact of, 178–80; UDHR against, 176, 177–78, 188. *See also* Racism/ racial violence

Hwang, Victor, 116

Identity development: guilty over, 136; harassment/bullying, 12, 21, 85; homophobic violence, 86–89; sexual, 34, 52, 90; shift in, 22; working class women, 54. *See also* "Coming out"

Iganski, Paul, 1–13
Illocutionary acts, 164, 166–67, 171
Illusion of invulnerability, 21–22
Immigrants/immigration: Asian Indians,
    109, 150–51; discrimination, 16; in
    gangs, 38; Latin Americans, 179–80;
    Muslims, 15, 129, 130, 151, 163. *See
    also* Asian Americans; ethnic violence;
    Foreigner issues
Individual *vs.* group fear, 179
"In-group" effects, 23–24, 86, 112
Intergroup violence, 15–16, 27, 118–19,
    180
Internalized homophobia, 130
International Victimology Conference, 60
In terrorem effect, 179

Jews, 114, 165, 168, 180
Justice personnel, 80–81

Kallen, Evelyn, 176
Knowledge systems, 62–63
Kubler-Ross model, 127
Ku Klux Klan (KKK), 111–15

Lagou, Spiridoula, 1–13
Latin Americans (Latinos), 179–80
Lawrence, Frederick, 12
Legislative reform, 188–90
Lesbian/gay/bisexual/transgender
    (LGBT): community support, 96–97;
    event fears, 93; free speech, 161;
    heterosexual behavior, 52–53, 59, 62,
    93; liberation, 32; narratives of abuse,
    38–46; support services, 135–36;
    victim survey, 31–32; well-being, 75,
    100. *See also* Antibisexual, antigay, and
    antilesbian; "Coming out"; Homophobia
Lim, Helen Ahn, 107–22
"Localism," 146–47
Loss feelings, 126–27

Maledictive hate, 162, 166–67, 172
Mason, Gail, 49–71
Mental health effects, 16, 25, 86, 101
Message crimes: avoidance behavior, 116;
    impact of, 111–20; narrative research,
    108–9; nonwhite targets, 109–11; as
    warning, 179

Mixed-heritage rural residents, 151
Motive criminality, 32
"Move-in" violence, 113, 180–81, 186
Muslims, 15, 129, 130, 151, 163

Narrative research, 38–46, 108–18
National Center for Victims of Crime, 20
National Coalition of Anti-Violence
    Projects (NCAVP), 77–78
National Incident-Based Reporting
    System (NIBRS), 107
Native Americans, 49–50, 179–80, 181, 186
Neo-Nazi skinheads, 28
Noelle, Monique, 73–105
Non–racially motivated crime, 9, 12
Nonreporting of victimization, 79
Nonwhite targeting, 109–11

Offenders: children as, 116–17, 118;
    dominant identity, 185; values, 12;
    vilification, 169–70. *See also* Victims/
    victimization; White offenders
Office for Juvenile Justice and
    Delinquency Prevention, 27
Olsson, Patrik, 175–91
Oppressive violence, 182
"Othering" process, 144, 146, 148, 153

"Parasitic construction" of self, 184
Performative speech acts, 163–68, 170
Perlocutionary frustration, 165–66
"Perpetual foreigner," 119
Perry, Barbara, 175–91
Physical harm: bias crimes, 179; body
    maps, 60; British Crime Survey, 1–2;
    crisis theory, 17–18; homophobia,
    38–39, 65, 75; *vs.* psychological, 20
Pilot Study (Sweden), 33–34
Police involvement/support: justice
    personnel, 80–81; reporting to,
    79–80, 138–39; response rate, 140;
    sensitive treatment by, 134; *vs.* support
    organizations, 138
Posttraumatic stress disorder (PTSD),
    19, 25, 119
Postvictimization experiences, 8, 19–21,
    25–26
Psychological harm: anti-BGL
    violence, 81–85; *vs.* emotional, 6–12;

homophobia, 37, 39–40; impacts, 20–24; implications/interventions, 24–27; of message crimes, 112; personal assumptions, 137; victims *vs.* offenders, 17–19. *See also* Emotional harm

PTSD. *See* Posttraumatic stress disorder

Punishing Hate (Lawrence), 12

Quality of life issues, 41–42, 125

Racism/racial violence: crime motivation, 9, 124; ethnic motivation, 4, 150; homophobia, 58–59; Latin Americans, 179–80; rural environments, 149–56; victim guilt, 129–30; village life, 146–49. *See also* African Americans; Asian Americans; Bias victimization; Discrimination; Ethnic violence; Stereotypes

Rai, D. K., 2

Rape crimes, 21, 56, 119, 134, 181

Register study (Sweden), 35–36

Religion/religious issues: anti-Semitism, 98, 168, 180; as barriers, 154; cultural violence, 112–13; fundamentalism, 132; homophobia, 42; Jews, 114, 165, 168, 180; Muslims, 15, 129, 130, 151, 163

Reporting/nonreporting: anonymous, 132; NIBRS, 107; retaliation fears, 128; UCR, 107; by victims, 78–79, 132–33

Research questions, 32–33, 123–24

Residential segregation, 187

The Response to Racial Attacks and Harassment (Home Office report), 6

Right to privacy, 49, 50–53

"Ripple effect," 6, 100

Romantic relationship issues, 95

Rural racism, 143–56

Safety issues: body maps, 54–60, 62–65; "safety maps," 55–56; in schools, 98; weapons, 82. *See also* "Coming out"; Danger issues

Sangrey, Dawn, 18–19

Secondary victimization, 26, 78, 79–80

Segregation, 187

September 11, 2001, 151

Serial victims, 32

Sexual assault, 25, 162, 171

Sexual behavior: homophobic violence, 52–54; identity issues, 34, 52, 90; monitoring, 57–58; salience, 97–98

Sexual orientation (SO) bias, 74–78

Silencing malediction, 164–66

Slippery slope, speech, 170–71

"Social cleansing" crimes, 183

Social Inequality and Social Injustice (Kallen), 176

Social network support: cross-cultural friendships, 152; from families, 24–25, 93–95, 100; hierarchical structures, 148; homophobic violence, 93–98; improvements for, 135–38. *See also* Family relationships

Sociopolitical context, 100, 185

Speech act theory, 168–70

Stereotypes: Asian Indians, 109, 150–51; bias crimes, 109; dominant, 144; Native Americans, 49–50, 179–80, 181, 186; negative associations, 21, 118. *See also* African Americans; Asian Americans; Lesbian/gay/bisexual/transgender; Racism/racial violence

Street children, 182–83

Stress management, 21, 119

Subordinating malediction, 164–65

Substance abuse, 83

Suicidal behavior, 92–93

Sweden, homophobic crimes, 31–46

Swedish National Institute of Public Health, 33

Systematic violence, 181–82

Targeted violence: anti-BGL crimes, 19, 50, 56, 77, 95; bias victimization, 16; against foreigners, 109–11, 115; hate crime as, 181–82; impact, 107–9; increase in, 15–16; intervention needed, 169; motives for, 84, 113, 116; SO crimes, 78, 80, 97; understanding, 21, 24, 90, 112, 119–20; against whites, 151

Task Force on the Victims of Crime and Violence (APA), 19

Terrorism: free speech issues, 161–62, 170–71; hate crimes as, 2, 86, 108, 113, 120; KKK, 111–15; legislation against, 175; London bombings, 129; September 11, 2001, 151; *in terrorem* effect, 179

Third-party reporting, 132–33, 140

Tiby, Eva, 31–48

Transgender issues. *See* Lesbian/gay/
bisexual/transgender (LGBT)

Traumatization effect, 24

Tribunal of the Equal Opportunity
Commission, 169

Trust issues, 43–44

Uniform Crime Reporting (UCR), 107,
119

United Kingdom, 143–56

United Nations, 176, 177–78

Universal Declaration of Human Rights
(UDHR), 176, 177–78, 188

U.S. Commission on Civil Rights, 113

U.S. Department of Justice (DOJ), 15

Verbal hatred: hate speech, 163–64;
illocutionary force, 166–67; speech act
theory, 168–70; subordination/silence,
164–66

Verdictive illocutions, 164

Vicarious traumatization effect, 24

Victims/victimization: anonymous,
183; chronic, 32, 127; genocide, 19,
175, 177–78, 180; human rights of,
178–79; "in-group" effects, 23–24;
nonreporting, 79; *vs.* offenders, 17–19;
with partner, 95–96; postvictimization
experiences, 8, 19–21, 25–26; quality
of life issues, 41–42; reporting, 78–79;
secondary, 17–19, 78, 79–80; serial,
32; stress management, 21; surveys,
3–4, 5, 31–32; as symbols, 107. *See
also* bias victimization; Homophobia;
Homophobic violence; Message crimes;
Offenders; Racism/racial violence

Victims/victimization, reactions: anger
response, 7–8, 98–99, 125, 128–29;
avoidance behavior, 8, 37–38, 116;
narratives of abuse, 38–46; physical,
17–18; process of, 145–46; racial
crimes, 7, 9, 10–11; social network
support, 24–25. *See also* Guilt feelings

Victims/victimization, support: crime
prevention, 133–35; key themes,
124–31; police, 138–39; reporting,
132–33; research on, 123–24; services,
135–38

Vilification, 169–70

Village racism, 146–49

Violence: animus-based, 175, 178, 185,
187; anti-BGL, 81–85; cultural,
112–13; genocide, 19, 175, 177–78,
180; intergroup, 15–16, 27, 118–19,
180; "move-in," 113, 180–81, 186;
oppressive, 182; retaliatory, 179;
systematic, 181–82; against women,
187. *See also* Ethnic violence;
Homophobic violence; Racism/
racial violence; Targeted violence;
Terrorism

Weapons, 3, 82

White Aryan Resistance, 114

White offenders: Gypsy Travellers,
149–50; KKK, 114; neo-Nazi groups,
28; oppressive violence, 182; racial
motivation, 6, 19, 106, 109–10

White supremacy movement, 114–16,
118

Wisconsin v. Mitchell (1993), 1, 179

Women's issues: feminism, 50, 56;
identity, 54; rape crimes, 21, 56, 119,
134, 181; sexual assault, 25, 162, 171;
sexual harassment, 56, 59; violence
against, 187. *See also* Lesbian/gay/
bisexual/transgender

Work/career issues, 42–43, 85